Ann Radcliffe

To her contemporaries, Ann Radcliffe was 'The Great Enchantress'. Her wild and stormy Gothic romances made her one of the most popular and successful writers of the later eighteenth century.

Radcliffe was lampooned by many for the excesses of her writing – the craggy mountains, gloomy forests, ghosts, orphans, fainting heroines, fantastic resolutions – and yet her influence was felt not only across England but throughout Europe. In recent years, her popularity as a writer is again on the increase with all her major works now easily available. The 1790s was a time of great political and social upheaval and Miles argues that Radcliffe should be read not as a conservative writer, but as one who creatively renders visible the power structures of her time, place, gender and class.

An essential book for all students of the period and for anyone interested in the Gothic genre and women's writing.

Robert Miles is Principal Lecturer in English at Sheffield Hallam University

The Ghost Story
engraving by R. Graves, 1874

Ann Radcliffe
The Great Enchantress

ROBERT MILES

Manchester University Press
Manchester and New York

distributed exclusively in the USA and Canada by St. Martin's Press

Published by Manchester University Press
Oxford Road, Manchester M13 9NR, UK
and Room 400, 175 Fifth Avenue, New York, NY 10010, USA

Distributed exclusively in the USA and Canada
by St. Martin's Press, Inc.,
175 Fifth Avenue, New York, NY 10010, USA

British Library Cataloguing-in-Publication Data
A catalogue record is available from the British Library

Library of Congress Cataloging-in-Publication Data
Applied for

ISBN 0 7190 3828 6 *hardback*

0 7190 3829 4 *paperback*

Phototypeset by Intype, London
Printed in Great Britain
by Biddles Limited, Guildford and King's Lynn

Contents

Abbreviations and bibliographical note

I have used the following abbreviations when quoting from Radcliffe's texts:

The Castles of Athlin and Dunbayne	*CAD*
A Sicilian Romance	*SR*
The Romance of the Forest	*RF*
The Mysteries of Udolpho	*MU*
The Italian	*I*
A Journey Made in the Summer of 1794, Through Holland and Western Frontier of Germany	*Journey*

See the bibliography for full details.

I have kept notes to a minimum, only using them in those rare instances where textual citation is insufficient to the purpose and where the point cannot be fitted into the main body of the text. The bulk of the bibliographical information is to be found in Chapter Nine (Further reading). When initially citing a text within each chapter I have supplied the date of first publication, but when quoting I cite the date of the edition used, if different. Where this is the case the original publication date may be found in the bibliography.

Acknowledgements and dedication

A number of people have helped in the writing of this book, Fred Botting, Leonora Nattrass and Phil Cox read portions of the manuscript: I want to thank them for their advice and encouragement. So, too, Elisabeth Bronfen, who not only read a section but kindly shared her ideas in conversation throughout the duration of the book's writing. The members of my 1993 Gothic seminar helped me considerably by volunteering to act as 'guinea pigs' for chapter 3, notating it for helpfulness and clarity; and a special debt is owed to Bryan Burns, who first of all suggested I write this book. But above all I want to thank my editor, Anita Roy, first of all for cultivating this project; for her unflagging support; and finally, for her superb editing skills. My fond hope is that I have been equal to them.

For Barb and Garry, Sean and Maureen

Introduction

I allude, Sir, principally to the great quantity of novels with which our circulating libraries are filled, and our parlour tables are covered, in which it has become the fashion to make *terror* the *order of the day* by confining the heroes and heroines in old gloomy castles, full of spectres, apparitions, ghosts, and dead men's bones. This is now so common, that a novelist blushes to bring about a marriage through ordinary means, but conducts the happy pair through long and dangerous galleries, where the light burns blue, the thunder rattles, and the great window at the end presents the hideous visage of a *murdered* man, *uttering* piercing groans, and developing shocking mysteries. If a curtain is withdrawn, there is a bleeding body behind it; if a chest is opened, it contains a skeleton; if a noise is heard, somebody is receiving a deadly blow; and if a candle goes out, its place is sure to be supplied by a flash of lightning. Cold hands grasp us in the dark, statues are seen to move, and suits of armour walk off their pegs, while the wind whistles louder than any of Handel's chorusses, and the still air is more melancholy than the dead march in Saul.

Every absurdity has an end . . . In the mean time, should any of your female readers be desirous of catching the season of terrors, she may compose two or three very pretty volumes from the following recipe:

Take – An old castle, half of it ruinous.

A long gallery, with a great many doors, some secret ones.

Three murdered bodies, quite fresh.

As many skeletons, in chests and presses.

An old woman hanging by the neck, with her throat cut.

Assassins and desperadoes, *quant. suff.*

Noises, whispers, and groans, threescore at least.

Mix them together, in the form of three volumes, to be taken at any of the watering-places before going to bed.

The Spirit of the Public Journals (1797: 227–8)

I must say I like Mrs. Radcliffe's romances better, and think of them oftener: – and even when I do not, part of the impression with which I survey the full-orbed moon shining in the blue expanse of heaven, or hear the wind sighing through the autumnal leaves, or walk under the echoing archways of a Gothic ruin, is owing to a repeated perusal of *The Romance of the Forest* and *The Mysteries of Udolpho*. Her descriptions of scenery, indeed, are vague and wordy to the last degree; they are neither like Salvator nor Claude, nor nature nor art; and she dwells on the effects of moonlight till we are sometimes weary of them; her characters are insipid, the shadows of a shade, continued on, under different names, through all her novels: her story comes to nothing. But in harrowing up the soul with imaginary horrors, and making the flesh creep, and the nerves thrill, with fond hopes and fears, she is unrivalled among her fair country-women. Her great power lies in describing the indefinable, and embodying a phantom.

William Hazlitt (1907: 164–5)

Twenty-four years separate the publication of Horace Walpole's *The Castle of Otranto* (1765) from Ann Radcliffe's first romance, *The Castles of Athlin and Dunbayne* (1789). During this interval a handful of novels appeared imitating Walpole's medieval setting.

After 1789 – after Radcliffe – the deluge. Europe was flooded with specimens of the 'terrorist school' of novel writing, with what we – following Walpole – have come to call the 'Gothic novel'. Literary crazes of such proportions by their very nature have complex origins. They do not have single 'authors'. And yet Radcliffe's contemporaries were clear in their views: it was she who had galvanised Walpole's moribund literary experiment, setting it stalking about the land, to the peril of young ladies. More than that, she was a huge, Europe-wide success. She was also one of the most influential novelists of her generation. The impression she made on fiction was more profound than any left by her contemporaries, with the possible exception of Jane Austen.

Nevertheless, attitudes towards Radcliffe and the Gothic have been, typically, ambivalent. This ambivalence is evident in the quotation from Hazlitt and is written deep into the structure of Jane Austen's contemporaneous *Northanger Abbey*. On the debit side, the Gothic novel is transparently formulaic, a point laboured by the first quotation's mock recipe. Anyone who has read even a single example of the genre will be familiar with its typical ingredients: the dilapidated castle, the winding corridors and dungeons, the distressed maiden, the pursuing, avaricious, and usually 'elderly' villain, the sublime landscapes, peculiar weather, spectres, bodies, banditti – not to mention discovered manuscripts, guttering candles or mysterious groans.

The genre has always been easy to guy. It was, for the young Jane Austen, irresistible sport. And yet she carefully distinguishes Radcliffe from the pack. Moreover, much of the depth of Austen's novel – beneath the satire – comes from the thematic conversation it opens with Radcliffe's texts, especially *A Sicilian Romance*, the Radcliffe novel that justifiably feeds Catherine Morland's suspicions regarding General Tilney's misogyny. It is as if Austen were saying: 'Radcliffe is good in spite of the absurdities of her chosen genre'. We see the same defensiveness in Hazlitt, who feels compelled to mention Radcliffe's deficiencies in the same breath as her virtues. Considerable virtues, too, for Hazlitt is telling us that Radcliffe has conditioned the way in which he sees the world, a prowess usually associated with the most profound art.

Modern assumptions about Radcliffe often display a version of Austen's and Hazlitt's double-mindedness. The sheer longevity and diversity of the genre – from Walpole to modern 'horror' – compels an acknowledgement that the form has tapped into something deep in the culture, but the formulaic nature of the writing invites the view that purveyors of modern Gothic scarcely know, themselves, what it is they have tapped. So, too, Radcliffe. Until recently – indeed, it is still often the case – the literary-historical reflex has been to acknowledge Radcliffe's formative role in the Gothic before dismissing her as a naive writer who could not get to the bottom of whatever it was she was up to.

As I explain in the opening chapter, one of the purposes of this book is to help scotch the view of Radcliffe as a literary primitive. I shall argue that Radcliffe's texts possess aesthetic depth, that they develop in interesting 'intentional' ways, and that she is properly seen in the context of her social origins. That is to say, she belongs to the Dissenting, critical, 'middling classes'.

I employ the phrase 'middling classes' frequently in the pages that follow, so I had best explain why. The phrase itself is Roy Porter's, who uses it as a way of cautioning against reading 'industrial' models of class back into the eighteenth century (Porter 1982). Porter's point is not that one has to understand that the middle class was smaller than present-day perspectives suggest. If anything, it was larger, and more dynamic, than we often condescendingly think. Porter goes on to remind the reader that the 'middling classes' were more varied, and more entrepreneurial, than the stereotype, and that their views of themselves were not fixed within a managerial, professional identity. Despite their respectability they were hostile to the upper classes, even if they feared the mob (such as the one unleashed by the Gordon Riots); they were often dissenters and non-conformists; they felt themselves to be self-reliant and did not identify their interests with the 'Establishment'; and they proudly saw themselves as the patriotic embodiments of Englishness, as the true repository of the qualities that made free-born Britons the most politically and commercially favoured of Europeans.

Radcliffe belonged to these eighteenth-century middling classes. Her parents were in trade in Holborn, and her husband was a small-time newspaper proprietor. Radcliffe was not a complacent member of the suburban middle classes, content to spin cotton-wool fantasies of a remote past. On the contrary, her words conceal a hard edge, one sharpened by the robust, liberal, critical energies of the dissenting 'middling classes' to which she belonged.

As the last sentence makes obvious, I am not ambivalent about Radcliffe. I believe her texts engage critically with her society and culture, and that they possess a teasing, satisfying complexity. In the rest of the book I explain why. But before beginning I want to say a few more, preparatory words about a vexed yet inescapable subject: patriarchy.

The typical terrain of the Gothic novel is the dysfunctional nuclear family; and the area within that – which Radcliffe made particularly her own – is the clash between fathers and daughters. Repeatedly in Radcliffe we encounter a daughter in flight from a father, or father substitute, who wishes to seduce, rape, murder or steal from her. Class and gender are the principle axes of power within Radcliffe, but they cross over something even more fundamental; patriarchy.

But having said that, one has said very little. Patriarchy did indeed typify eighteenth-century society, but that hardly needs pointing out. In referring to it I certainly do not mean to suggest that Radcliffe conceived of patriarchy as a wicked system of male dominance in which poor victimised women skulked about in terror of the lord of the castle. It enters the frame of her fictional explorations in a far more interesting, if also elusive, way.

One way of thinking about the social history of the last two hundred years – that is to say, of Romanticism and after – is that is has constantly recurred to the issue of individual rights. As regards gender this has meant the struggle for sexual equality. In the eighteenth century this struggle was frequently couched in terms of romantic love, of marriages based on love, respect, equality and companionship, as opposed to marriage based on family convenience or dynastic ambitions. The ideal of 'companionate marriage' was particularly associated with the middling classes. The conflicts of Radcliffe's romances are less those of tyrannical fathers versus craven daughters and more a case of a new, liberal order set up in opposition to a regressive, feudal (and in that respect) 'patriarchal' one. No less than any other sophisticated novelist, Radcliffe does not simply advocate one over the other. Rather, the opposition is a *donnée* she explores.

It is no accident that over the last twenty years the Gothic in general, and Radcliffe in particular, have come back into the public view. An aspect of the postmodern is that class has (relatively speaking) slid down the agenda, while gender and race have leaped up. Radcliffe, of course, has little directly to say about race (beyond the stereotype of the southern 'Oriental' European), but she has a lot to say about gender, as does the Gothic. In my view, it has been the liberal mission over the last two hundred years or so to seek a less invidiously destructive distribution of power within our society. Patriarchy has not been uniformly strong over this period, nor has it been uniformly weak, but is has been consistently (if unsteadily) opposed. During the last two decades a great deal of effort has gone into questioning issues of power and gender: traditional paradigms of identity have seemed (perhaps only seemed) to crumble. The 1790s were another period of vigorous questioning and evident transition, where accustomed models of identity could no longer, apparently, be instinctively relied upon. A sense of change, and changing identity (what I call in the following pages the 'Gothic cusp'), was very much Radcliffe's fictional point of departure. It is owing to the depth of her explorations – and the familiarity of the terrain she explores – that she reaches us again.

In writing this book I have had a student audience primarily in mind, but another has also beckoned me on: Radcliffe's first readership, which was huge, and hugely appreciative. Radcliffe is once again making contact with the larger reading public; in this she can be entrusted to secure her own audience. Nevertheless, I have tried to assist the process by helping to make Radcliffe more accessible. In particular, I have worked at 'assessing' the intriguing complexities that lie behind the conventional facade of 'Mrs Radcliffe'. With this ambition in mind I have kept to the romances published during Radcliffe's lifetime, which is the work on which her reputation rested (and will continue to rest).

I

The Great Enchantress

The Shakespeare of Romance writers.

> Nathan Drake (1800: 359)

Mrs Radcliffe has a title to be considered as the first poetess of romantic fiction . . .

> Sir Walter Scott, 1826 (Williams 1968: 103)

Mrs Radcliffe has long borne undisputed, and almost solitary sway over the regions of romance . . .

> *The Edinburgh Magazine*, 1826 (McIntyre 1920: 50)

Ann Radcliffe – 'Mrs Radcliffe', as she used to be – was once regarded as the writer of conventional, if hair-raising, romances, whose proper place was the bibliographical hinterland of the 'rise' of the novel. It was felt that she bore some responsibility for the 'Gothic' tale, a fictional sub-genre featuring pursued maidens, dingy castles, and a lot of bad weather. 'Mrs Radcliffe' required a footnote, but the books themselves need detain no one long, save specialists. But recently her romances have come back into critical fashion. Indeed, so radically have tastes changed – together with the bases on which we judge such things – that it is now plausible to argue that she was one of the most significant writers of the 1790s, the troubled decade in which all but two of her romances were written (the first and last).

But as the opening quotations attest, this change in critical fashion merely restores Ann Radcliffe's reputation to what it once was. The literary establishment of the day placed her in the front rank of contemporary English fiction. The reviews were not always uniformly complimentary, but their criticisms were more in the way of noticing minor faults within an overall structure of achievement deemed unique, and uniquely impressive. Critics might cavil over her leaden humour, the prolixity of her 'comic' characters, the repetitiousness of her style or her use of the 'explained supernatural'. But for every review reproving such features, another praised her for them. In the main, contemporary critical opinion confirmed her position as the presiding genius of prose romance. But her success was not simply critical – it was also popular. She was far and away the best-selling English novelist of the 1790s; the most read, the most imitated, and the most translated. As the *Gentleman's Magazine* proudly noted, not only were Radcliffe's romances among the best ever to appear in the English language, they were translated into every 'European tongue' to the 'honour of the country' (1823: 87). She was a huge, Europe-wide success. The experienced publisher Thomas Cadell found the reputed sums paid for her novels (£500 for *Udolpho* and £800 for *The Italian*) so incredible he wagered £10 that the stories were false. He lost.

Such popularity begs comparison with modern day best-selling romance writers. Barbara Cartland may spring to mind but this would be misleading, as the analogy invokes modern stereotypes of literary hierarchy. We instinctively classify Henry James, James Joyce or Marcel Proust as up-market; 'popular culture' (meaning Cartland, Mills and Boon, graphic novels, or thrillers) as bargain basement, Stephen King and P. D. James as something in between. There is a further tendency to map these divisions on to class structures. But in the 1790s restricted literacy and the high cost of books (despite the rapid growth of lending libraries) militated against a novel-reading 'popular culture' (Punter 1980: 25). Perusing romances, as Jane Austen's *Northanger Abbey* attests, was still largely the prerogative of the 'middling classes', that is to say, of that group of people retrospectively known by social historians as the 'bourgeoisie'. To be sure there was a vigorous publishing trade in comparatively inexpensive 'chap books', pirated, paperbacked, sensationalised, thirty-page versions of novels such as Radcliffe's, or those issued by the Minerva Press, and these were undoubtedly consumed by the 'great unwashed'. But Radcliffe's readership was mainly the same as those who were later avidly to consume Byron and Scott.

This is not to say that this readership was homogenous. There were tensions, but they were between the self-appointed guardians of traditional literary values – a canon privileging tragedy and epic, genres inscribing hierarchical differences – and a new, rapidly expanding readership: women. Tragedy and epic were largely 'male' genres: they charted the plight of kings and heroes. This new readership preferred novels and romances where women figured centrally, albeit ambiguously. The familiar scorn heaped upon these genres by male critics, with their strictures on the danger of turning the ductile minds of young women – turning them, usually, upwards beyond their station – may give the impression that such critics feared an uprising of discontented scullery maids and fishwives, comparable to the female 'mob' that had recently menaced Marie-Antoinette in Paris (Schama 1989: 456–70). But it would be more accurate to say that they had in mind the Jane Eyres of their social world, women from the poorer end of the middling classes, newly educated, but also frequently disenfranchised by primogeniture (by the legalised right of the first son to inherit the bulk of the family estate) and other mechanisms of a patriarchical order.

There was, then, in the 1790s a newly enlarged readership whose creative divisions were those of gender and (in the limited fashion I have been arguing) class politics. Radcliffe had an unparalleled success with all sections of this readership, with both its consumers and critics (unlike Barbara Cartland, whose success has been limited to readers). In the rest of this introductory chapter I want to probe further into the origins and character of Radcliffe's critical and popular success as a way of understanding her art. Her contemporary reception will help us catch a glimpse of Radcliffe fresh, unencrusted with the prejudices of a hundred years of frequently patronising criticism.

With one or two exceptions, critics saw Radcliffe's success in straightforward aesthetic terms: 'Mrs Radcliffe, as an author, has the most decided claim to take her place among the favoured few, who have been distinguished as the founders of a class, or school' (Williams 1968: 110). This claim, by Sir Walter Scott, was a critical commonplace. It may seem dubious, given the manifest nature of her 'Gothic' influences. As the *Critical Review* noted as early as 1792, her manner resembles '*The Old English Baron*, formed on the model of *The Castle of Otranto*' (1792b: 458). *The Old English*

Baron, by Clara Reeve, dates from 1777; *The Castle of Otranto*, by Horace Walpole, was published in 1765. To these sources we can add Sophia Lee's *The Recess* (1783–85), and the early novels of Charlotte Smith, which in various ways anticipate Radcliffe's work, as do Friedrich Schillers' *The Ghost-Seer* and *The Robbers* (although here the translation dates, and Radcliffe's poor German, leave the issue of influence less than clear-cut [Tompkins 1921: 92–110]). *The Critical Review* cites 'the ruined abbey, a supposed ghost, the skeleton of a man secretly murdered' (1792b: 458) as borrowed particulars, but there are other 'avatars'. Montoni and Schedoni (from *The Mysteries of Udolpho* [1794] and *The Italian* [1797], respectively) and Radcliffe's persistent, lowering castle echo Horace Walpole's Manfred in his decaying Gothic pile. Clara Reeve and Sophia Lee also use this Gothic *mise-en-scène*, Sophia Lee adding the figure of two sisters imperilled in a lawless chivalric world (to be adopted in *A Sicilian Romance* [1790]), while in the early works of Charlotte Smith we find versions of Radcliffe's lone heroine of sensibility suffering in the midst of the aristocratic detritus of a feudal culture (albeit in a contemporary setting).

Striking off items on a generic check-list may indeed undermine Scott's claim that Radcliffe was the founder of a distinct class of romance. But for Scott these 'items' represented so much inert novelistic scenery, dead props only flickering to life with the arrival of Radcliffe's animating genius. Her sum was greater than the parts borrowed, a synergy Scott termed 'enchantment' (Williams 1968: 105). The great English critic William Hazlitt emphatically supported Scott's views. 'The *Castle of Otranto* (which is supposed to have led the way to this style of writing) is, to my notion, dry, meagre, and without effect'. *The Recess* and *The Old English Baron* were 'dismal treatises'. It had taken Radcliffe to invest the genre with the 'spirit of fiction or the air of tradition'. 'She makes her readers twice children' (Hazlitt 1907: 165–67). To the general public, she was the 'Great Enchantress' (cf. McIntyre 1920: 49).

In one respect the argument over whether Radcliffe originated the Gothic romance is academic. The notion that writers of genius are completely original is a myth. All texts draw upon their predecessors. If this was not the case, we would not be able to make sense of literary works. As in other language acts, texts mean by virtue of difference, and difference signifies by virtue of

deviation from a recognisable norm. But in another respect Scott
and Hazlitt do have a point. It may be that we can find the
components of Radcliffe's narrative art scattered among her pre-
cursors, but in her work they come together with a particular
force. As Scott put it 'She led the way in a peculiar style of
composition, affecting powerfully the mind of the reader...'
(Williams 1968: 110). The judgement finds its verification in the
diverse series of texts in some degree or other lying within
the shadow cast by her *oeuvre*: from Coleridge and Byron to the
Brontës, Mills and Boon and Harlequin.

In pondering the sources of Radcliffe's powers of enchantment
critics referred to her poetic sensibility, her pictorial, scenic art, or
her ability to duplicate a sense of the supernatural, here visionary,
there phantasmal. In modern critical terms we may say that she
helped create a new 'topography of the self' and a new 'readerly
hermeneutics' (phrases I shall elaborate upon in subsequent
chapters). The Lake Poets, opined the *Quarterly Review*, are
nature's

> humble worshippers. In her silent solitudes, on the bosom of her lakes,
> in the dim twilight of her forests, they are surrendered up passively
> to the scenery around them, they seem to feel a power, an influence
> invisible and indescribable, which at once burthens and delights, exalts
> and purifies the soul (1814: 181).

Nature worship has a long pedigree during the 'Romantic' period
– it did not spontaneously materialise with William Wordsworth
(whose 'Tintern Abbey', incidentally, is here paraphrased by the
Quarterly Review). For instance, such 'pre-Romantic' poets as
William Collins (1721–59), Thomas Gray (1716–71) and James
Beattie (1735–1803) all celebrated the encounter between a receptive consciousness and the world beyond the fence. Surrounded by
'scenery of a stupendous and solitary cast', writes Nathan Drake,
those who possess genius, especially where civilisation has made
little progress, 'will eventually be the sons of poetry, melancholy,
and superstition' (1800: 81). Drake's list and his 'primitivist' quali-
fication glances, not at the new poetry of *The Lyrical Ballads* (1798),
but at the work of a previous generation of writers. Primitivism
itself recalls that complex of ideas, values and attitudes, associated
in the popular mind with the figure of Rousseau, which formed

a dominating aesthetic of the period. Dates here are necessarily imprecise (aesthetics do not have set life histories) but we can say that this valorisation of nature had already taken shape by the mid-eighteenth century, and that a case can be made for saying that it was still obscurely (if problematically) at work a hundred years later.

And yet there is a difference between the representations of the commerce between self and nature of the 'Lake Poets' and those of their pre-Romantic predecessors. The difference (partially validating the notion of Romanticism itself) is notoriously difficult to pin down, but it flutters in-between the lines of the quotation from the *Quarterly Review*. Unlike the pre-Romantic one, the Romantic encounter is not between an observing self and a stimulating nature, between two discrete entities or realms which meet and separate. On the contrary, the observing self is shown to be constituted in and through nature. To be more precise, self and nature are revealed as sharing the same constituent terms, the same metaphors, turns of phrase, figures of speech. In short, they are constituted by the same shaping rhetoric. This sensed reciprocity between the rhetoric and the self and the rhetoric of nature is radically more important than it may first appear, for what it suggests is that the self has come unmoored from its traditional paradigms. The self is now no longer defined by a priori notions of identity but enters a free-floating, conditional realm of signification. Language is notoriously ambiguous, multi-dimensional, shifting rather than shiftless. In setting out to constitute itself through the *rhetoric of nature* the Romantic self discovers itself grounded in the *nature of rhetoric*. For the purposes of self-discovery rhetoric is slippery ground, to say the least.

When earlier I used the phrase 'a new topography of the self' I meant precisely this ambiguous state of signifying affairs, one later to be stigmatised by John Ruskin as the 'pathetic fallacy'. Ruskin wished to reinstate a boundary between the figures of speech used to express subjective experience and those used to express nature, between inside and outside. In his view, what a character feels and the metaphoric potentialities of nature description ought not to be confused. But through the whole of Romantic poetry they are constantly confused. To cite an example, Coleridge's *The Rime of the Ancient Mariner* is, among other things, a nature

poem. Much of its complexity hinges on its persistent use of
the 'pathetic fallacy'; we are constantly invited to speculate on the
relationship between the metaphoric life of the natural world –
here inexplicably teeming, there suddenly inert – and the inner life
of the Mariner. Such reciprocity does not simplify, but multiplies
meaning. Ruskin's stigmatising 'pathetic fallacy' was a rationalist
attempt to shut the stable door after the Romantic horse had
bolted.

I earlier cited Nathan Drake's list of the dispositions of natural
genius: to poetry, melancholy, and superstition. As a largely undistinguished belletrist Drake serves as a reliable guide to the common
taste of the immediately preceding 'age'. Proneness to superstition
and melancholy may seem surprising characteristics for the age to
have esteemed. In one respect melancholic superstitiousness merely
points to a deeper fashionable value: sensibility. According to the
tenets of sensibility, only the spiritually inert will remain unmoved
by the current fashion for Graveyard Poetry, will show themselves
up as bestially indifferent to the piteousness of death or to the
terrors of the immaterial world. Fashion is frequently the battle-
ground for class politics, and that is undoubtedly the case here.
But it is also the case that these fashionable affectations signalled
profound shifts in attitudes. This is perhaps clearest in the case of
superstition, a mental weakness traditionally reviled as the chief
instrument of Catholic obscurantism and oppression. Why was
this prime transgression in the Protestant list of mortal Catholic
sins now considered a redeeming virtue? It had been used to
figure the Catholic as dangerous and Other. Why was it now
employed to represent the English and 'homely'?

Many things may be said in response to this. The feature I
want to pick out here concerns the decay in traditional theological
structures. Theological points of difference were increasingly
giving way to national, secular ones; by the same token differences
in dogma no longer signified in the way they had once done. In
terms of value, spiritual 'instinct' took precedence over its theological codifications: what was important was sensitivity to the immaterial world. Here superstition and religiosity found common
ground. This revaluation of superstition can be placed in the
context of the Great Awakening, that upsurge in religious feeling
which, in its diverse ways, distinguished much of the later eight-

eenth century, although, historically, it is probably true to say that
it found its most concrete manifestation in the ministry of John
Wesley (1703–91), in his evangelical, 'methodistical' mission. But
paradoxically this upsurge in religious feeling did not signify a
greater security in religious faith. On the contrary, the very multi-
plicity of socially licit beliefs served to underline the absence of
any authoritative base.

At least, one is likely to take such a line if one follows the
French social historian Michel Foucault in reading the late eighteenth century as a period of 'epistemic' disruption, a moment
when the epistemes – the deep structures of knowledge – of what
Foucault calls the Classic and Modern periods discontinuously
overlap (Foucault 1970). Such a juncture naturally produced general feelings of unease. This reading has its attractions for understanding the origins of Radcliffe's popularity, as she was the great
poet of the aesthetics of uncertainty. *The Mysteries of Udolpho*,
says Coleridge, is unmistakably Radcliffe because of its trademark
features: 'the same mysterious terrors are continually exciting in
the mind the idea of a supernatural appearance, keeping us, as it
were, upon the very edge and confines of the world of spirits, and
yet are ingeniously explained by familiar causes . . .' (Raysor 1936:
356). Although the device of the explained supernatural was not
Radcliffe's invention it was indelibly associated with her in the
public mind. Some critics praised her use of the device, others
deprecated it; generally it was misunderstood. As Coleridge suggests, Radcliffe's art was to leave the reader on a borderline
between the phantasmal and the real, between superstition and
common sense, the supernatural and nature. As Hazlitt put it, 'All
the fascination that links the world of passion to the world
unknown is hers, and she plays with it at her pleasure; she has all
the poetry of romance, all that is obscure, visionary, and objectless
in the imagination' (Hazlitt 1907: 165).

Radcliffe's use of superstition and the supernatural – the 'visionary' – keys her into the taste of her age, but she played upon this
taste in a manner that clearly moved her readership. There is a
difference between texts which 'reflect' contemporary tastes in
fairly straightforward ways and ones that mediate these tastes in a
more complex fashion, capable of addressing – of speaking to –
the subjectivity of their readership. Radcliffe's books, I want to

suggest, fall into the second category (and not the first, which is where she used to be put). Radcliffe's visionary art – her teasing use of the spectral – created a blurring across a set of boundaries: between inside and outside, nature and self, life and death. The 'spirit of the age' (to use Hazlitt's phrase) found in this 'blurring' a powerful enchantment.

When Radcliffe's critics approvingly refer to her as 'the Great Enchantress', we should not simply register that she told good stories. We should recognise that her powers of enchantment draw upon her ability to create what I have called the Romantic 'topography of the self', a nexus of subjectivity, nature and language. Radcliffe's 'descriptions of scenery', Hazlitt reminds us, are neither 'nature nor art' (Hazlitt 1907: 165). Her descriptions are not scenic windows but peculiar acts of artifice, acts conjuring an emotional terrain for which her readership had a special affinity. And just as we recognise in such a 'topography', when sketched by the Romantic poets, evidence of a deep shift in sensibility, so we should with Radcliffe.

Of course cultural shocks did not end with the fragmentation of those deep structures underpinning conventional notions of the 'real'. There were also shocks of a more immediate, historical kind. The Gothic novels of Radcliffe and Matthew Lewis, says De Sade, 'became the necessary fruit of the revolutionary tremors felt by the whole of Europe' (Sage 1990: 49). Scott's comments confirm that De Sade's was not an isolated view: it was 'the cry of the period . . . that the romances of Mrs Radcliffe, and the applause with which they were received, were evil signs of the times' (Williams 1968: 111). Scott goes on to say that the romances of her inferior imitators were the true sinister portents, not her works (distinguishing between Radcliffe and her imitators, the one as excellent as the others were poor, was another critical commonplace). But the real interest comes with the metaphors Scott employs in his defence of Radcliffe. The rage for Radcliffe 'argued a great and increasing degradation of the public taste, which, instead of banqueting' on the masterpieces of Richardson, Smollet and Fielding 'was now coming back to the fare of the nursery, and gorged upon the wild and improbable fictions of an overheated imagination' (Williams 1968: 111). Scott's metaphors echo the English response to the revolutionary events in France: consuming Gothic fictions somehow becomes the literary equivalent of relishing the works of the guillotine, the final, regressive expression of a fatally overheated public imagination. Aristocratic 'banqueting' has become plebeian 'gorging'. Scott's strategy is to allow that in the case of her imitators comparisons with the revolutionary, incontinent French may very well be just, but not in Radcliffe's: the 'servile' copyists, unable to follow the 'clear, precise, and distinct' outline of the original, produce childish monstrosities, and these – the implication runs – might reasonably be considered 'evil signs of the times'.

The views of De Sade and Scott agree up to the point where they encounter Radcliffe. Scott appears to allow De Sade's characterisation of the Gothic novel as 'the necessary fruit of revolutionary tremors' but bridles at Radcliffe's inclusion. Once again Scott's language indicates why. The tenor of 'servile', or 'crowd of copyists', is to construct Radcliffe's imitators as a scarcely literate mob, too dim to be original, and too uneducated to write properly. In the public mind, at least, the 'mob' was associated with revolutionary violence. Scott is clearly concerned to cleanse Radcliffe's reputation of a tainted association with 'proletarian' turmoil.

This raises a central, troubling question in Radcliffe criticism: How conservative was Radcliffe? Judging by her reception, she was deemed reassuringly orthodox in her views. A few half-hearted attempts were made to lump her damagingly with the 'terrorist school of novel-writing' (a phrase explicitly linking the Gothic fad with revolutionary excess), the usual ploy being to query the correctness of her style and the sophistication of her knowledge: if she could be found wanting in these, she could be safely consigned to the category of the unwashed, deeply suspect 'mob'. On the whole Radcliffe's first critics repudiated such aspersions, defending her 'propriety', purity of style and correctness.

Thomas Mathias is a case in point. An otherwise doughty scourge of political and literary uncorrectness, he singles out Radcliffe for praise after disparaging several of her sister novelists:

> Though all of them are ingenious ladies, yet they are too frequently whining and frisking in novels, till our girls' head turn wild with

impossible adventures; and now and then are tainted with democracy. Not so the mighty magician of *The Mysteries of Udolpho*, bred and nourished by the Florentine muses in their secret solitary caverns, amid the paler shrines of Gothic superstition, and in all the dreariness of enchantment; a poetess whom Ariosto would with rapture have acknowledged as,

La Nudrita
Damigella Trivulzia Al Sacro Speco.

(Sage 1990: 58)

In framing his compliment (it could hardly have been higher, cf. Sage 1990: 58) Mathias implicitly contradicts De Sade: Radcliffe enchants, not because she registers revolutionary tremors, but because she does not. Her work belongs in the transcendental realm of the sacred, not the terrestrial one of 'democracy' and social revolt.

The apogee of Radcliffe's early fame was probably 1826, the year of *Gaston de Blondeville*'s posthumous release, an event which allowed critics the opportunity for a final, appreciative summation of her career. After that her fame quickly tarnished, although it is worth noting that it was her female readers and critics who endeavoured to keep it burnished. For instance, around the turn of the century the best George Saintsbury could say of Radcliffe was that, although the literary value of the Gothic was 'low', she herself was 'not without glimmerings' (Saintsbury 1906: 44). During the same period Lucy Harrison stoutly maintained that Radcliffe possessed 'a distinction of her own' (1916: 203), her novels giving her 'a unique place amongst the prose writers of the Romantic school' (1916: 185). Radcliffe 'was superseded but not eclipsed; no one who could hold her generation spell-bound, as she undoubtedly did, can pass into oblivion, and her name will always be one to conjure with' (1916: 202–03).

If George Saintsbury is the spokesman of a canon that endured until relatively recently, then Harrison is the spokeswoman of the present. In the modern reformulation of the canon, Radcliffe's importance has once more been re-established. It is doubtful whether Radcliffe's books have ever been more available than they are at the present, with all the major novels now in paperback.

But if they are more physically (and financially) available than they were, say, in 1800, they are certainly less accessible. In one

respect Scott was wrong: her readership did 'gorge' themselves on
her texts. Readers may have been meant to husband the treasure
of a new Radcliffe, savouring the narrative at the leisurely pace
demanded by a four-decker, but many, such as Catherine Morland,
unable to contain themselves, bolted the fare down at once. Modern
readers apparently find Radcliffe less digestible.

There are many reasons for why this should be so. But one of
them seems to be the very quality of her contemporaries esteemed
her for: the conservatism noted by Matthias. The main impetus
behind the re-evaluation of Radcliffe has come from feminist
critics who have invented and theorised the category 'female
Gothic': 'Feminist critics have read the female Gothic as a narrative
about mothers and daughters, in which a daughter who has lost
her mother either discovers that she is not dead or finds mother
substitutes in her place' (Heller 1992: 2). Radcliffe has been read
as providing a crucial narrative matrix, not because she destabilises
patriarchal structures, but because she articulates a conventional
norm from which later female writers challengingly depart. Radcliffe's 'female Gothic' − her tales of lost mothers and searching
daughters − may hold a radical message, but to get at it the
modern critic has to read against the grain of Radcliffe's apparent
intentions.

In this book I have three principle aims. Firstly, I want to draw
out the context in which Radcliffe's romances were first produced
and consumed, with the express purpose of making Radcliffe more
accessible for the modern reader. In particular, I want to show
what was radical and different about her romances, what it was
about them that induced her grateful readership to call her the
'Great Enchantress'.

Secondly, I want to argue against the preconception of Radcliffe
as a 'conservative' writer. This means leaning back from Scott's
assessment towards De Sade's, but on a point of general theory,
one concerning the way in which novels are approached and
understood. If one were looking for names to attach to the oppos-
ing factions of the theoretical argument, they would be Mikhail
Bakhtin and Michel Foucault. At its simplest the argument goes
like this. For Bakhtin the novel is a site of 'heteroglossia', a place
where many diverse discourses intersect. Bakhtin likens this babel

to the tradition of European carnival: in these moments of licence,
values – ideologies – are turned upside down, are liberated by
rites of reversal which sanction transgression. The dialogic novel
– the novel which teems with socially diverse voices – exploits just
such a licence to create subversive, liberating artefacts. Bakhtin's
theories are interestingly buttressed by the attitudes taken by eighteenth-century conservative commentators attending to the 'rise of
the novel'; such commentators particularly deplored comic novels,
as such texts depicted high people in low situations, a reversal they
saw as a serious threat to existing social hierarchies (for instance,
see Hurd 1811). Other critics, taking their cue from Foucault,
argue that Bakhtin's model is hopelessly Utopian. Just because a
figure of low station is allowed subversive utterance in the pages
of a novel does not mean power structures outside shift in fact.
The purchase hierarchy has on subjectivity is more than secure
enough to withstand the depiction of aristocrats in compromising
positions. As Foucault puts it, power is everywhere and nowhere:
what from one vantage point may appear a subversive act, from
another may transpire as yet another expression of an indeterminate, *oppressive* power.

But there is a point where the two views meet. I italicised
'oppressive' because, for Foucault, the word in itself is misleading.
One should not think of the flow of power as from the top down.
On the contrary, power – as expressed through discourse – is
inherently unstable. Discourses may turn either way, either in
support, or against the status quo; for Foucault, *power* has an
irreducible duplicity (Foucault 1979: 100–01). Bakhtin's 'heteroglossia' pushes in the same direction, or it will do if we see it, not
only as a descriptive term, but as an aesthetic one. As an aesthetic
term 'heteroglossia' registers the way in which texts render visible
the ideological double-sidedness of language through the 'dialogic'
(through the destabilising techniques of juxtaposition). This is
what I, for one, find aesthetically satisfying about novels. What
effects the aesthetic may have on society at large is another, imponderable issue.

My argument, then, is that Radcliffe's texts belong within the
category of the 'aesthetically satisfying': they make power visible
in unexpected ways. Radcliffe's mature texts possess an irreducible
duplicity, one engaging both Scott's and De Sade's viewpoints. As

such they avoid the narrow categorisation 'conservative'. But they
do not do so by virtue of simply belonging to what is arguably an
inherently dialogic genre – the Gothic romance.

This takes me to my third purpose. I want to show how
Radcliffe's art develops, and in several ways: by 're-inventing' the
Gothic romance; by working through a response to the French
Revolution; and by changing internally through the invention of
more sophisticated narrative techniques.

This final purpose naturally raises the issue of intention. In my
view Radcliffe is a conscious artist; conscious in the sense that
there is a deliberation – a guiding purpose – behind her textual
modifications and changes. Whether this deliberation was ever
articulated in so many words by Radcliffe is an imponderable; the
final appeal must be made to the texts as we have them, and it is
in comparing one with another that we begin to sense the motiv-
ations and purposes of her writing. But to acquire this sense we
need to rid ourselves of the narrowly intentionalist prejudices that
have grown up round the public figure of 'Mrs Radcliffe'. The
knowledge we have of Radcliffe's life is certainly helpful for
understanding her textual apprehension of the issues of class,
power and gender; but for that knowledge to be useful we have
to separate biographical 'facts' from the myths, presuppositions
and prejudices that dogged Ann Radcliffe from the very beginning.
We need to see past – or at least include within our vision – the
figure of 'Mrs Radcliffe'.

2

The gentlewoman
and the authoress

The fair authoress kept herself almost as much incognito as the Author of *Waverley;* nothing was known of her but her name on the title page. She never appeared in public, nor mingled in private society, but kept herself apart, like the sweet bird that sings its solitary notes.

Edinburgh Review, May 1823 (McIntyre 1920: 6)

She was ashamed, (yes, ashamed) of her own talents; and was ready to sink in the earth at the bare suspicion of any one taking her for an author; her chief ambition being to be thought a lady!

Literary Gazette, 3 June 1826 (McIntyre 1920: 24)

[Had Ann Radcliffe mixed more in liberal society] she might also have divested herself of the idea, probably acquired from the early impressions of her education, and of the somewhat primitive and old-fashioned society with which she associated when young, of the incompatibility of the gentlewoman and the authoress.

Mrs Elwood (1843: II, 169)

Despite being born two hundred years later, Ann Radcliffe runs Shakespeare a close second for the distinction of being the best-known English writer with the most obscure personal history. But whereas Shakespeare's scanty biography was the product of the inattentiveness of the times, Radcliffe's was the result of deliberate policy. So successfully did she keep her private life separate from her public one that when, half a century after her death, Christina Rossetti attempted her biography, she abandoned the project for want of information. However, while the knowledge we have is meagre, it is also highly suggestive.

The bare facts are these. The only child of William Ward and Ann Oates, Ann Radcliffe was born Ann Ward on 9 July 1764, a year before the publication of the first Gothic romance, Horace

Walpole's *The Castle of Otranto*. Her parents were engaged in 'trade' and had the *déclassé* address of Holborn, but Ann Oates in particular possessed distinguished relatives, a fact underlined in Radcliffe's obituary notices. The *Annual Biography and Obituary*, conceding that the Wards were 'nearly the only persons of their two families not living in handsome, or at least easy independence', takes great pains to trace Radcliffe's respectable genealogy, mentioning such worthies as Colonel Cheselden; her maternal grandmother, Ann Oates ('the sister of Dr Samuel Jebb of Stratford, who was father of Sir Richard', who was in turn the King's surgeon); Dr Halifax, the Bishop of Gloucester; and the DeWitts, who came to England during the Civil War, settling in a 'mansion near Hull', before giving birth to a daughter 'Amelia', the 'mother of one of Mrs Radcliffe's ancestors'.

An aunt married Thomas Bentley, the partner and friend of Josiah Wedgwood, the famous potter. Although she died around the time of Ann's birth, another aunt kept house for Bentley until his second marriage in 1772. In 1769 Bentley moved to Chelsea where Ann, a favourite niece, was a frequent visitor. Bentley was reputed to be a man of wide culture. An expert in Greek and Etruscan art, he 'negotiated with Flaxman for design for the Wedgwood ware' (Tompkins 1921: 2). He had travelled widely, held liberal opinions, and published articles in the *Gentleman's Magazine* and the *Monthly Review*. Intriguingly, in one of his letters Wedgwood reproaches Bentley 'for not publishing a manuscript on female education' (McIntyre 1920: 9). Many members of the intelligentsia of the day visited Bentley at his home, including Hester Thrale, the friend of Johnson and future travel writer, historian and critic (as Mrs Piozzi); Elizabeth Montagu, the famous 'bluestocking' and author of the *Essay on the Writings and Genius of Shakespeare;* and Anna Laetitia Barbauld, editor, poet, dissenting radical intellectual, as well as future critic of Radcliffe.

Of her formal education we know little and once again have only a tantalising snippet to go on. In 1781 Sophia and Harriet Lee opened a school in Bath for 'young ladies'. The Lee sisters were also writers of note. Sophia wrote *The Recess* (1783–85), an historical novel having an important bearing on the development of the Gothic romance, while Harriet produced, in collaboration with her sister, *Canterbury Tales*, a collection of novellas that included *Kruitzner*, a minor masterpiece later adapted by Byron as his play *Werner*. The *Annual Register* for 1824 in its obituary notice of Sophia Lee says the following: 'It is to be remarked that Mrs Radcliffe (then Miss Ward), resident in Bath, and acquainted in Miss Lee's family, though too young to have appeared herself as a writer, was among the warmest admirers of *The Recess*' (McIntyre 1920: 11). The question of whether Ann Ward attended the Lee sisters' school naturally springs to mind. That her family were then resident in Bath does not present strong evidence either way.

The next definitive sighting we have of Ann is in 1787, the year she married William Radcliffe, an Oxford graduate and law student. The ceremony was also in Bath, but shortly after that they moved to London, where William embarked upon his journalistic career as proprietor and part-editor of the *English Chronicle*. The only physical description we have of Ann refers to her at around this period. It comes from the *Annual Biography and Obituary*, and was probably written by William:

> This admirable writer, whom I remember from about the time of her twentieth year, was, in her youth, of a figure exquisitely proportioned; while she resembled her father, and his brother and sister, in being low of stature. Her complexion was beautiful, as was her whole countenance, especially her eyes, eyebrows, and mouth.

T. N. Talfourd's memoir, prefaced to the posthumous *Gaston de Blondeville*, represents the other authoritative source we have for facts regarding Ann Radcliffe's life (Talfourd seems to have been closely briefed by William). According to Talfourd, Ann was strongly encouraged to write by her husband. As a young woman she had adopted the fashionable practice when travelling of recording her impressions of picturesque scenery through verbal sketches. William was duly impressed. Editorial business frequently kept him away during the evenings so Ann now had three very congenial conditions for sustained writing: privacy, quiet, and an appreciative – if somewhat limited – audience. *The Castles of Athlin and Dunbayne* appeared in 1789, two years after her marriage. *A Sicilian Romance* followed in 1790. Both books were welcomed in positive, if lukewarm, tones. *The Romance of the Forest* (1791) revealed a new maturity in Radcliffe's writing, a fact duly and appreciatively registered in the reviews. The publication of *The Mysteries of Udolpho* in 1794 established her reputation, not just in Britain, but also in Europe. In the summer of 1794 she and her husband travelled down the Rhine as far as the Swiss border, where they were denied entrance on bureaucratic grounds. The Radcliffes were by this time fatigued with European travel – part of their journey had taken them through what had recently been a war zone – and rather than pressing the matter they returned to England, where they toured the Lake District. The closest Ann Radcliffe got to the mountain scenery she had written so much about was a distant outline on the horizon. There is a certain pathos in her forlorn supposition that the English lakes as 'an exhibition of alpine grandeur, both in form and colouring . . . compose a scenery perhaps faintly rivalling that of the lakes of Geneva' (*Journey:* 378). But then her scenery drew its impact, not from the accuracy with which it depicted nature, but from her understanding that landscapes were 'archetypes' (*Journey:* 419) of human emotions, a fact soon to be rediscovered by the Lake Poets. Her travel writing was published as *A Journey Made in the Summer of 1794, Through Holland and the Western frontier of Germany, With a Return Down the Rhine: To Which Are Added Observations During a Tour to the Lakes of Lancashire and Westmoreland, and Cumberland. The Italian* was the last work published during her lifetime. It appeared in 1797.

In the absence of any personal knowledge, numerous rumours circulated as to why Radcliffe should have suddenly stopped writing. She was, after all, only thirty-three, and at the height of her fame. Some believed her sensibilities had received a mortal wound by the adverse comment meted out to *The Italian*. This is a scarcely credible theory. The worst criticism was mildly hostile. Most of the notices were positive and even when they were critical it was in the context of acknowledging Radcliffe's fictional pre-eminence. Coleridge's notice in the *Critical Review* of 1798 is typical: 'In reviewing the Mysteries of Udolpho, we hazarded an opinion, that, if a better production could appear, it must come only from the pen of Mrs. Radcliffe . . .' (Raysor 1936: 378). Coleridge goes on to say that Radcliffe struggles with the law of diminishing returns, despite some local triumphs. It is true that there was one purely hostile review, in *The Anti-Jacobin Review and Magazine*

(1801), which insinuated that Radcliffe had a foreign, and therefore sinister, sensibility (her mysteries are 'rather German than English'), but this was four years after *The Italian*, by which time Radcliffe would have had another book out, or two, if she had maintained her pace.

Others conjectured that she was so appalled by the excesses of her imitators – such as Lewis's *The Monk* – that she lost the will to write. Her obituarist and first biographer ascribe a more prosaic reason: a legacy that left her financially independent. As Talfourd put it, 'To the publication of her works, she was constrained by the force of her own genius; but nothing could tempt her to publish *herself;* or to sink for a moment the gentlewoman in the novelist' (Tompkins 1921: 7). Money allowed her to quit the embarrassing environs of the romance-writer's Grub Street, where few proper ladies were to be found.

Radcliffe spent the next quarter-century travelling at home and writing for pleasure, leaving the historical romance *Gaston de Blondeville* and the narrative poem *St Alban's Abbey* among her papers. Her seclusion during this extensive period engendered many rumours. The anonymous *Ode to Terror* said she died in 'the horrors', while other reports confirmed that the morbid exuberance of her imagination led either to her early death or to the alienation of her wits. The story that she was confined in Haddon Hall in Derbyshire at least has the merit of being resonant. Haddon is near Hardwick, which Radcliffe visited during her travels in 1794, drawn by the fallacious story that Mary Queen of Scots had been imprisoned there – a lore that had earlier inspired Sophia Lee's *The Recess*. Haddon is also close to Hathersage, a place subsequently visited by the future Gothicist Charlotte Brontë, who supposedly found her inspiration for Thornfield (with its imprisoned 'madwoman') in a nearby hall. These anecdotes do not add up to concrete evidence, but they do begin to resonate somewhat when we recall that the central, recurring motif of Radcliffe's romances is an imaginatively resourceful woman imprisoned in a decaying Gothic pile, such as Haddon was thought to be. Her fiction and life were consolidating as myth.

Ann Radcliffe died on 7 February 1823. Although the obituaries were laudatory, the old rumours of her disoriented wits resurfaced. The *Monthly Review* claimed that 'she died in a state of mental desolation not to be described' (McIntyre 1920: 19). Radcliffe had thought it indecorous for living writers publicly to correct rumours of their death or mental derangement. Ann's demise cleared the way for William to come to the defence of his wife's reputation. In response to the *Monthly Review*'s claim he gave Talfourd a statement by the family physician to append to the memoir, the gist of which was that Ann was clear-minded up until the last few days of her life, and even then what disorientation there was had physiological causes. Far from suffering from morbidity, she 'enjoyed a remarkably cheerful state of mind'. Moreover, she 'possessed a quick sensibility, as the necessary ally of her fine genius', but this quality increased rather than impaired 'the warmth of the social feelings' (McIntyre 1920: 20).

But if Radcliffe's social wits were not alienated, they were, to say the least, hypersensitive. Radcliffe's biographer in the *Annual Biography and Obituary* (almost certainly William) set out to clear up two matters which had apparently weighed heavily on Radcliffe's mind. In one, Anna Seward had confided in a letter her belief that the *Plays on the Passions* (by Joanna Baillie, but at the time anonymously published) were in fact by Radcliffe; furthermore she had heard that Radcliffe had 'owned' them. Baillie's *Plays* were a literary sensation; people wondered who the genius was. Radcliffe was mortified by the imputation that she had let out it was her. Decorum prevented her from contacting Baillie directly, once Baillie's authorship was known. Radcliffe accordingly suffered in silence for the next quarter-century. The subject, says her biographer, was 'a great one with the deceased', William obviously feeling the matter had to be cleared up before the shade of his departed wife could find final rest. In the other incident, a note was appended to one of Mrs Carter's published letters saying 'Mrs Carter had no personal acquaintance with Mrs Radcliffe'. Radcliffe was burdened by the fear that the reader would take this as implying a snub, that she, Mrs Radcliffe, was in some way unfit to be known by Mrs Carter. William once again came to the rescue of his wife's tortured shade, supplying documentary evidence that the note simply referred to an attempt by Mrs Carter to visit Radcliffe while she was out.

These 'facts' tell us a number of significant things about Ann

Radcliffe while conclusively proving practically nothing. For a start, they remind us that Radcliffe's is the *oeuvre* of a young woman; her major novels were published between the ages of 25 and 33. During these years Radcliffe was, to say the least, prolific, writing five novels – three of them of substantial length – plus a travel book. The years involved (1789–97) were historically highly significant. It was a period of upheaval, excitement and anxiety – turmoil we find registered in her romances. That her *oeuvre* was the product of a vibrant young novelist – De Sade speaks appreciatively of 'the bizarre flashes of the brilliant imagination of Radcliffe' (Sage 1990: 48) – tends to be obscured by her fusty cognomen: 'Mrs Radcliffe'.

In actual fact it was in the advertisement to the second edition of *The Romance of the Forest* that a name first appeared (her first three novels were initially published anonymously), and the name used was not 'Mrs Radcliffe'. The writer of a notice in the *Critical Review* comments: 'In the advertisement . . . she styles herself Ann Radcliffe, and we have no authority for prefixing Miss or Mrs' (1792b: 458). This is suggestive on a number of accounts. It reminds us that at that time it was thought significant for women writers to appear in print with their names unadorned with the signification of their principal relation to men. Was the bare 'Ann Radcliffe' a 'statement'? Shortly after Ann Radcliffe was to be subsumed within 'Mrs Radcliffe'. 'Mrs Radcliffe', it seems, was acutely aware of the incompatibility of (to use Mary Poovey's phrase) the proper lady and the woman writer (Poovey 1984). But for this we have to rely on William Radcliffe, the jealous guardian of Mrs Radcliffe's reputation, and the principal conduit of information about her. We are told that William encouraged Ann to write (by William through Talfourd). But by the same token it may have been William who urged her to stop, given that the school of writing with which Mrs Radcliffe was associated was now, by 1797, identified in the public mind with sanguinary and lascivious *Schauerroman* ('shudder-novels'), such as Matthew Lewis's *The Monk* (1796), Karl Grosse's *Horrid Mysteries* (1796), or W. H. Ireland's *The Abbess* (1799). Similarly, William takes great care to remove the public blots from his wife's career (such as they were). But we have only his word for it that it was she, and not himself, who was most scandalised by them.

The point here is not that we should belatedly pillory William
Radcliffe for oppressing his wife. There may have been no
oppression, only genuine, even politically correct, companionable
assistance. But that is just the point: what information we have
leans towards no firm conclusions of any kind, but is, rather,
suggestive in its indeterminacy and open-endedness. The Radcliffe
story – as it is carefully structured by William Radcliffe and
Thomas Noon Talfourd – is rich in ideological nuance, not least
because of its very managed quality.

For instance, take Ann's family background. On the one side
there is the liberal, intellectual circle of Bentley and Wedgwood,
on the other, Ann's 'superior' relatives. There is an obvious class
tension here, one exemplified in Jane Austen's novels, where it
runs through her work like a fault line. It is the conflict between
Elizabeth Bennet's aunt and uncle, engaged in trade, and Lady
Catherine; between Mrs Elton and Mr Knightley; between Catherine Morland and General Tilney; between the Wentworths and
the Elliots; between Fanny Price's socially exalted extended family,
and her socially disgraced immediate one. It is, in other words, a
tension between a middle class and an aristocracy; or, to be more
precise, between new wealth and/or a materially degraded gentry,
and a gentry who take their cue in manners and values from an
aristocracy they would join, if they could. The reports we have of
Radcliffe's desire to be thought a 'gentlewoman' suggest that her
sympathies lay with the latter, a supposition reinforced by the
genealogy of her respectable family found in the *Annual Biography
and Obituary*.

But to reiterate, this was probably written by William, and may
simply reflect his snobbish values. The issue gains in importance
when we recall the refracted, and therefore ambiguous, nature of
class representation in Radcliffe's romances. Their European
nobility and settings suggest a social world far removed from
England's. But in the later romances especially, one finds a pastoral
world of minimised class differences and liberal sensibility – the
milieu of the heroine – pitched against a decadent, proud, luxurious, lawless, rapacious, violent aristocracy. To put the matter into
perspective, if Elizabeth Bennet were to indulge her early prejudices against the likes of Lady Catherine (or General Tilney, if
she had known him) in impressionistic fantasy, while idealising

her own family background, she might very well produce the kind of contrast we find in *The Mysteries of Udolpho*, between Emily's benevolent father and the intemperate Montoni. In the biographical terms before us, we might recast the conflict as between the bourgeois liberal-humanism of Bentley's circle, with its dissenting attitudes to the established church, its support for the anti-slavery campaign, its sympathy with the American Revolution, its principled individualism, and the social snobbery manifest in William Radcliffe's genealogy. If one were to take her first biographers at face value, one would assume that 'Mrs Radcliffe' did successfully sink the 'authoress' in the 'gentlewoman', that her social vision was conservative, that criticism of her betters was the last thing in the gentlewoman's mind, and that it would be quite improper to read into her depiction of European social disharmony refracted images of tensions closer to home. But the face value offers bogus authority, and one is entitled to suppose that the writer did not give in to the proper lady – at least, not without a struggle. The writer may very well have sharpened her critical wits in the 'dissident' milieu of the Bentley household, to the proper lady's discomfort.

The story of Radcliffe's education is equally suggestive. As Mary Wollstonecraft famously complained, standards of female education of the day seemed designed to produce accomplished ornaments. The ability to play the piano, some skill in needlework, a smattering of continental languages, a modicum of polite learning – in other words enough education to make a young woman tolerable company but not enough to make her useful, knowledgeable, or so empowered as to put her on a par with men (Wollstonecraft 1985). Too much education, it was felt, would 'masculinise' woman, destroying the fascinating modesty that was the source, both of her attraction to the opposite sex, and the respect it accorded to her. Given preconceptions such as these, it seemed quite natural that women should be excluded from the public schools and Oxbridge with their Latin and Greek curricula. As the classics formed a kind of lingua franca for cultural transactions, women were, as a consequence, in this respect unvoiced and powerless.

At this point the Gothic romance interestingly impinges upon the issue. Before there was such a thing as the 'Gothic novel' there was, gathering pace sometime around mid-century, a Gothic taste, a revival of antiquarian interest. It was also a nationalist movement in that 'Gothic' designated, not just the 'Middle Ages', but the racial past that gave birth to Englishness. According to the outlook of the later eighteenth century, the Middle Ages came to an end with the death of Queen Elizabeth; Shakespeare and Spenser were 'Gothic' (i.e. English) writers uniquely expressing the national genius. Shakespeare and Spenser were not only set beside the ancients, such as Homer and Virgil, but at times, patriotically, above them. Gothic romancers, such as Clara Reeve, quickly seized the advantage offered by this cultural transvaluation, of raising the Gothic above the classic, Shakespeare above Homer (Reeve 1785). The classics were not accessible to women, but Shakespeare was; the higher his stock rose, the greater the potential for female cultural literacy and power. Moreover, given that Gothic values were also associated with chivalry, women could advance their 'Gothic' education without injuring their modesty or threatening propriety (one has to keep in mind that this argument was made before the 1790s and the appearance of the *Schauerroman*).

Given their literary interests, it is probably safe to assume that the Lee sisters established the curriculum of their school for young ladies on just such principles of 'Gothic' education, on English, Englishness, and English writers. Radcliffe's allusions and epigraphs demonstrate that she was well versed in the fashionable English pre-Romantic poets and deeply imbued with Shakespeare. Her few adverse critics attempted to cast aspersions on her education, one reviewer sneering that in *The Mysteries of Udolpho* she ignorantly had tripods suspended from the ceilings (*Spirit of the Public Journals* 1797: 227), but for the most part her critics acknowledged the purity and correctness of her style. From whom, then, did Ann receive her 'education'? Was she a student of the Lee sisters? Was Ann the beneficiary of Enlightenment notions of female education prevailing in the Bentley household? Either one would work against the received image of 'Mrs Radcliffe' as the voice of late eighteenth-century conventionality.

The ideological character of the biographical material reaches down to the levels of words, as we see from the language used to describe the conflict between the woman writer and the proper lady (as, for instance, in the epigraphs to this chapter). The conflict has a long history, but if we look at it around 1790 we can see that it expresses itself as a series of paradoxes implicit within the figure of the 'proper lady', ones bound up with the commensurate 'rise' of sensibility and the sentimental.

A proper woman was a 'modest' one, but modesty was 'providentially' designed both to stimulate and quell male sexual desire, to awaken it while keeping it within bounds. For a woman to effect modesty was simultaneously to announce and deny herself as an *object* of desire. The paradox worked from the other direction in that modesty also figured women as paradoxical *subjects* of desire. Modesty defined the 'feminine', which meant that femininity was conceived as an obliquitous state. Modesty forbade direct self-expression (by definition masculine); the female self, on the contrary, announced itself by its receptivity, its 'sensibility'. Women were conceived of as intuitive, sentimental beings who arrived at the heart of the matter sideways, through the senses. But by the same token they lacked inherent rationality; nature left woman unequipped with a brake on her senses. In such circumstances, sense is always on the verge of deteriorating into the sensual. Women were thus, simultaneously, thought of as ethereal and animal; in touch with emotional nuance perhaps, but it was a 'touch' which, by its very irrationality, could degenerate into gross physicality. Modesty, although woman's natural state, had to be nourished and cultivated – vigilantly watched – because it contained the seeds of its own destruction: sexual desire. The 'finishing school' notion of female education was based on this paradigm of 'modesty', whereby it was not women's brains that needed training, but their sexuality, an educational state of affairs deemed scandalous by Mary Wollstonecraft in her *A Vindication of the Rights of Woman* (1792).

A number of historical developments sharpened such paradoxes. During the late eighteenth century an abundance of rich mercantile daughters, together with a dearth of land-rich, money-poor upper-class bachelors, imparted new value to women as objects of marital exchange. This mismatch of supply and demand pushed up dowries. Women were associated with increasing values, but as they were monetary ones this merely underlined their status as potential commodities. In such circumstances, for a woman to prosper on the marriage market she had to be richly endowed, not only with cash, but with a tractable, modest manner and good looks. At the same time it was a period distinguished by what we now call 'the rise of bourgeois individualism', a complex of related values having its deepest roots in the very classes that attached cash rewards to their daughters.

From the point of view of women, individualism assumed its most potent and attractive expression as the cult of romantic love, a cult predicated on the dispositions of the heart, not titles and bank balances. This cult was ably supported by the fashion for sensibility. Sensibility declared a democracy of the heart, an egalitarian world of feelings where all were equal who wept before scenes of tragic benevolence, or who shuddered with delightful terror before sublime manifestations of the divine power. As such, sensibility constituted a language of equal emotional entitlements, a democracy of feeling hearts that greatly assisted women in defending their personal interests. The view that women were – by virtue of their vocation for modesty – the natural embodiments of sensibility had the further merit of empowering women to at least a relative degree. It was felt that the progress of society required the spiritual nurture of women: through their gifts of sensibility, women operated on mankind as a softening, civilising influence. This at once enhanced the position of women (compared to what it had formerly been), while putting a limit upon it: women were only effective if they remained within their own, self-effacing sphere. In other words, the state of women in 1790 was well on its way to entering that condition – prevalent from 1800 on – we now designate as 'the angel in the house'.

All this was, of course, in direct conflict with the vocation of writer, which is, after all, a fundamental act of self-assertion. Radcliffe is an obvious case in point. The collision between the woman writer and the proper lady may be put in any number of ways, each with a different edge: it is a conflict between id and super-ego, desire and conformity, rebelliousness and convention, self-expression and self-sacrifice, Ann and Mrs Radcliffe. In Radcliffe's case – at least in the case of Radcliffe the writer – we should not see these tensions as debilitating. On the contrary, such contradictions helped produce her art.

As we have seen, the 'facts' of Radcliffe's life are not, in themselves, authoritative; on the contrary, they form a context – both as we have them and as they are transmitted to us – which nudges interpretation in various directions. But biography only presents us with the broad canvas of a writer's life. I now want to turn to the scene of writing as Radcliffe encountered it in the late 1780s. It is here, in the realm of circumscribed choices, that Radcliffe's textual decisions begin to take on the character of informative particulars.

3
The aesthetic context

It would be wrong to think of Ann Radcliffe as a 'Gothic novelist' – at least, it would be if one were judging her by the critical lights of the eighteenth century. To her readers, she was a writer of romances. In eighteenth-century discussions of the 'progress' of fiction clear distinctions were made between 'romance' and 'novel', even if the terms were often deployed in inconsistent ways. For instance, one will encounter commentators using the terms *romance* and *novel* as if virtual synonyms where the totality of long prose fiction is meant, but when it comes to literary history – and nice distinctions have to be made – differences once again emerge. This is particularly true of writers themselves. Romance and novel were separate wings of the house of fiction: whether one called one's work a 'romance' or 'novel' often flagged significant differences in intention, especially given the ideological nature of the debate surrounding the decision.

The purpose of this chapter is to sketch the aesthetic context of Radcliffe's decision to enter the 'wing' of 'romance'. My contextual discussion is in three parts. The first part reviews the eighteenth-century romance/novel debate as it impinges on Radcliffe's Gothic art; the third reviews the general aesthetic background. The second part is more polemical, in that it is designed to lay to rest a long held but unhelpful view of Radcliffe's intervention in the 'development' of Gothic writing. According to this view Radcliffe's principal contribution was to marry Horace Walpole's Gothic with the novel of sensibility. There are two things wrong with this. Firstly, it implies that Radcliffe was too timid to follow in Walpole's footsteps without equipping herself with the armour of fashionable, feminine sensibility; secondly, it invites the further inference that Radcliffe's Gothic did not have an agenda of its own. The first point may contain some substance, but it is put in an entirely unhelpful way. The second I believe is simply wrong.

1. Novel/Romance

> Romances are a dangerous recreation. A few, no doubt, of the best may be friendly to good taste and good morals; but far the greater part are unskilfully written, and tend to corrupt the heart, and stimulate the passions. A habit of reading them breeds a dislike of history, and all the substantial parts of knowledge; withdraws the attention from nature, and truth; and fills the mind with extravagant thoughts, and too often with criminal propensities. I would therefore caution my young reader against them; or, if he must, for the sake of amusement, and that he may have something to say on the subject, indulge himself in this way now and then, let it be sparingly, and seldom.
>
> James Beattie, 'On Fable and Romance' (1783: 573–74)

One wonders why Beattie doesn't mention going blind while he's at it. Although Beattie's comments may strike us as faintly comical, they typify the lowly status attached to fiction during the mid to late eighteenth century. Poetry and tragic drama were the prestigious literary forms, partly for historical reasons and partly because they were the province of men. The reputation of fiction – seen as entertainment for women and children – suffered accordingly. In defending themselves writers of romances and novels often fell into fratricidal warfare. But their real aim was often not to wound each other but to impress the guardians of public morals, such as Beattie, who doubted the value of fiction no matter what its shape. Champions of romance, say, would readily concede the dangers of novel reading, dangers naturally distinct from the virtues of their particular form. I want to look further at Beattie's essay, partly for the typical hostility it displays, but mainly because its animadversions on fiction help us understand the ideological undertones of arguments deployed in the defence of romance.

In Beattie's genealogy of fiction, there never was a golden age. From the beginning story-telling was sinister. Even the 'fable' – Beattie's earliest form of fiction – is presented as a product of an inherent human 'weakness' for marvellous tales. This weakness may be utilised responsibly, or not; Christian parables of religious instruction did, *The Arabian Nights* did not.

Beattie's argument eventually brings him to 'new' and 'old' romance, which is where our interest in him begins. Old romance was the product of the Gothic societies of the Middle Ages. The Goths were distinguished by a number of positive qualities:

> The true Knight was religious, valiant, passionately fond of strange adventures, a lover of justice, a protector of the weak, a punisher of the injurious; temperate, courteous, and chaste; and zealous, and respectful, in his attentions to the fair sex. And this is the character assigned him in all those old romances and poems, that describe the adventurers of chivalry.
>
> (Beattie 1783: 549)

Unfortunately, the knight errant was also lawless and prone to indiscipline. During the feudal period a society of contending fiefdoms maintained its integrity as long as it was focused on the Crusades, but without an external, religious object Gothic society threatened to break up into anarchy. All over Europe kings began to exert the rule of law: questing knights, with their own, chivalrous agenda, were now deemed social pests (while 'false' knights, taking advantage of the concealment offered by armour, committed actual rapine). But the suppression of knight errantry was hampered by the fact that old romance, glamorising chivalry's fantastical and marvellous adventures, was then at its height. Thankfully 'the final extripation of chivalry and all its chimeras was now approaching. What laws and force could not accomplish, was brought about by the humour and satire of one writer . . . the illustrious Miguel de Cervantes'. *The History of Don Quixote* 'brought about a great revolution in the manners and literature of Europe, by banishing the wild dreams of chivalry, and reviving a taste for the simplicity of nature'. Cervantes' book represented 'an important era in the history of mankind' (Beattie, 1983: 562).

An anonymous writer in the *British Critic* provides a conventional reading of the significance of this new 'era' as it impinged on 'novel' reading:

> The fictitious histories produced in Europe followed the manners of Europe; when they delighted in chivalry, and believed in enchant-

ments, they were full of knights-errant and enchanters: when tastes grew more refined, they were formed in imitation of real life for the delineation of passions and characters, such as might combine probability with interest.

(*British Critic* 1798: 61)

Another reviewer sharpens the point: the 'more reasonable, modern novel' has succeeded the 'improbable' old romance; the novel draws its characters from 'actual observation', and presents, not just a captivating, but an 'accurate' view of 'real life' (*British Critic* 1796: 527).

Beattie's phrase for the modern novel is 'new romance', which he sees as a direct reflection of the social progress the *British Critic* refers to. He has the schools of Richardson and Fielding particularly in mind. Although he sees them vested with adult, mature virtues – more probable, more truthful – he nevertheless returns to his starting point: delight in fictitious histories is a regressive pleasure. Given the imperfect state of present affairs it behoves Beattie to take cognisance of the case of fiction; but he does so in order to expedite the process which will replace storytelling – no matter how true to nature – with history and philosophy.

The debate gives rise to three important points. The first is that despite the confusion of terms, such as Beattie's 'old' and 'new', a clear-cut distinction had emerged between novel and romance, as Clara Reeve's definitions from *The Progress of Romance* (1785) show: 'The Novel is a picture of real life and manners, and of the times in which it is written. The Romance in lofty and elevated language, describes what never happened nor is likely to happen' (Allott 1959: 47). 'Romance' looked to the past, was 'a military fable of the middle ages, a tale of wild adventure in war and love' (*Critical Review* 1796: 146). The novel, by contrast, was 'contemporary' or modern.

The second important point is that the novel/romance debate found itself entangled in notions of progress. This was partly due to the Enlightenment temper of the period, but it was also a strategy whereby writers sought to defend themselves against the kind of animus we saw typified by Beattie. This meant that writers were defensive, and being defensive they frequently attempted to steady their arguments by piling in ideological ballast.

As a case in point, here is Samuel Richardson defending the 'novel' (his 'new species of writing') by attacking 'romance':

> I thought the story, if written in an easy and natural manner ... might possibly introduce a new species of writing, that might possibly turn young people into a course of reading different from the pomp and parade of romance-writing, and dismissing the improbable and marvellous, with which novels generally abound, might tend to promote the cause of religion and virtue.
>
> (Allott 1959: 85)

Richardson's remarks come from the preface to *Clarissa*, published in 1747–48. Tobias Smollett clarifies Richardson's ideological references in his preface to *Roderick Random*, also published in 1748. Romance originally arose 'when the minds of men were debauched by the imposition of priestcraft, to the utmost pitch of credulity ...' (Allott, 1959: 43). The novel/romance debate of the 1740s was embroiled in anti-Catholicism. It was, after all, the time of the Jacobite rebellions. Romance here is implicitly linked to feudal, regressive Catholicism, the novel to English Protestantism.

Smollett's language is also inflected by the Enlightenment's self-conscious tones. The 'novel' is seen to belong to the general drift of improving modernism; in an English context, this meant a Whiggish reading of Britain, where political, philosophical and aesthetic affairs continue their improving drift. According to the critical lights of the mid-century, the novel – meaning a 'truthful' representation of contemporary manners – appeared to be one of the improving inventions of a Protestant age.

However, by the 1780s, faith in the Enlightenment project was anything but firm. The decade was haunted by a sense of social and metaphysical dislocation, a natural breeding ground for nostalgia. Progress may continue its inevitable upward march but the Middle Ages now seemed a period uncursed with the modern 'dissociation of sensibility'. The Goths with their superstitions may have been childish and credulous, but they were also steeped in faith, were simpler, closer to nature, had imaginations untrammelled by the ambiguous gifts of reason.

In this context, Richardson's and Smollett's earlier arguments against 'old romance' no longer seemed so compelling. The seminal figure here is Horace Walpole, who in his second preface to *The Castle of Otranto* sketched out a theory of fiction that would combine the best of both modes, as Clara Reeve explains in her preface to *The Old English Baron* (1778):

> [*The Castle of Otranto*] is an attempt to unite the various merits and graces of the ancient Romance and modern Novel. To attain this end, there is required a sufficient degree of the marvellous to excite attention; enough of the manners of real life to give an air of probability to the work; and enough of the pathetic to engage the heart on its behalf.
>
> (Reeve 1977: 4)

Which brings us to the third point. As a fictional type the Gothic romance comes into being during the latter half of the eighteenth century as a self-conscious intervention in an earlier debate between romance and novel. We thus have three terms with which to juggle: old romance, the novel, and 'new' or Gothic romance, which initially sets itself up as an improved version of the old.

Clara Reeve has a seminal place in the construction of this new, 'Gothic' romance, in theory and practice, through *The Progress of Romance* (1785) and *The Old English Baron* (1778). In the former she joins forces with Walpole's nationalist defence of the Gothic 'classics'; Spenser, Shakespeare and Milton. She took the theory of Walpole's new kind of romance to an extreme. Mindful of criticisms such as Beattie's, she argued that new romance should do more than combine the best of both modes: it would also remedy their failings. Modern Gothic romance would nullify the charge of improbability levelled at 'old romance' by situating superstitious impulses in a Gothic society closely observed in the manner of the 'novel'. The presence of ghosts would be justified because the people of that remote time believed in them. As this was an aspect of their manners, novelistic fidelity would be satisfied: at the same time, the reader would recognise and so dismiss superstitious belief as a weakness belonging to the infancy of the nation.

The salient charge against the novel was that as it charted the progress of love among the quality, it lifted the sights of young readers above their station, made them impatient with their lot, and by constantly dwelling on sexual desire, depraved their minds. Gothic romance would obviate this, too. For by again dwelling novelistically on the chivalrous manners of Gothic society an ideal picture would emerge of the proper relation between the sexes, one based on a due regard for feminine modesty. And although Gothic romance must necessarily represent the quality, it does so with the feudal hierarchy rigorously intact. There would be none of the novelistic tendency to erase class lines or to show the quality in familiar contact with their inferiors, as one finds in the scandalous *Pamela*.

At this point it is worth asking why women writers such as Reeve eagerly developed Walpole's intervention. A preliminary answer is that here, too, there was an ideological dimension: behind Reeve's aesthetic discussion there lies a hidden, 'feminist' agenda. In the last chapter we glanced at how the conception of 'Gothic classics' (Spenser, Shakespeare and Milton) empowered women by elevating texts written in English. Further advantages were to be secured from Beattie's typical representation of Gothic society. Beattie's attitudes are deeply ambivalent. He divides his subject into true and false knights. True knights are courteous, chivalrous, adventurous, liberty-loving, patriotic, Christian, patriarchal: false knights, hiding behind their vizars, appear to be the antithesis of all these things, except the last. At the same time as Beattie idealises the Goth, he ruefully accepts the necessity of their historical passing. Reeve internalises this schema in *The Old English Baron*, but by setting her romance during a period in which Gothic society was still vigorous, the true knight easily (and so didactically) vanquishes the false. In doing so she embraces the ideal values of the Goths.

Here it is worth attending further to what Beattie has to say on Gothic manners. He begins by drawing a comparison between the Goth and the Oriental. Among the latter, 'the condition of the female was little better than slavery',

> But the Gothick warriors were in all their expeditions attended by their wives; whom they regarded as friends and faithful counsellors, and frequently as sacred persons, by whom the gods were pleased to communicate their will to mankind. This in part accounts for the

reverence wherewith the female sex were always treated by those
conquerors...

(Beattie 1783: 527)

Beattie goes on to link 'that polite gallantry, which distinguishes our
manners' throughout Europe to these Gothic origins. He then further
develops his Goth/Oriental opposition politically. 'Warm and fruitful
countries, by promoting indolence and luxury, are favourable to the
views of tyrannical princes...' In contrast, Goths are distinguished
by 'an invincible spirit of liberty... All the Gothick institutions
were, in their purest form, favourable to liberty' (Beattie, 1783: 527).

Beattie here is, in fact, reproducing a widespread myth of the
Goth. At its core one finds the opposition between Goth/Oriental,
where the Oriental is Other (Said 1978: 198). One way of thinking
about the significance of the Other is that it represents a projection
of characteristics one fears within oneself, or, collectively, within
the 'body politic'. If so, then the figure of the Oriental signifies
English fears of desire and tyranny. The Goth, by contrast, is a
'homely' figure of national characteristics, one synonymous with
our best features. Indeed, Whig apologists in particular were eager
to link together the liberty-loving instincts of our Gothic ancestors,
the Magna Carta, the Glorious Revolution of 1688, and the constitutional monarchy, which happily divided us from our benighted,
'Oriental' neighbours (Kliger, 1952). As Edmund Burke famously
argued in his *Reflections on the Revolution in France* (1790), these
features were all of an organic piece.

The myth proved highly durable. Here is an expression of it
thirty years after Beattie's, from S. T. Coleridge's lecture on 'The
General Character of the Gothic Mind'. This is J. H. Green's – a
member of the audience – report of Coleridge's lecture:

He also enlarged upon the influence of the female character on our
education, the first impressions of our childhood being derived from
women. Amongst oriental nations, he said, the only distinction was
between lord and slave. With the antique Greeks, the will of everyone
conflicting with the will of all produced licentiousness; with the
modern descendants from the Northern stocks, both these extremes
were shut out, to reappear mixed and condensed into this principle or
temper; – submission, but with free choice, – illustrated in chivalrous
devotion to women as such, in attachment to the sovereign, &c.

(Raysor, 1936: 8)

Here Coleridge adds a new element to the familiar duality so that the Goths now become a mediating term in a triadic structure. The 'antique Greeks' are clearly a figure for democracy (a society of independent wills) and are rhetorically meant to signal the calamity of Revolutionary France, where democracy – to English eyes – had literally run riot. The Goths represent a transcendent 'medium' between the tyranny of Oriental despots and the licentiousness of the revolutionary mob. 'Submission, but with free choice' is effectively an expression of the ideology of constitutional monarchy, and as such is a patriotic assertion of the English political status quo in the face of threats from abroad, and from within.

Coleridge's formulation of the Gothic myth bears the marks of recent events, and yet it retains an essential feature present since (and long before) Beattie: the inextricable linking of the liberty-enhancing institutions of the Goths (through veneration of the sovereign) with the Goths' chivalrous devotion to women. In one respect this is another expression of the ideology of sensibility, where women are understood to have an important though peculiar sphere of influence. As Coleridge puts it in another of his Gothic lectures, maternal care and instruction are instrumental 'in forming our character, in repressing all our evil tendencies, and encouraging every good and amiable sentiment . . .' (Raysor 1936: 9). As we saw in the previous chapter, this construction of the feminine was for women an ambiguous boon, as it served both to empower women while reducing them to a passive role: it is by being an object of 'chivalrous devotion' that women work their influence.

But in another respect the Gothic myth empowered women in a quite different way, for the myth insisted upon female equality. In Gothic society, women were the 'friends and faithful counsellors' of men, their partners and equals. Here the opposition Goth/Oriental worked to the advantage of women, as it was based on a comparison of the Goth, who recognised that women had souls, with the Oriental, who did not. Furthermore it stigmatised the Oriental treatment of women as sexual objects, while turning 'companionate marriage' into an ideal.

The first Gothic 'novel' – the first self-conscious 'modern romance' – may have been by a man, but women quickly took control; and one way of understanding the interest of Clara Reeve and others is that the Gothic myth behind the romance offered women numerous political benefits. The fact that these benefits were inextricably linked with a patriotic nationalist myth was all to the good, as it presented ammunition with which to fend off male critics. The myth's conservative values – chivalry, the cult of feminine modesty, patriarchy – concealed forms of empowerment.

'Concealed' is perhaps the operative word. Ideological matters tend to be shadowy, complicated, or duplicitous. The myth of the Goth was first and foremost an ideological construction; and as the myth moved from a political device to a new type of fiction its ideological significance tended to take on a subtextual life. At first glance the meaning of the 'Goth' may be entirely obscure, but once we become familiar with the contours of the ideological conflict motivating the myth the subtextual elements become very clear indeed. This is especially true once we realise the Goth/ Oriental dualism has not just a gender, but also a class vector. For Radcliffe no less than Coleridge, the spiritual 'Goth' is a cipher for middle-class values; and by the same token 'Oriental' is a byword for aristocratic abuse and luxury. Beattie's Goth/Oriental dualism lives on in Radcliffe, but it does so as the contrast between benevolent fathers and suitors with middle-class sensibilities (founded on chivalrous respect for women), and despotic feudal lords (such as *Udolpho*'s Montoni) with their flagrant, 'Oriental' disregard of women's rights.

2. Horror/Terror

Mrs. Radcliffe was decidedly the originator of her own peculiar style of writing, which, may, perhaps, be considered as holding a sort of middle class, between the romance of chivalry and the modern tale of terror, though equally remote from both.

Mrs Elwood, *Memoirs of the Literary Ladies of England* (1843: 171)

In order to appreciate fully the merit and originality of Radcliffe's books the reader needs 'an exact knowledge of what preceded and what followed them'.

Julia Kavanagh, *English Women of Letters* (1863: I, 251)

So far we have examined the aesthetic context of Radcliffe's art in terms of the contemporary debate between romance and novel,

with Gothic romance appearing as a late, self-conscious, ideologically nuanced intervention. To reduce the issue to a phrase,
Gothic romance as a genre was fit enough for a proper lady to
dabble in, and roomy enough for a woman writer to explore. I
now want to approach the state of the 'novel' during the late
1780s (when Radcliffe was preparing to write) from the opposite
direction, from the vantage point of, say, 1800, as this will enable
us to clear up several chronological misconceptions while establishing a few more of the guiding principles of Radcliffe's Gothic.

As we saw in the first chapter, Radcliffe's critics took pains to
draw a distinction between Radcliffe and her imitators, while Scott
carefully says that Radcliffe was at the head of a school of her
own. Carefully, because his remarks allow that there might be
other schools of Gothic writing into which her imitators might
fit. Critics have subsequently adopted this division, separating
Radcliffe's 'female Gothic' from the German *Schauerroman*
(literally shudder-novel). In the first, extreme violence is only
threatened. In the second, it is delivered in spades (as good an
example as any is the scene in Lewis's *The Monk*, where Agnes
awakes in the convent crypt with the putrefying body of her
dead baby, whilst in earshot of the monk Ambrosio raping and
murdering his sister). The distinction between Radcliffe's 'school'
and the other implies that the female Gothic was bound by feminine timidity, whereas the *Schauerroman* – largely written by men
– had the courage of its generic convictions. If for no other reason,
the distinction is invidious for resting on an anachronism. As J.
M. S. Tompkins established early on (Tompkins 1921), and as
recent criticism has confirmed (Hadley 1978), with the exception
of *The Italian* (1797) and the posthumous work, Radcliffe's *oeuvre*
predates the English appearance of the *Schauerroman*. There is
even a plausible argument that the *Schauerroman* only assumed its
characteristic shape after the German consumption of Lewis's *The
Monk* (1796), itself not published until after *The Mysteries of Udolpho* (1794). It is wrong to imagine Radcliffe writing in coy opposition to the infamous but popular 'shudder-novels', for the simple
reason that such novels did not appear in English (if anywhere)
until 1794 at the earliest.

Of course, it is still possible to argue that Radcliffe's Gothic and
the *Schauerroman* shared the same agenda despite the chronological

difference, and that it required uninhibited male writers to make explicit what was only implicit in the conservative Radcliffe. Feminist critics have recently set about demolishing the basis of this prejudicial reading. They point out that male critics have taken as their epitome of the Gothic post-Radcliffean texts by male writers (such as those by James Hogg, Charles Maturin, Nathaniel Hawthorne and Herman Melville), where the central conflict is an Oedipal one betweens sons and fathers, between the 'id' and the 'ego-ideals' of church and state, between (to use William Blake's more germane terminology) Orc and Urizen. Feminist critics have countered by saying (as mentioned in the first chapter) that the female Gothic has its own agenda, one based on a daughter's search for an absent mother.

But this is only to say, with Walter Scott, that Radcliffe is at the head of a school of her own, and it is unhelpful to read her texts as failed examples of something else. As mentioned in the Introduction, it would be wrong to imagine Radcliffe performing an astounding act of literary prestidigitation – conjuring the Gothic romance out of thin air. Her literary invention was more by way of an act of 'bricolage', of assembling existing parts into something new. If Horace Walpole provided the narrative skeleton and Clara Reeve the ideological flesh, then Radcliffe contributed the aesthetic *esprit* that made the whole thing move. It was her contribution that galvanised the Gothic movement. To understand the nature of her 'school' one has to set aside the others, if only for the moment.

Shortly before the publication of the posthumous *Gaston de Blondeville*, an 'excerpt' appeared in the *New Monthly Magazine* entitled 'On the Supernatural in Poetry'. One should not discount the obvious purpose – an appetiser for the main fare – but it does seem that once again William Radcliffe has come to the defence of his wife's reputation, in this instance by judiciously leaking *Blondeville*'s intended introduction. Presented as a dialogue, the excerpt sets out the aesthetic justification of Radcliffe's art, directly tackling the sore subject of her imitators and the infamous shudder-novels. One character, 'W – ', making a case for the ghost of Hamlet's father having a greater sublimity than Banquo's, argues that

'The Union of grandeur and obscurity, which Mr. Burke describes as
a sort of tranquillity tinged with terror, and which causes the sublime,
is to be found only in Hamlet; or in scenes where circumstances of
the same kind prevail.'

'That may be,' said Mr. S – , 'and I perceive you are not one of
those who contend that obscurity does not make any part of the
sublime'.

(Radcliffe 1826: 149)

The reference is to Edmund Burke's *A Philosophical Inquiry Into
the Origin of Our Ideas of the Sublime and Beautiful* (1757), a key
aesthetic work of the period. For Burke, terror – fear of pain –
was the basis of the sublime, but it was a terror mixed with a
paradoxical delight. Ostensibly, this was because the sublime
viewer is not actually threatened – safety in the midst of danger
produces a countervailing pleasure. In his study *Sublimity in the
Novels of Ann Radcliffe*, William Ware lists the sources of the sublime mentioned by Burke and utilised by Radcliffe: in both we
encounter images of obscurity, power, privation, vastness, infinity,
difficulty and magnificence. 'Mr. S – ' in his riposte alludes to
those who took umbrage with the notion that obscurity belonged
in the list. An instance, here, would be William Blake. For Blake,
obscurity and the mystifications of codified religion amounted to
much the same thing. W – , who appears to represent Radcliffe's
views, has no time for such Jacobinical notions. He warmly
embraces the sublime value of obscurity:

'They must be men of very cold imaginations . . . with whom certainty
is more terrible than surmise. Terror and horror are so far opposite
that the first expands the soul, and awakens the faculties to a high
degree of life; the other contracts, freezes, and nearly annihilates them.
I apprehend, that neither Shakespeare nor Milton by their fictions,
nor Mr. Burke by his reasoning, anywhere looked to positive horror
as a source of the sublime, though they all agree that terror is a very
high one; and where lies the great difference between horror and
terror, but in the uncertainty and obscurity, that accompany the first,
respecting the dreaded evil?'

(Radcliffe 1826: 149–51)

Banquo's ghost appears unambiguously on stage; the ghost of
Hamlet's father, off-stage, is by contrast uncertain and obscure. Is
he a trick of the devil? A 'legitimate' shade? Or Hamlet's halluci-

nation? The very uncertainty leads the observer's imagination into awful mysteries.

But there is more at stake than which of Shakespeare's ghosts is the most sublime. Radcliffe's discrimination between 'terror and horror' virtually encodes the difference between her style of Gothic, and, say, Matthew Lewis's. His is full of 'positive horror'. Nothing is left to the imagination; all is shown. In Radcliffe very little is 'shown'; hers, rather, is an art of suggestion. Terror occurs in the minds of her characters, whereas in Lewis terror leaves its literal imprint on his characters' mutilated bodies.

Radcliffe, then, differentiates between her school of writing and that of her successors: theirs is the false sublime of horror, hers the true sublime of terror. She is also trying to educate her audience into the aesthetic rationale behind this difference. To do so she reaches back to 'On the Pleasure Derived from Objects of Terror', an influential essay by her childhood acquaintance Ann Laetitia Aikin (later known as Mrs Barbauld). Aikin had set out to explore a 'paradox of the heart': 'the apparent delight with which we dwell upon objects of pure terror' (Aikin 1773: 120). She produces two possible sources. The first is echoed by 'W –' in Radcliffe's excerpt. Aikin argues that the unknown produces the most intense experience of aesthetic terror. The agony of 'suspense' – the 'irresistible desire of satisfying curiosity' (Aikin 1773: 123) – is more painful than the emotional discomfort of observing events transpire, with the result that we avidly 'dwell upon objects of pure terror' rather than turn away, wondering.

Aikin was dissatisfied with her first solution. It was, after all, negative, a question of the lesser unpleasure predominating. Her second possible source is more positive. The first had failed to satisfy her

> with respect to the well-wrought scenes of artificial terror which are formed by a sublime and vigorous imagination ... A strange and unexpected event awakens the mind, and keeps it on the stretch; and where the agency of invisible beings is introduced, of 'forms unseen, and mightier far than we', our imagination, darting forth, explores with rapture the new world which is laid open to its view, and rejoices in the expansion of its powers. Passion and fancy co-operating elevate the soul to its highest pitch; and the pain of terror is lost in amazement.
>
> (Aikin 1773: 125)

Aikin's essay was published in 1773. Nathaniel Drake, in his *Literary Hours* of 1800, glosses and refines Aikin's aesthetic, which he sees exemplified pre-eminently in Radcliffe. Drake divides objects of terror into those whose origins bespeak supernatural agency and those with material causes. In Drake's scheme Aikin's 'well-wrought scenes of artificial terror' refer to the latter. Such terror, based on material causes, cannot 'induce that thrilling sensation of mingled astonishment, apprehension and delight' that accompanies 'those mysterious incidents which indicate the ministrations of beings mightier far than we'. Non-preternatural terror – meaning the threat of terrestrial GBH – accordingly risks producing 'horror' and 'disgust'. 'To obviate this result, it is necessary either to interpose pictoresque description, or sublime and pathetic sentiment, or so to stimulate curiosity by the artful texture of the fable, or by the uncertain and suspended fate of an interesting personage' that a compensating pleasure mitigates what would otherwise shock and appall (Drake 1800: 354). For Drake, Radcliffe excels all moderns in the delicate production of artificial terror. Never degenerating into horror, her scenes of sublimity are 'wrought up in so masterly a manner that every nerve vibrates with pity and terror' (Drake 1800: 359–60).

Aikin and Drake are helpful for the way they explicitly identify the conflicting tensions of Radcliffe's aesthetic. According to the lights of this aesthetic, obscurity – the unknown – is the most fecund source of sublime terror. By contrast, materialised violence produces 'horror'; more, by satisfying curiosity, it paradoxically undoes the very mechanism of sublimity. To avoid this one may turn to the ministrations of mightier beings, as these screw wonder to its most sublime pitch. This is unproblematic in the case of scenery as the grandeur of oceans and mountains shadows God's omnipotence, indicates a divine, invisible ministry. But in the case of supernatural beings it is problematic indeed. Pagans and possibly Catholics might believe in the preternatural, but certainly not Protestants. For them the notion of an animistic nature obscurely working God's will – through signs, portents, or interventions – is anathema. This leaves the 'material' sublime, which, as we have seen, holds palpable dangers. One resolution lies in the direction of the 'explained supernatural' – where preternatural events prove to have physical causes – another in the area of what Drake calls an 'artful texture' (Drake 1800: 354) of scenic description, narrative tension, and pathos to alleviate the horrifying shock of actual violence. As Drake argued, Radcliffe excelled in both resolutions.

3. Associationism, sensibility and travel-writing

Aikin and Drake disclose the explicit principles of Radcliffe's 'terrorist' art. But they reveal implicit ones, too. In particular, the language they use to describe aesthetic experience consistently implicates a stimulus/response model. For Aikin, a 'strange and unexpected event awakens the mind, and keeps it on the stretch' (Aikin 1773: 125); for Drake, sublime events 'wrought up' in a masterly manner, cause every nerve to vibrate 'with pity and terror' (Drake 1800: 360). This is essentially the language of 'association-ism'. As a model of mental functioning it stood to the eighteenth century much as Freud's does to our own: its assumptions were so deep-rooted as to have become second nature. Its origins lie in British empiricism, particularly in John Locke's metaphor of the *tabula rasa*. According to Locke, the mind is a blank tablet on which experience leaves its marks. The residue of these 'etches' aggregate in the mind along three possible associative paths: simi-larity, contrariety and contiguity. That is to say, one thing will remind us of another because it is similar, or because it is different, or because the residues are adjacent to each other in the memory. During the period the single most influential work on association-ism was David Hartley's *Observations on Man* (1749).

In the eighteenth century associationism underwent a number of modifications without losing its basic stimulus/response charac-ter. In particular, associationism increasingly relied on the figu-ration of the mind as a kind of vibrating machine, where the 'nerves' stood as the individual strings. These vibrations allow associations to follow their destined paths. As a psychological paradigm associationism suddenly lost its prestige around the turn of the century. Where it was a compliment to call someone 'ner-vous' in 1790 (the term suggested one was robustly yet finely strung, in the manner of a well-tuned instrument), by 1810 it had taken on its modern overtones of being fractiously 'highly-strung'. This sudden loss of prestige is obviously a complex matter, but a number of superficial aspects stand out. The mechanistic assumptions of associationism were out of tune with the more organicist ones of the 1790s and after, when all of creation was deemed, not a smoothly ticking clock, but a respiring living organism. In the public mind associationism was linked with the free-thinking Enlightenment. As the bloody events in France were increasingly seen as the logical conclusion of Voltaire's and Rousseau's intellectual meddling, to be identified with Enlightenment hubris – as David Hartley's system was – was bound to be fatal. More particularly, radical philosophers, such as William Godwin, had enthusiastically built upon associationist premises to produce what was called 'necessitarianism' – basically, the belief that, as all actions are determined (in the way that associative paths are predictable) given the proper social foundations, a Utopian super-structure will naturally follow. As necessitarians were perceived as atheistical Jacobins intent on destroying Christian and 'family' values, they tended to bring associationism into disrepute.

It would be wrong to think of associationism as a clearly articulated philosophy; it was more a set of assumptions that found different expression in different areas. In socio-political philosophy it could produce necessitarianism; in aesthetics, sensibility. Sensibility shared necessitarianism's spectacular reversal of fortune. Whereas 'sensibility' was a universal language of aesthetic response in the pre-Romantic period, by 1800 it was being systematically reviled. It, too, had been tainted by its perceived connections with the French Revolution. Its democracy of the heart now appeared dangerously radical.

Despite the democratic slur levelled against it during the reactionary 1790s, sensibility was essentially conservative in vision. It may have envisaged a democracy of the heart, but it was a democracy where some were definitely more equal than others. Equality may subsist among the fine-tuned. But not between refined instruments and those whose receptive mechanisms were coarse or loosely strung, or those whose instruments were furnished with fine 'cat-gut', but so irregularly tuned as to produce unpredictable or ungovernable emotions. The conventional figure for the first was the merchant whose coarse nerves imparted vigour, but who, owing to their obtuseness, was egocentrically oblivious to the events around him and was, as a result, aesthetically dead to the world. The typical figure for the second was the loyal servant: the natural fineness of his strings made him a congenial – and loyal – companion of his master, but their irregularity deprived him of judgement and moderation, pre-requisites for true equality. The latter figure is especially common in Radcliffe's fiction; one thinks, for instance, of Annette in *Udolpho*, or Paulo in *The Italian* (cf. Todd 1982).

When Aikin and Drake talk of the sublime as keeping the mind 'on the stretch', or of causing every nerve to vibrate 'with pity and terror', they speak the language of sensibility, and behind that, of associationism, where the reader is a detached observer waiting for her receptive mechanism – her 'nerves' – to be played upon. It is, says Drake, the aim of the writer 'to stimulate curiosity by the artful texture of the fable'. Radcliffe's art is to work upon the nerves of her reader with the utmost dexterity. As Coleridge put it, Radcliffe aims to excite curiosity by artfully 'escaping the guesses of the reader' (Raysor 1936: 356). Beyond that, it amounts to a whole economy of readerly stimulus. If Radcliffe places the reader on the rack, so that the reader's nerves, tightly strung, vibrate, she will loosen them again through a comic interlude. If through the sublime she elevates 'the soul to its highest pitch', she will bring it down again through the tranquillity of the picturesque. If she darkens her picture by drawing upon the wild landscapes of Salvator Rosa, she will lighten them again through the soft pastoral hues of Claude. The references here are primarily visual, and that is because the aesthetic paradigm is also visual: its presupposition is that the reader is an observer before whose gaze the world unfolds. One could say, with some justification, that Radcliffe's art was 'cinematic' before the fact, for her art is geared to producing in the reader a visual train of association, a series of images on the picture screen of the reader's mind. Her narrative art, to an extent, lies in producing a chain of tableaux.

At the same time that Radcliffe shows herself attuned to readerly rhythms, she implicitly flatters the reader by implying that our receptive machinery belongs in the category of the finely tuned. Such flattery contains a moral justification. It was one of the tenets of sensibility that human beings are providentially disposed to react with horror and disgust to representations of malevolence, and with empathetic pleasure to scenes of goodness. Human beings were providentially equipped with an innate moral sense, to which

fiction was admirably suited, for it was the virtue of fiction vividly
to recreate touching or revolting scenes for the reader, the first to
stir their benevolent instincts, the other to sharpen their censorious
ones. Radcliffe's artful texture subordinates itself to this moral
regime. As Clara Reeve said of the new, 'Gothic' romance, it was
to contain 'enough of the pathetic to engage the heart on its behalf'
(Reeve 1977: 4).

But behind the moral justification there was also commercial
shrewdness. Drake's list of what ought to compose an artful texture
('picturesque description, or sublime and pathetic sentiment')
reminds us of the other fashionable genre Radcliffe draws upon:
travel literature. The picturesque, the beautiful and the sublime
formed a triad of landscape description. To an extent each was
defined against the other. The beautiful was understood in terms
of smooth, undulating lines. The picturesque, by contrast, was
defined as unevenness and irregularity, as, for instance, the 'sport-
ive hedgerow run wild'. The sublime involved nature on a grand
scale, and was, in contrast with the other two, the epitome of the
rugged and untamed. The movement from the beautiful to
the sublime is in fact a movement towards a raw, primitive nature,
and away from the artifice of 'beauty'. The picturesque, which
stands somewhere in between, implies a mix of art and nature, of
human and natural presence. The picturesque trope of an ivy-clad
ruin suggests this harmonious conflict of human continuity and
nature's supremacy, of time and tide, where particular tokens pass
across the face of an unchanging archetype. Its pastoral vision
(classically summed up in the first movement of Wordsworth's
'Tintern Abbey') is in sharp contrast with the sublime scene, where
the grandeur of nature is meant to overwhelm the solitary spectator
– either the one actually depicted in the scene, or the consumer
herself.

The picturesque and the sublime were not without ideological
meaning. The picturesque was principally elaborated by William
Gilpin, whose sketch and travel books met the demands of a new,
mainly urban, leisured class. Gilpin's 'picturesque' guides served
as aesthetic instruction manuals for enriching the experience of
this novel breed of tourist. In effect, they sold a way of seeing,
one that rendered invisible the miserable plight of the inhabitants
of that landscape: irregular rags were now picturesque. Enclosures

were progressive, but it was the rural poor who paid the price. Enclosures allowed economies of scale, which boosted production, which provided a surplus, which enabled a leisured middle class to emerge from the cities furnished with the latest Gilpin. And this, in its turn, conveniently masked the human costs of their good fortune under the guise of a higher aesthetic (Barrell 1980; Bermingham 1987).

The ideological meaning of the sublime was somewhat different. An oppositional figure such as William Blake is helpful here. In 'Tyger Tyger' (from the *Songs of Experience*) Blake sets out to puncture the ideological force of the sublime. The 'experienced' speaker, in fashionable abject terror before the beast, rhetorically asks 'what hand or eye could frame your fearful symmetry?'. The whole point of this fashionable sublime is for the sublime witness to feel that he or she is a mere nothing in comparison with the awe-inspiring absent-presence of God. Blake's trick is to frame this very abasement before an inscrutable authority (registered in the rhetorical question) as an aspect of the 'fallen' condition of experience. In doing this Blake turns the fashionable sublime on its head: feeling it no longer signifies spiritual fitness, but unfitness. Blake attacks the fashionable sublime for encoding a hierarchical structure of authority. To Blake's jaundiced view, feeling the sublime emotion of intimidation looking on a mountain or a regal beast is much the same thing as having a sublime experience in response to the mystery and majesty of church and state: both represent a lamentable abdication of the task of self-becoming.

For all Blake's tilting, the sublime remained fashionable, as did the picturesque. Before Radcliffe, travel literature conceived itself as a worthy labour, akin to history, where the gradual accumulation of knowledge of men and manners of other societies would contribute to the progress of one's own. One studied landscape, because it offered a clue to the culture it sustained (Butt 1979: 244–308). This mission is residually present in Radcliffe's own travel book, where she comments on the law-abiding, orderly but ponderous Dutch, or the slovenly, fractious Germans. But on the whole she devoted herself to simple landscape description, and here she pleased her readership. In reviewing *A Journey*, the *Critical Review* tells us that the 'character of Mrs. Radcliffe's pen, for a peculiar

felicity in the descriptions of objects of fancy, has been acknowledged by universal suffrage.' The repeated proofs of her ability

> excited a public wish that she might engage in a work where the
> same talent should be necessarily employed to delineate the grandeur,
> beauty, or sublimity of real scenery . . . Such a work is now before us,
> and we have not been disappointed . . .
>
> Her language, it must be owned, is in some respects peculiar and
> unfamiliar, but it is the language that has been formed by all writers
> who have made picturesque description a study. It is partly the lan-
> guage of poetry and partly of painting; but the *feeling mind* acquiesces
> in its propriety, and its greatest beauty is that the means are pro-
> portioned to the end, that the grandeur of the thought is expressed
> with the least possible diminution, and that the enthusiasm of the
> author is in a great degree imparted to the reader. Language cannot
> do much more in a supposed state of perfection. – Her scenery is a
> grand combination of moving and fixed objects: – the effect of the
> rising or setting sun – the remote and indefinite wood – the obscure
> summit – the rocky promontory – the varied hues – the towering
> stem – the feathery branch – the heavy foliage – the spreading lawn
> – the abrupt break – the mouldering tower – the rushing torrent –
> and the many objects that are lost to a common eye, or neglected by
> an impatient one, are here brought together, enriched with successive
> images and nervous expression, and contribute to raise in the mind
> the highest emotion of perfect grandeur or sublimity.
>
> (*Critical Review* 1795b: 241–2, my italics)

the *Critical Review* explicitly links Radcliffe's popularity with her
ability to create painterly effects, her talent for finding verbal
expressions for essentially visual material, for creating spaces into
which the reader can effortlessly project herself. If this descriptive
talent ensured her success as a purveyor of vicarious 'tourism'
through her fictional jaunts through the Alps and Pyrenees, at a
time when foreign turmoil made 'grand tours' difficult, it also
remained the case that her ability to play upon the *feeling mind*
unlocked more meanings than those fashionably encoded within
the sublime and picturesque. The multidimensional nature of her
'artful texture' ensured that she was part of two processes: one
where landscape was commodified, and another whereby this process was itself rendered visible.

In his review of Matthew Lewis's *The Monk*, Coleridge echoes

Radcliffe's terror/horror distinction, but with a difference. In Drake's terms, Coleridge approves of the preternatural sublime, miracles wrought by inscrutable powers. It is in defining the opposite term, 'horror', that Coleridge introduces a difference. What particularly disgusts readers are not descriptions of *physical* but *moral* violence. Ambrosio's transformation from abstemious monk to murderous lecher is a 'moral miracle' so outlandish as to violate our sense of the natural (Raysor 1936: 372–3).

Coleridge's criticism suggests the following gloss. Lewis's horror fiction makes explicit what the 'terror' school leaves obscure: the discontinuity of the self, the notion that the self is not a unity but a set of discontinuous desires, in 'normal' circumstances held in check, but prone to a disastrous fragmentation, to 'moral miracles', when placed in extremis. Whereas the novel – stressing probability – tends to conspire with the process of naturalising the self, of making it seem a tidy unity, Gothic romance does the reverse by focusing on monstrous division.

To re-interpret Radcliffe's distinction in the light of Coleridge's review, we may say that in 'On the Supernatural in Poetry' Radcliffe is at pains to establish that her brand of romance sides with the 'novel', at least in being antithetical to the horrific *Schauerroman* with its dislocating explicitness. But to use our earlier terminology, these are the protests of the 'proper lady' anxious to establish that her works fall in with the polite tenets of fashionable literary modes, such as travel-writing. But as we shall see, the very complexity of her language and narratives tends to sketch in a position closer to Lewis's. In holding the middle ground between the romance of chivalry and the modern tale of terror, Radcliffe's novels do not fall short because they lacked courage to be explicit. It is rather that her peculiar art was steadfastly to remain on transgressive borders without crossing them, to hold the excesses of desire in sight without being explicit.

Radcliffe's preferred wing of the house of fiction accommodated her practice of this 'peculiar art'. By choosing new, Walpolian romance (recently made respectable by Clara Reeve, Charlotte Smith and Sophia Lee), Radcliffe ostensibly avoided the political controversy endemic in the novel's realistic depiction of modern manners; and yet, subtextually, there was ideological advantage to

be had from the myth of the Goth. The sublime and the picturesque codified conservative values, but by the same token these
values were now placed within the unstable realm of representation, where interpretation becomes ungovernable. Radcliffe did
not flirt with the transgressive because she was, deep down, a
subversive. Her oppositional sensibilities were rather those of the
dissenting 'middling classes'. But Radcliffe wrote at a time when
even fence-sitting could look dubious. To see why requires an
historical focus.

4
The historical context

The title of romance still invigorates our spirits. [I]t recalls ... the stories in which our youth delighted, of wandering knights, tilts, tournaments, enchanted castles, formidable giants, sea monsters, distressed damsels, tremendous fights, and impossible valour. We forget, however, that 'the days of chivalry are gone'; and that, in the *present day romance*, we must expect little other amusements than the oglio[1] of the modern novel supplies: consisting of unnatural parents, – persecuted lovers, – murders, – haunted apartments, – winding sheets, and winding stair-cases, – subterraneous passages, – lamps that are dim and perverse, and that always go out when they should not, – monasteries, – caves, – monks, tall thin, and withered, with lank abstemious cheeks, – dreams, – groans, – and spectres.
Such is the outline of *modern* romance.

The Monthly Review (1801: 203)

When has Europe been so inundated and overwhelmed with fanaticism, as in our own age? Who has not heard of the devils of Loudun? of hobgoblins, sylphs, convulsionaries, magnetists and cabbalists? What is the object of the freemasons, and those phrenetic societies called the illuminated with their plots, their secrets, their invocations, and their ridiculous rites?

Preface to *The Life of Joseph Balsamo* (1792: v–vi)

A metropolis harrowed and subdued by the perpetual terrors and dungeons of a Bastille, the horrid cemetery of the living; their only *Habeas Corpus*, either for life or death, being a *lettre de Cachet*.

David Hartley, *Argument on the French Revolution and the Means of Peace* (1794: 13)

In the last chapter we saw that in order to appreciate fully the

---

[1] An 'oglio' is a hotchpotch, a medley of heterogeneous material.

originality of Radcliffe's romances one needed 'an exact knowledge
of what preceded and what followed them' (Kavanagh 1863: I,
251). Gaining the measure of her texts' ideological meanings
requires an equally precise understanding of their historical context. Showing how Radcliffe's romances formulate a response to
the changing ideological climate will be the task of a later chapter.
The purpose of this one is to sketch in matters of historical and
ideological detail.

Ann Radcliffe's first romance, *The Castles of Athlin and Dunbayne* appeared in 1789; *The Italian*, her last during her lifetime,
in 1797. The year 1789 saw the convening of the Estates-General in
France, the beginning of the French Revolution and the fall of
the Bastille. By 1797 a lot had happened. 1792 witnessed the
September massacre, in which scores of the Republic's prisoners
were murdered in an orgy of mob violence. The King was executed
in the January of the following year. The terror reached its
height in 1793, not just in Paris but throughout the larger cities
of France. The *European Magazine* of 1794 reports that over 2,000
people had been executed in the previous month, nationwide, with
the guillotine failing to live up to its promise as the scientific
answer to execution on an industrial scale – the reporter grimly
notes that cannon and grape-shot were used instead (1794: 324).
This was the year in which Robespierre, the leader of the Jacobins
and chief pilot of the Terror, himself went under. The Directory
took control in 1794. By 1797 Napoleon had entered the world
stage. On the Continent French armies continued with their suc-
cesses. In England a central debate was whether France ought to
be opposed on principle or policy. Edmund Burke was the leading
voice of principle, arguing that the Revolution was an abomination
that ought to be expunged, and the monarchy restored. The more
cautious Pitt favoured pragmatic containment linked to the protection of British commercial interests, with Pitt naturally prevailing
(Schofield 1992). By 1797 Britain was involved in a military policy
aimed at keeping the French off balance by attacking them around
the fringes of their expanding 'empire'.

In terms of Radcliffe's romances the importance of these dates
is not the events they signal but the changing attitudes they chart.
In the early years the French Revolution and the fall of the Bastille
were greeted with great enthusiasm, but mounting violence in

France soon led to reaction in England. Burke's *Reflections on the Revolution in France* began the process of demonising radical politics, but in 1790 (the year it was published) it expressed a minority view. Burke's central tactic was to defend the British Constitution as the hallowed product of history. By implication, all those who questioned the status quo were Jacobinical meddlers. Over the next two years there raged a pamphlet war, with reactionaries arguing that, constitutionally, whatever is, is right, with radicals adopting a more or less opposite position.

George Thompson's *The Spirit of General History* (1791) illustrates some of the crucial points of ideological difference. Burke would wholeheartedly agree with Thompson's assessment of the British Constitution as the best 'which has yet been seen upon the earth'. He would also embrace Thompson's reading of the Glorious Revolution of 1688 as the seminal event in the evolution of the Constitution:

> The Revolution was the epocha [sic] of true liberty to England. The nation, represented by its parliament, obtained the bill of Rights for the people, fixed the prerogatives of the crown, so long contested; and having prescribed to the Prince of Orange the conditions on which he was to reign, chose him for king . . .
>
> (Thompson 1791: 406)

According to this conventional reading of English history, Magna Carta was, to use Hester Thrale's phrase, 'the embryonic atom' within which there grew 'to full maturity the animated aggregate since known to all the world, as the British *House of Commons*' (Piozzi 1801: I, 334). English history was seen as an organic process in which the 'tyranny of the crown' and the impulse for a 'free constitution' gradually found themselves reconciled in the perfected shape of the British constitutional monarchy, the organism gloriously bursting out of its shell in 1688.

But Burke would not have been so happy with Thompson's reading of French history, which Thompson also sees as taking a significant turn in the seventeenth century, one immeasurably for the worse. Then it received 'the form which it had till the late revolution; that is, the form of an absolute monarchy. The feudal administration disappeared. The states general ceased, and with them the shadow of liberty, which those assemblies had preserved'

(Thompson 1791: 409). This tale of two monarchies, one constitutional, the other absolute, was summed up in the popular mind
as the story of two 'castles': the Tower of London and the Bastille.
M. Linguet's *Memoirs of the Bastille*, written in 1783 and translated
into English in the same year, makes the case. Louis XVI did
indeed institute Enlightenment measures, such as banning 'putting
the question' (the 'question' was generally put with thumbscrews
or other like appliances). Yet, says Linguet, there is still the Bastille,
in itself an instrument of barbarous torture. It may spare the body,
but it racks the mind. At the whim of the King, or worse, his
minions, a *lettre de cachet* may consign a Frenchman to an 'oubli-
ette', to virtual live burial. By contrast, the Tower of London is
under the scrutiny of Parliament. On top of that, an Englishman
may depend upon habeas corpus to protect his liberties. From this
patriotic redoubt Thompson directly attacks Burke for having
given succour (in his *Reflections*) to the absolute monarchy of the
ancien régime:

> Unfeeling souls, who with competent and independent fortunes, live
> at a distance from court and its numerous agents, may think this form
> of government the most proper to obtain and promote the happiness of
> a nation, because the general tranquillity is the result; but persons
> of more sensibility, who still preserve some energy of character,
> whether they are the victims of tyranny, or only the witnesses of it, can
> see nothing in such a government but slavery, shame, the abasement of
> all virtues, and the degradation of the human race ... It must be the
> wish of every friend to the rights of mankind, that the present
> revolution in France, in favour of liberty, may triumph over all
> opposition; that an enlightened nation may make a code of equitable
> and just laws ...
>
> (Thompson 1791: 410)

Until the shock of the massacres of 1792 and the beheadings of
Marie Antoinette and Louis Capet began to shift it, intellectual
opinion in England was more exercised by the shape of the old
France than worried by the character of the new. The spectre of
royal despotism had after all been used to prime public opinion
during the recent wars with France (1756–63 and 1778–83). As a
result the French Revolution was welcomed on a broad front,
from the liberal middling classes and dissenters to out and out
radicals. *The Spirit of the Public Journals*, instituted in 1797, set

out to collect 'the most exquisite essays and *Jeux d'Esprits*' published over the previous years. Recent events had stimulated the conservative genius of satire, but the editor felt compelled to conclude that the pieces collected favoured Burke's regretful observation that 'the balance of intellect is entirely on the side of the Jacobins' (*The Spirit of the Public Journals* 1797: iv).[2] Until 1792, the tide of English intellectual opinion favoured the French 'experiment'.

Up until about 1793 opinion towards France defined itself between two poles: Burke's *Reflections* and Tom Paine's *The Rights of Man* (1791–92). The British Constitution was at the heart of the debate. As we saw, Burke regarded the Constitution as a kind of providential growth initially sown by the Magna Carta, a living organism to be blessed and left alone. According to these lights, the French Revolution was a catastrophic intervention in the French historical process, an example to be eschewed at all costs. Paine, a believer in the 'Normal yoke', saw both King John and the barons as so many banditti who had subverted our Anglo-Saxon liberties (cf. Thompson 1968; 94–5). For Paine, Magna Carta was a rogues' charter. We were, as a result, not bound by the Constitution, and were free to design a new one based on the rights of man, with France leading the way. The full Paine argument was deemed seditious – in approaching it one had to tread carefully. But in the first year or two of the decade it was still possible for the English Revolutionary Society to defend itself by arguing that it wished for France no more liberty than was granted Englishman by the Glorious Revolution.

A Journey Made in the Summer of 1794 provides the most emphatic evidence of Radcliffe's own political opinions at a juncture when the public mood had shifted sharply against the opti-

[2] But one has to be careful here. *The Spirit of the Public Journals* presents itself as an unbiased collection of the wittiest pieces from the popular press. But according to *The Anti-Jacobin Review and Magazine: or, Monthly Political and Literary Censor, The Spirit of the Public Journals* is dyed deep in Jacobinism, is indeed one of the journals the *Anti-Jacobin* has come into being in order to censor (1798, I: 324–31). Against that one has to set the satiric, wrecking tactics of *The Anti-Jacobin*, which included so confusing the issue no middle, liberal position would be possible. And the main device here was to accuse every other journal of rank radicalism irrespective of their actual politics.

mism of 1791 and 1792. In Kendal she visited a monument to the Glorious Revolution of 1688:

> At a time, when the memory of that revolution is reviled, and the praises of liberty itself endeavoured to be suppressed by the artifice of imputing to it the crimes of anarchy, it was impossible to omit any act of veneration to the blessings of this event.
>
> (Radcliffe 1795: 389)

It was a brave view her uncle Bentley would have heartily endorsed. By 1794 the reaction against French Revolutionary atrocities had reached a fever pitch. The hopeful mood of 1791 had turned very sour indeed. Habeas corpus was suspended; in 1794 the radical intellectuals John Thelwall and Horne Tooke (plus sundry others) were tried for high treason (Thompson 1968: 20–2). This 'show trial' failed in its ostensible intent – gaining convictions – but it succeeded in creating a repressive atmosphere in which radical intellectuals found it difficult to survive (McCalman 1993). Citizens could find themselves in sudden jeopardy. John Frost, an attorney, in 1793 was overheard to say that 'he was for equality, and saw no reason why any man should not be upon a footing with another; that it was every man's birthright; and that he was for no kings' (*Critical Review* 1795: 107). For uttering his seditious words Frost was imprisoned for six months, pilloried, bound over for good behaviour for five years at the risk of a £500 bond, and struck off the role of attornies. It hardly helped to know that Frost was a noted Jacobin who had served as an English delegate to the French convention, and that the charges were in fact fabricated (Thompson 1968: 124).

Although published in 1801 Hester Thrale's sketch accurately reflects the overheated, mid-decade view of revolutionary France:

> Contagious phrenzy seemed to seize mankind ... Infants of three years old were taught *literally* to suck their fellow-creature's blood, – ladies wore little guillotines as ornaments ... members of the political assembly leaped from their seats, and danced the carmoghole, like frantick bacchanals, their partners dressed in priest's vestments, and their musicians habits like satyrs ... Our own fools here in England, sung plant, plant the tree, the glorious tree, 'midst blood and bones and slaughter.
>
> (Piozzi 1801: II, 511)

The public mood was now, to say the least, paranoid. Conspiracy theories proliferated. One of the more sinister was that an international network of Freemasons, styling themselves the 'Illuminati', having formed cells throughout Europe, were busily fomenting bloody revolution. *A Letter to the Reverend John Erskine, D.D., One of the Ministers of Edinburgh: On the Dangerous Tendency of his Late Sketches of Church-History: By His Counternancing The Authors, and Promoting the Designs, of the Infamous Sect of the Illuminati* (1798) is a typical pamphlet of the period. We hear of a deeply suspect Nicholai from Berlin: 'After having been successively free-mason, Rosycrucian, Deist, Materialist, and Atheist, Nicholai has finally distinguished himself as chief of a sect, whose diabolical plots and execrable mysteries must make every honest mind thrill with horror' (*Letter*: 6). Hester Thrale joins in the task of finding scapegoats in foreign free-thinkers. She tells us that the Cardinal de Bernis

> dreaded and justly the effects of Jacobinism; he knew that clubs existed throughout Europe, of men afterwards known by name of Jacobins: when they obtained in Paris an old convent belonging to that order for their meeting-place; they were now called Encyclopedists, Philsopher-Adepts, &. *Illuminati* of different shapes appeared, and nought was seen in Germany or France at least, but by the red glare of their Asphaltick torches.
>
> (Piozzi 1801: II, 496)

According to this radical demonology, liberty and libertinism were virtually the same thing. To be a free-thinker was also to profess free love and anarchy. According to the anti-Illuminist novel *Horrid Mysteries*, by Karl Grosse (1796), it was a favourite tactic of Deistical Masons to debauch their victim, hardening his heart through promiscuous sex, an indifference to family values being an obvious preparation for the terroristic job of levelling church and state. Needless to say, such scaremongering had a salutary effect on English Freemasons, who surfaced, protesting their innocence against such charges as those levelled by Thrale: 'Our London Corresponding Societies saw not so far, *Free-Mason's Hall*, the proper scene for such debates, resounded with seditious blasphemies . . .' (Piozzi 1801: II, 508).

Given the political hysteria, Radcliffe's comments on the Kendal monument stand out as a brave defence of bourgeois freedoms, one bringing to mind her dissenting ancestry.

> We are met to thank God for that event in this country to which the name of the Revolution has been given; and which, for more than a century, it has been usual for the friends of freedom, and more especially Protestant Dissenters, under the title of the Revolution Society, to celebrate with expressions of joy and exultation.
>
> (Price 1790: 31)

These words by Richard Price were provocative in 1790. Radcliffe's cool reaffirmation of Price's dissenting principles in 1795 may be taken as an index of deep political belief.

In retrospect it is easy to see the belief that Illuminists lurked under beds as so much reactionary witch-hunting. But to contemporaries the existence of Illuminist sects was further evidence that Europe was 'inundated and overwhelmed with fanaticism' (*Balsamo*: v). Peter Will – the translator of Cajetan Tschink's anti-Illuminist novel *The Victim of Magical Delusion* (1795) – in his preface cites the case of Richard Brothers as proof that in 'introducing the present work to the English Public' he does not join battle 'with a phantom of his own imagination' (Tschink 1795: vi). Public fanaticism was real enough: witness Richard Brothers, the self-styled prophet. The title of Brothers' book is instructive in itself:

> *A Revealed Knowledge of the Prophecies and Times Particularly of the present Time, the present War, and the Prophecy now fulfilling. The year of the World 5913. Book the Second. Containing, with other great and remarkable Things, not revealed to any other Person on earth, the sudden and perpetual Fall of the Turkish, German, and Russian Empires. Wrote under the Direction of the Lord God, and published by his sacred Command: it being a second sign of Warning for the benefit of all Nations. By the Man that will be revealed to the Hebrews as their Prince and Prophet.*

The *Critical Review* lists Brothers' pretensions:

> the *nephew of the God almighty*, the man who is to be revealed to the Jews as a second Messiah to attend them to their own country, and who is to supercede our own monarch, and indeed all the kings of the earth. It is owing, it seems, to *his* intercession that this wicked city of London was not destroyed two years ago.
>
> (1795a: 458)

By 1795 millenarian sects abounded. The *Critical Review*'s notice of an anonymous pamphlet offers a possible explanation. The author of the work 'appears to have been once pleased with the French Revolution; but now considers it a *visitation from God* upon account of the *sins of nations* . . .' (*Critical Review* 1795a: 223). That is, as radical hopes for terrestrial solutions to despotism were washed away by French blood, so supernatural ones bred in their place. One has to be careful here, however, for as the reviews suspiciously attest, an apparent method lurks within the prophetical madness. Given that repression now gripped the nation, were radicals disguising their rational hopes as irrational visions, maintaining a public voice through 'code'? Even if this were so, it still does not explain the enthusiasm for Brothers, which was widespread enough to reduce one reviewer to despair. It was 'a humiliating consideration for those who wish to feel proud of their country, or of human nature' (*Critical Review* 1795a: 459).

The fact that Revolutionary France appeared to be – and styled itself as – the acme of modernity increased English perceptions of contemporary dislocation. As Hester Thrale sarcastically put it, alluding to the French mania for scientific flight, the French republic was 'gazed at by Europe as an air-balloon' (Piozzi 1801: II, 504). They were, said Burke, acidly, 'aeronauts'. The implication here was that the Jacobins were Faustian meddlers piloting the ship of state they knew not whither. The Republic obviously thought otherwise. In order to consolidate its identity the new state sponsored 'republican' exhibitions on a grand scale, largely drawing on a Graeco-Roman semiology for political style and a 'futuristic' one for architecture. The purpose of both was to delineate the face of modernity (Schama 1989: 169–74).

In some respects England and France were indeed 'modern', technological societies. The 'information revolution' – the speedy dissemination of text and images – had already begun. In both England and France pamphlets and illustrated tracts appeared with bewildering rapidity. Books, in particular, were produced with a speed impressive even by current standards. For instance, the French Protestant Jean-Jacques Calet's history of his imprisonment in the Bastille, together with a bogus account of its fall in July, hit the bookstands in an English translation within three months (at most) of its original French publication date. In it, Calet contrasts the medieval, Gothic horror of the Bastille, with its secret dungeons and crypts where men were capriciously confined and tortured, with modern, enlightened England, which was 'Blessed in its climate, in its productions, in its liberty, religion and laws: blessed in its inhabitants, in its constitution and king' (Calet 1789: 60).

Those who praised the British Constitution echoed this language of unique blessings, of unrivalled contentment and liberty. But one did not have to look very far beneath this gloss of a happy modernised state to discover a brutal reality. Here the propaganda was somewhat deflated. The *European Magazine* of 1788, under its regular feature, 'Executions', provides a startling vignette of the casual ordinariness of English state violence just before the French Revolution:

> The three following malefactors, viz. Richard Carrol, a blind man, for breaking open the house of John Short, in the parish of St. Botolph, Aldgate, and stealing a quantity of wearing apparel, &. George Roberts, for assaulting Benjamin Morgan on the highway near Finchley, and robbing him of one guinea and some silver; and Thomas Kennedy, for stealing a quantity of silver buckles, plate, jewels, and other goods, to the amount of £100 in the dwelling-house of Richard King, where he was shopman; were brought out of Newgate, and put into a cart, which drew them under a temporary gallows fixed in the middle of the Old Bailey opposite Newgate, when they were immediately tied up and hanged.
>
> (*European Magazine* 1788: 137)

The visually challenged Richard Carrol may indeed have been a hardened clothes-burglar. Then again, he may have been trying to stay warm.

We saw how Linguet identified a paradox in Louis XVI's position, at once banning torture in keeping with Enlightenment principles yet retaining other instruments of 'medieval oppression'. In 1789, England was a similar, paradoxical mix, a society that ideologically looked both ways, forwards towards greater 'enlightenment', as well as backwards to its feudal past (Punter 1980). Habeas corpus may have given England the advantage over 'medieval' France, but England, too, had its expressions of 'feudal' violence. As the Revolution wore on, and as France, the modern, and fanaticism were increasingly seen as the same thing, so the English 'paradoxical mix' intensified into something like schizophrenia. By mid-decade – with habeas corpus itself suspended – the serene, Whiggish certainties of England's blessed history were shattered, even as they were loudly insisted upon. The public mood – looking both ways at once – had become deeply confused. As the reactionary literature had it, it was an 'age' of fanaticism and 'convulsionaries', credulity and violence. It was also a period when the past and the future – remnants of medievalism and harbingers of industrialisation – confusingly overlapped.

What, then, was the ideological meaning of Gothic during this period of upheaval? The constitutional debate that raged during the first years of the decade is once again a helpful place to begin, as it cues us into the political overtones of the word 'Gothic'. In his *Reflections* Burke turned the history of the Constitution into a kind of Gothic romance – an 'old romance' in Beattie's terms – one idealising the Constitution's cultural origins. Radicals attacked precisely here. Just as the Bastille was a French touchstone for feudalism, an icon denoting the unjust survival of aristocratic prerogatives into the present, so the British Constitution was a feudal 'mansion of idolatry' for the radical left. Thomas Christie attempts to undermine the effect of Burke's rhetorical support for the Constitution's mystical perfections:

> As the apologist of Ancient prejudice, he is without a rival ... But what avail his tuneful periods, that only cheat us into error and deception? What avail his brilliant colours, that only varnish the deformity of folly and oppression. With majesty and grace ... he conducts us to the Temple of Superstition, and the magic of his language soothes our hearts into holy reverence and sacred awe. But when we enter the consecrated portal, and behold a miserable deformed gothic idol ... set up as a god for our adoration ... we turn with disgust from the false splendor of the mansion of Idolatry.
>
> (Christie 1791: 5)

For English radicals, the British Constitution (as construed by Burke) was a 'gothic idol', a verbal Bastille, one concealing the oppressive realities of English life. One can gauge the official sensitivities towards criticisms of 'things as they are' by the fact that in 1789 an opera conflating the stories of the fall of the Bastille and the man in the iron mask was censored: 'when it came to the Licenser, every part of the piece that bore immediate resemblance to late popular events in Paris was from political considerations forbidden' (*European Magazine* 1789: 379).

The debate about the 'Gothic' origins of the Constitution – itself a debate about 'Englishness' – hinged on the role of the Normans. One anonymous contribution of 1791 makes a stiff defence of the British Constitution against Jacobinical calumnies, but in a way that signals liberal sympathies. The writer sees political history developing between two poles: royal despotism and popular freedom (government through free consent of the people). The Normans tended to despotism: only under the 'Saxon princes' and 'the Revolution of 1688' have we enjoyed 'any settled state of constitutional liberty' (*Critical Review* 1792: 166). This position is liberal because it demystifies the authority of the Crown: there is no authenticating continuity in Hanoverian rule, only periods when the people have been able to assert themselves against the inherently oppressive monarch. By contrast, Richard Warner two years earlier concluded that 'although the Saxons might have formed the *basis* of the edifice' of English traditionary law, 'yet the greatest part of the *superstructure* was the work of the Norman artists' (Warner 1789: xxxiii). Although Warner appears to adopt a studied neutrality, his reading of the Saxons as Goths who brought their ancient customs – the foundations of ours – from the woods of Germany moves him closer to Burke's conservative position of the Constitution as the product of organic accretion. His positive view of the Norman contribution is merely icing on a Tory cake.

It was on the subject of the aristocracy that the issue really began to bite. For example, David Hartley, writing in 1794 in belated support of the Revolution, represents the French aristocracy in the following way (note, too, the echoes of Radcliffe's *Romance of the Forest*):

> Feudal superiorities, with monopolizing and all-grasping entails, possessed by an oppressive nobility, entrenched within their own impregnable castles and forest laws; and insolently exempt from the common burdens of the state, in proportion to the extent of those feudal and territorial monopolies.
>
> (Hartley 1794: 11–12)

'Entails' refers to the legal practice of ensuring that estates in their entirety descend to the next lineal male heir (it is for this reason that the all-daughter Bennet family are in such distress in *Pride and Prejudice*). Entails kept aristocratic families strong and powerful. The Marquis de Montalt in *The Romance of the Forest*, lording it over his forested domains, is just such a feudal baron.

But as a writer in the *Critical Review* acknowledged two years earlier, 'manorial rights' was, in the English context, a touchy subject. The question was 'whether it would be just or even popular in England to abolish all prerogatives of lords of the manor, the remains of a Gothic legislation' (*Critical Review* 1792a: 443). For Burke the answer would have been that it was unquestionably unjust to abolish ancient privileges, for such Gothic 'remains' were the very source of English liberties. But for others, of a more radical disposition, English aristocrats – with their manorial rights – were no different from French ones: they enjoyed a life of 'uninterrupted indolence', their privileges equipping them with 'the means of commanding every gratification of a luxurious and vitiated fancy' (*Critical Review* 1798: 117).

Where, then, did the Gothic romance stand regarding the ideological meaning of 'Gothic'? There is no set answer to this for the basic reason that the figure of the Goth is ideologically overdetermined: one encounters a number of conflicting positions crowding around it. Given the radical 'take' on the Gothic mythology as so much Establishment obscurantism, to present images of an ideal chivalric society was to adopt a 'reactionary' position. As one writer put it, chivalry, late the laughing stock of Europe, was thankfully popular again: it gave tone to 'the love sick whine of modern romances' (*British Critic* 1796: 448). Moreover, by mid-decade, French fashions had given Gothic imagery a patriotic éclat by virtue of being the antithesis of a French republican style drawing upon the iconography of the 'ancient' republics of Greece and Rome. Helen Maria Williams reported that 'Stately silken beds, massy sophas, worked tapestry, and gilt ornaments, are thrown aside as rude Gothic magnificence, and every couch resembles that of Pericles, every chair that of Cicero' (*British Critic* 1796: 25).

But Gothic romances also teamed with representations of the dark side of chivalry, with rapacious counts and plundering barons.

To equate these with their French counterparts signalled liberal sympathies; to invite comparisons with their English ones would certainly have been deemed seditious by mid-decade, if provable. But matters were not as clear-cut as that, as we can see by referring to the prison literature of the Bastille. The Bastille was typically figured as an instrument of Gothic live burial – it was a 'cemetery of the living'. In Gothic romances representations of institutionalised oppression, such as the Inquisition, resonate with the Bastille imagery generated by the prison literature. To represent the Bastille in such a way that it invoked the imagery of a Gothic dungeon, or vice versa, would have been unexceptionable in 1788: it would simply have endorsed Calet's flattering contrast between the Enlightened Tower of London and the feudal – French – Bastille. By 1792 such a representation would have acquired a seditious edge: it could be read as implicit support for the Revolution, for it was, after all, the Jacobins' own reading of the Bastille (Schama 1989: 410). By 1797 it would be idiosyncratic. The prisons of the Terror had by this time erased the image of the Bastille in the European mind, replacing it with the image of another kind of nightmarish enclosure. In Germany, in particular, the claustrophobic spaces of torture and confusion were now the Jacobinical cells of the Illuminati, often figured as crypts or caves. To persist with Inquisitional imagery under the circumstances (as Radcliffe did in *The Italian*) could be construed as die-hard radicalism, given that anti-Catholic attacks had been a mainstay of Jacobinical propaganda.

Except that the prison literature of the Bastille adds another level. Much of it was produced by Huguenots, French Protestants who explicitly equated the abuses of the French monarchy with the absolute power of the Catholic church: the Bastille and the Inquisition were, for the Protestant imagination, virtually the same thing. To dwell on the horrors of the Inquisition in 1797 could thus be read as a patriotic assault on Catholicism, and in comparison with the 'Illuminist' Gothic novels, as a ladylike alternative to matters current and political.

But only if the reader was determined to see it that way. Gothic texts of the 1790s in a certain respect resemble those visual puzzles where, for instance, a picture looked at in one manner produces a vase, in another, two faces in profile. Representations of profligate

European aristocrats or Inquisitional dungeons could be seen as patriotic British attacks on the lamentable state of manners and society across the channel; or they could be seen as coded assaults on aristocracy and institutional despotism everywhere. This last way of 'seeing' would be sharpened by a latent irony: that a form that had initially sought ideological protection by wrapping itself in the Whig myth of the Goth – where ideal aspects of Gothic society were seen as coextensive with the blessings of the present – should now dwell, almost exclusively, on feudal society's disastrous failures. This irony moved the Gothic romance perilously close to the position advanced by the radicals in their critique of Burke.

Representations of the Bastille or the Inquisition as images of institutional despotism had a further, 'radical' resonance, as we can see here in a hostile review of a feminist tract entitled *An Appeal to the Men of Great Britain, in Behalf of Women*. The reviewer complains that radicals attribute current miseries, not to their real cause – 'the wickedness and mischievous passions of human nature' – but to 'the *incorrect organization* of society, and the abuses of established institutions'. For them, 'whatever is, is wrong'. The unfortunate result of this radical poison is that women see men as 'her tyrant and superior; that odious subjection to his powers is the cause of all her misery' (*British Critic* 1799: 206). In 1790s Gothic romances, dungeons of a castle/Bastille or of the Inquisition are typically presided over by a single, male, 'tyrant' and 'superior'. In their duplicitous way, these texts leave it open whether such monsters are the product of human nature's 'mischievous passions' or whether they are the result of the '*incorrect organization* of society'. The conservative and radical views are left in unstable irresolution.

The first epigraph with which I began this chapter nicely sums up the fate of Gothic romance during the 1790s. The reviewer first lists the features of romance, as it was supposed to be, and then enumerates them as they actually are. The review is shrewder that it may at first seem; according to it, the difference hinges on the fact that 'chivalry is dead'. This is, in fact, a quotation of one of the most influential, or (depending on one's politics) infamous passages from Burke's *Reflections* (Burke 1910: 73). Thomas Paine's *The Rights of Man* pays special, critical, attention to the phrase (Foot and Kramnick 1987: 211), as does Wollstonecraft (1790: 61).

Burke blames the outrages performed against the queen (by a mob of women) on the absence of chivalry in revolutionary France, the implication being that the flame still lives in England, one that lights up our civil and constitutional decencies (an implication vigorously attacked by Paine). In quoting Burke the reviewer is registering that the ideal shape of Gothic romance – as evinced by Clara Reeve in both her theory and practice – was fundamentally shattered by the shock of contemporary events. To write a Gothic romance after 1789 was very different from writing one before. And as the reviewer indicates, what emerges from the aftermath is dystopic: innocent enchantments have turned to nightmares. Gothic romances echo the cultural convulsions that increasingly racked the decade.

5

The early works:
The Castles of Athlin and Dunbayne
and *A Sicilian Romance*

Mrs. Radcliffe's 'enchantments drear', and mouldering castles, derived part of their interest, no doubt, from the supposed tottering state of all old structures at the time . . .

William Hazlitt (1907: 161)

1. *The Castles of Athlin and Dunbayne*

In her first two romances Ann Radcliffe was learning her art. This is especially true of *The Castles of Athlin and Dunbayne* (1789), which in comparison with her later works is not just short, but 'thin'. The 'artful texture', praised by Nathan Drake, is only discoverable in embryonic form, as are Radcliffe's famous techniques for delaying rational explanations. Such delays work upon the reader's expectations, but Radcliffe's mature romances work their enchantment through more profound devices than simple uncertainty. They have, for their foundations, narrative structures capable of bearing numerous complex meanings. These structures are only partly formed in *The Castles of Athlin and Dunbayne*. In looking at Radcliffe's first romance I want to examine what it is she later abandons, and what she develops, as these choices and changes key us into her dominant themes.

The plot of her first romance is comparatively simple. The castles of the title refer to the ancestral seats of two families in feudal Scotland. The hero and heroine of the noble houses of Athlin are Mary and Osbert; both are on the verge of embarking on their adult lives, Mary as wife, Osbert as the Earl of Athlin. We learn that their father was murdered in a cowardly ambush by Malcolm, the wicked lord of Dunbayne. With the forces of

Athlin routed, Osbert and Mary live a retrenched life in the castle
with their mother, Matilda, plus sundry retainers. Osbert is torn
by two conflicting passions: the desire to revenge himself upon
Malcolm and sentimental compassion for his mother and sister.
Meanwhile, Mary and Matilda fall prey to melancholy as they fear
they shall lose not just the father, but the son.

It is on this scene that the story opens. The plot thickens with
the addition of Alleyn, a 'noble' young peasant who crucially assists
Osbert in his campaign to destroy Malcolm. Mary and Alleyn fall
in love, creating tension within the family. Osbert and Matilda are
sensible of the services Alleyn has rendered the house of Athlin,
but through the 'darkness of prejudice and ancient pride' (*CAD*:
269) they reject out of hand a family alliance with a peasant.
Mary's conflict is somewhat different. Love has overpowered her
prejudices, but as a dutiful daughter she refuses to bring shame
upon her family. The brother's patriarchal 'no' is a prohibition she
is unable to transgress, even in the extreme of passion.

The complication is untied in a predictable way. While imprisoned in Dunbayne Osbert discovers a secret panel opening into
chambers occupied by two fellow prisoners, the Baroness Malcolm
and her beautiful daughter, Laura. The Baroness, it transpires, is
Malcolm's sister-in-law. She and her daughter have been imprisoned in Malcolm's castle for eighteen years, ever since the death
of the Baroness's husband on his return from a visit to her ancestral
estates in Switzerland. In a paroxysm of greed Malcolm confiscates
the Baroness's titles and revenues, protecting his claims by 'burying
alive' the Baroness and her daughter deep within Dunbayne, and
by dispatching the male heir. Foolishly, he does this by putting
the child out for adoption among nearby peasants. The missing
heir is naturally 'Alleyn', a truth disclosed by Malcolm in a death-
bed repentence. With Malcolm gone, and Alleyn restored, the way
is clear for a double wedding (Mary and Alleyn, Osbert and
Laura), a wedding which not only restores order, but which binds
together the formerly antagonistic houses with indissoluble ties of
kinship and property.

The trajectory of the plot – as we can see – is towards the
death of the usurping Malcolm, and the recognition of the true
heir, Alleyn. But this neat arc is interrupted by another story
clumsily tucked into the text. The Count Santmorin, a relative of

the Baroness, comes from Switzerland to investigate the peculiarities of her financial affairs and is coincidentally shipwrecked off the coast near Athlin. Rescued by Osbert, the Count contracts a passion for Mary. Although Osbert and Matilda strongly support his suit, they respect Mary's right to choose – at least, to the extent of respecting her right to say 'no'. After Malcolm's death, when all should be at peace, and on the day of Osbert's and Laura's wedding, Mary is mysteriously abducted – by the disappointed Count, as it turns out. Alleyn followed by Osbert, comes to the rescue in the nick of time.

The episode has a 'tacked on' feel. In her later work such necessary stories will be interpolated as inset tales, as narratives of, or by, subsidiary characters. Such stories are 'necessary' because they enforce important contrasts, here, between Santmorin's and Malcolm's courtship of Mary. Malcolm's is of course a travesty of 'courtship', of the mechanisms of the duties of alliance, of marriages arranged for dynastic purposes. Malcolm displays Osbert's enchained body from the parapets, threatening his instant death if Mary is not delivered to him for marriage. Twin lusts spur Malcolm on: to possess Mary's body, and then Osbert's mind. Malcolm sadistically envisages Osbert 'retiring in an anguish more poignant than that of death' (*CAD*: 115) from the scene of his father's murderer enjoying the body of his sister. Mary decides to sacrifice herself to save Osbert, in her mind's eye significantly seeing herself 'entombed' (*CAD*: 105) in the arms of Malcolm.

Santmorin's courtship occupies a completely different register, that of sentimental love. The juxtaposition of the two stories subverts this difference. In abducting Mary, the man of sensibility, Santmorin, has become like Malcolm. This is partly a comment on male rapacity (in which light differences in courtship styles are delusional); but more importantly, Mary's language of submission takes on a new meaning. In preparing to sacrifice herself for Osbert Mary puts her fortunes at the disposal of her brother, preparing to 'entomb' herself in order to free Osbert from his chains. The episode provides an exaggerated representation of the kind of dynastic pressures placed on women in the interests of primogeniture; the enchained Osbert is, as it were, a nightmare version of the emotional blackmail endured by Clarissa when she is urged to marry the dreadful Mr Solmes in the interest of her brothers. Beneath the velvet glove of Osbert's sentimental toleration of Mary's refusal of Santmorin lies the iron fist of social reality. As later in Radcliffe, 'parallelism' is used to undermine differences between the sentimental and its opposites.

Radcliffe's plot structures change radically after *The Castles of Athlin and Dunbayne*. Perhaps the most notable thing she abandons is the Beattie/Reeve story-line. As we saw in Chapter 3, in *The Old English Baron* (1777) Clara Reeve adopted James Beattie's split between the ideal Goth and his dark other as a narrative principle. As the 'ideal' won, so did conservative, chivalric values prevail. In Reeve, too, the struggle between ideal and wicked Goths is resolved through a noble 'foundling' who has his usurped rights restored; restored, moreover, by providence. Here plot and divine order coincide. And so it is in *The Castles of Athlin and Dunbayne*. Osbert makes the case at the denouement. He is describing the upshot of Alleyn's noble pursuit of virtue: 'It is now seen, that those virtues which stimulated him to prosecute for another the cause of justice, mysteriously urged him to the recovery of his rights' (*CAD*: 280). The machinations of the plot are also the machinations of a divine power working to establish a 'throne of Justice' (*CAD*: 280).

Radcliffe here comes close to Reeve's position of identifying the supernatural with providence, where the mysterious powers we do not understand are God's. This is, of course, an intensely conservative vision. As a form of romance it looks back to (for instance) Shakespeare's late plays, where, typically, noble children are lost or usurped. Despite their rustic environments, the 'class' of noble foundlings naturally shows. After several providential interventions, the proper social order is restored, and the tale ends in harmonious marriage.

In her later works Radcliffe moves decisively away from the plotlines of conservative romance, with their providential closures. In *The Romance of the Forest* and *The Italian* we do have the plot of the noble foundling whose rights and property are restored, but by making the foundling female (Adeline in *Romance*, Ellena in *The Italian*) Radcliffe alters the plotline's centre of gravity. As we shall see, what is installed is not glorified feudalism but an order based on the progressive promises of female sensibility. Here the bourgeois values of individualism and 'companionate marriage' triumph over the prejudices and vices of a passing aristocratic, patriarchal regime.

Of all Radcliffe's texts her first is closest to Reeve's; but even here one finds destabilising nuances. It is a tenet of conservative romance that class differences are divinely sanctioned. *The Old English Baron* does not challenge this tenet, but *The Castles of Athlin and Dunbayne* does. The text is shot through with the language of meritocracy. Osbert tries to think his way through to accepting the 'peasant' Alleyn: 'he wished to reward the services and the noble spirit of the youth, with the virtues of Mary; but the authority of early prejudice silenced the grateful impulse, and swept from his heart the *characters* of truth' [my italics] (*CAD*: 217). What these *characters* signify is decidedly uncertain. They could refer to the marks of Alleyn's nobility, meaning Osbert intuitively recognises (but only intuitively) the truth of Alleyn's noble class. Or they could signify the reverse, that class differences are unreal, something the unreconstructed Goth Osbert is incapable of understanding. This ambiguity – typical of the later Radcliffe – is not the only dissonant note, for the language of 'equitable' government also anachronistically creeps into the romance. This contemporary inflection invites the reader to associate Malcolm's despotism with the abused, Gothic prerogatives of a present aristocracy.

Perhaps the most significant change made by Radcliffe concerns the narrative structure of present mother/absent father. In the next four romances we have the reverse pattern: present father/absent mother. This proved a more productive structure, for three reasons. An absent mother is more suggestive. An actual mother presents a fixed image of cultural identity; a missing one provides scope for redefinition, for a plurality of meanings and shades. Secondly, and by the same token, a present father provides a fixed set of cultural values; as the daughter finds these values imposed upon her, resistance to stereotyping is sharpened. And thirdly, it cleared the way for a revamped version of Beattie's opposition. The duality now becomes, not the ideal 'Goth' and his dark other, but an 'ideal' father (in some of the romances, literally so) and his dark other. The significance of this change is that it helped bring patriarchy under scrutiny.

Having abducted Mary, Santmorin's party encounters 'the ruins

of an abbey, whose broken arches and lonely towers arose in
gloomy grandeur through the obscurity of evening. It stood the
solitary inhabitant of the wastes – a monument of mortality and
of ancient superstition . . .' (*CAD*: 252). Given that *The Castles of
Athlin and Dunbayne* depicts a world in which there is no other
law besides the might of feuding barons, it is reasonable to assume
that the romance is set some time in the Middle Ages, certainly
before the Reformation. Abbeys, then, would have been new,
rather than in ruins, and they definitely would not have been
regarded as monuments of ancient superstition. This lack of historical specificity obscures the fact that the feudal has collapsed
into the present: the ruined abbey signifies a present day, Protestant
view of Catholicism.

In her later romances Radcliffe will take greater care with her
historical settings, for a reason which may explain the final deviation her later career takes from her first romance: from now on,
the settings of all but her posthumous work will be European
rather than British. For what can be said of ruined abbeys can
also be said of ruined castles; that they are a parasitical survival of
the past into the present. 'Parasitical', because in Radcliffe's Gothic
(and indeed, in the Gothic in general) castles are structures of
oppression, of confinement and curtailed liberties ('cemetaries
of the living'), their very dilapidated condition signifying such
'manorial' powers as feudal vestiges, with no energy of their own,
save for what they extract from their immured victims. As if by
reflex Thomas Paine links together the 'arbitrary power' of 'the
Pope, and the Bastille' (Foot and Kramnick 1987: 212). For
the English, Protestant, bourgeois imagination there was a natural
connection between feudal, aristocratic power and Catholicism.
The coded anti-aristocratic animus of Radcliffe's first romance
touched a class nerve that became ever more raw as the decade
progressed.

Of course, Radcliffe may have switched to European settings
for the greater exoticism they offered. Considering the tradition
of female Gothic romances before Radcliffe will give us pause.
The most significant of them – Clara Reeve's *The Old English
Baron*, Sophia Lee's *The Recess* (1783–85) and Charlotte Smith's
Emmeline (1788) – all have British settings. In this context, Scotland
would have been a not unnatural choice for her first romance,

doubly so, given the prestige lent to Celtic 'medievalism' by James Macpherson's *Fingal* (1762), Thomas Percy's *Reliques* (1765), Thomas Gray's *The Bard* (1757), or James Beattie's *The Minstrel* (1771–74). Europe was not the automatic choice, especially for an English sensibility which, like Catherine Morland, was apt to see in the Celtic fringe plenty that was attractively, sinisterly exotic (Austen 1972: 202). That Europe became the only choice after 1789 suggests that even in *The Castles of Athlin and Dunbayne*, the most black and white of Radcliffe's romances, one finds shades of grey. Her first romance's representation of a dubious British aristocracy became less sustainable as the public mood sharpened. As in other times of great political sensitivity, writers of indeterminate ideological texts have had to seek out displaced settings in order to find scope for their dissonances. And so it seems with Radcliffe.

Although Radcliffe revamped the plot and setting for her next romance, in other respects *The Castles of Athlin and Dunbayne* very much anticipates the direction and concerns of her later work.

It is in the area of Nathaniel Drake's 'artful texture' in particular that we encounter Radcliffe developing her craft. It is as if, in writing her text, Radcliffe was beginning to discover the means for prolonging suspense, for giving her narrative emotional layers. Compared to her later work, Radcliffe barely touches upon the supernatural, and when she does, the explanations are never far behind. Her first use of the supernatural occurs at the start of Chapter VIII. Osbert passes through the secret partition

> when by the faint gleam which the fire threw across the apartment, he perceived, indistinctly, the figure of a man, and in the same instant heard the sound of approaching armour. Surprise and horror thrilled through every nerve; he remained fixed to the spot . . . A fearful silence ensued: the person whom he thought he had seen, disappeared in the darkness of the room; the noise of armour was heard no more: and he began to think that the figure he had seen and the sound he had heard were the phantoms of a sick imagination, which the agitation of his spirits, the solemnity of the hour, and the wide desolation of the place had conjured up.
>
> (*CAD*: 161–62)

A series of delaying tactics interrupts the flow of information. Isolated perceptions are doled out in a discontinuous fashion;

information is filtered through conjecture; while the animated armour and eerie setting strongly suggest a ghost. It is, in fact, a friendly, but frightened, guard. Radcliffe refines these methods of controlling the reader's perceptions in her later romances by holding back explanations, increasing suspense and, as we shall see, meaning.

Another area where we can observe Radcliffe's artful texture in embryo is in her use of the sublime and picturesque. In the first chapter we are told that Osbert's

> warm imagination directed him to poetry, and he followed where she led. He loved to wander among the romantic scenes of the Highlands, where the wild variety of nature inspired him with all the enthusiasm of his favourite art. He delighted in the *terrible and in the grand, more than in the softer landscape*; and wrapt in the bright visions of fancy, would often lose himself in awful solitudes [my italics]
>
> (*CAD*: 8–9)

This pre-Romantic *gestalt* – of a lone wanderer among the scenic hills – appears to have been lifted wholesale from James Beattie's *The Minstrel*. Radcliffe's originality lies in what she does with it. The scene develops with Osbert wandering through his favoured sublime landscapes. He finds himself lost on a distant heath from 'whence the eye was presented with only the bold outlines of uncultivated nature, rocks piled upon rocks, cataract and vast moors unmarked by the foot of traveller' (*CAD*: 9). Osbert wanders for some time through this desolate landscape, without a 'vestige of a human being', until an 'abrupt opening in the rock suddenly presented him with a view of the most beautifully romantic spot he had ever seen. It was a valley almost surrounded by a barrier of wild rocks, whose base was shaded with thick woods of pine and fir' (*CAD*: 10). A picturesque landscape opens up, in the manner of a Constable: 'Far on the margin of the stream were scattered a few neat cottages' (*CAD*: 10–11).

The movement between the sublime and picturesque becomes the strophe and antistrophe of Radcliffe's art, a rhythm giving her narratives emotional depth as well as thematic meaning. A set of obvious contrasts immediately arise: wild/domestic; individual/ society; nature/nurture.

More important still are the latent contrasts. 'Terrible and grand'/'softer landscape' suggest that the sublime and picturesque are gendered. The sublime appeals to Osbert's masculinity in the same way that the martial arts are 'congenial to the nobility of his soul' (*CAD*: 9). The picturesque is comparatively 'feminine' (it is a 'softer landscape'). In addition, the picturesque is a version of pastoral, as Radcliffe's bucolic scenes make clear. The pastoral traditionally mediates between two contrasting terms: barbarous nature and the corrupt city. In Radcliffe's Gothic, a single term emerges to oppose the pastoral: the castle. The castle condenses the traditional contrasting terms within itself: it is at once a corrupt city – a labyrinth of sinful spaces – and something which is barbarous and wild, a humanity feudal and untamed.

The castle is opposed to the pastoral, the sublime to the picturesque. Despite the symmetry, the pairs do not match. Picturesque and pastoral correspond, but not, apparently, sublime and castle. In *The Italian* we encounter the heroine, Ellena, 'gazing upon the stupendous imagery around her, looking, as it were, beyond the aweful veil which obscures the features of the Deity, and conceals Him from the eyes of his creatures' (*I*: 90). Conventionally, the sublime moment affords the viewer just such an intimation of a divine order. As such the sublime is the antithesis of earthly power, of castles. 'Sublime castle' is oxymoronic (it mixes the sacred and profane in a single phrase). Evil Dunbayne is just such an oxymoron: 'proud sublimity' plays around its 'lofty towers' (*CAD*: 26). The castle and the sublime are linked again through Osbert. His preference for the sublime, the martial exercises congenial to the nobility of his soul, and his exemplary status as the master of the feudal castle, are all of a piece.

The significance of this oxymoronic linkage sharpens when we consider two further contrasts invited by castle/pastoral: power/anti-power; history/Utopia. In *The Castles of Athlin and Dunbayne* the action moves from an ideal castle to a corrupt one; but in Radcliffe's mature romances it moves from pastoral to castle. This movement from bucolic idyll to the dystopic has the tendency of deepening the castle's associations with the processes of history and the mechanisms of power, which makes the sublime's association with the castle all the more disturbing; what, the reader wants to know, has the transcendental sublime to do with the squalid power of a feudal castle? Rather than a paradigm of religious experience, the sublime now appears as something else – something terrestrial and compromised.

Analogically, this is evident in the Alleyn/Osbert contrast. Alleyn is associated with the pastoral world of the picturesque valley (his apparent place of origin); Osbert, with the sublimity of the castle. The valley is associated with meritocratic values; the castle, with feudal class consciousness, a pagan sense of revenge, and a patriarchal order. The reader is invited to dismiss these worrying undertones to Osbert's character as the primitive manners of the times; but the narrative's historical slippage re-introduces them. Within a modern time frame Osbert appears less a harmless Goth, and more (to use Matthew Arnold's phrase from *Culture and Anarchy*) an aristocratic 'barbarian'. This ambiguity also attaches to the sublime, to the extent that it finds itself associated with the feudal order. Malcolm in Dunbayne uncomfortably parodies God in his heavens.

As mentioned in the previous chapter, Radcliffe's style of representation is suffused with the language of associationism; in *The Castles of Athlin and Dunbayne* it is already a pronounced presence. According to this 'language', the mind is a 'screen' that passively anticipates a process of inscription, one determining the mind's character. For instance, we hear of the young Osbert and Mary that 'Impressions would soon be formed which would stamp their destiny for life' (*CAD*: 7). The conflict between Osbert's desire for revenge and Matilda's maternal solicitude is represented in a similar deterministic way: matters are fixed 'when the figure of [Osbert's] dying father arose to his imagination, and stamped his purpose irrevocably. The anxiety of a fond mother presented Matilda with the image of her son bleeding and ghastly' (*CAD*: 21). The point of this language is that it figures the mind as something helplessly bearing impressions: images no sooner pop into the purview of consciousness than they stamp themselves on the mind. Sense data appear to be incorrigible (nothing stops them), and this includes those produced by the mind itself. The 'ardour' of Osbert's impulse to revenge his father finds itself instantaneously 'checked' as the 'image of his weeping mother' crosses his mind (*CAD*: 14). Mary discovers 'the generous and heroic qualities' of Alleyn bursting 'upon her memory' (*CAD*: 90). Such irrepressible interventions are not always so welcome. Mary finds that the idea of her imprisoned brother 'would often obtrude itself on her imagination, with an emphasis that almost overcame her reason' (*CAD*: 33). Matilda's mental theatre is worse: 'the bleeding figure of her beloved son, pale and convulsed in death, started on her imagination, and stretched her brain almost to frenzy' (*CAD*: 102–03).

It is not just that the characters are unable to stop images from assaulting their minds, leaving lasting impressions: they cannot get rid of them either. Mary 'saw in the eye of fancy the long train of inquietudes and sorrows which were likely to ensue. She sought to obliterate from her mind every remembrance of the past' (*CAD*: 74). Lovestruck with Alleyn, Mary 'solicited her mother to assist in expelling the destructive image from her mind' (*CAD*: 90). She believes that 'she had taught herself to forget' (*CAD*: 91), but such acts of will inevitably fail against the incorrigible power of mental impressions.

The court physicians 'pronounced the malady of the Countess to be seated in the mind, and beyond the reach of human skill' (*CAD*: 86). The mind in Radcliffe has just this paradoxical character. It is at once mysterious ('beyond the reach of human skill') and 'mechanical' or deterministic (because bound by set associative processes). The mind operates as a stimulus/response machine in which associations happen, as they will.

A number of consequences flow from this. Firstly, as we have seen, it gives rise to a highly visual style as Radcliffe describes the trains of associations that haunt the minds of her characters. Secondly, it means that identity – selfhood – is represented as something highly tenuous. I mean 'selfhood' as it is common-sensically understood, where the self is conceived as a decision-making agent, one formulating choices as it seeks to shape its destiny. We tend to think of these choices as emerging out of what, deep down, we really are. But in Radcliffe's Gothic world, selves are shaped by the impressions that incorrigibly stamp themselves upon them. Radcliffe's 'selves' are less agents, more recipients. Not only does this give rise to a pervasive sense of the instability of the person, but it leads to a blurring of the real and unreal, life and death (Castle 1987).

We are told that 'fancy gave [Mary] the horrors of reality' (*CAD*: 105). Exactly so: in Radcliffe's associational world, from the point

of view of the mind's experience, there is no difference between
fresh sense impressions, those bursting out of the memory, or those
involuntarily conjured by the fancy. In the phantasmal world of
our inner theatre, the dead live again. Osbert is haunted by the
'glowing image of his father' (*CAD*: 39). Memory alone – over
which characters have scant control – is enough to produce spectral
presences. The same also holds for futurity. Malcolm 'exulting in
his scheme' forcibly to possess Mary, already beheld her 'at his
feet, and the Earl retiring in an anguish more poignant than that
of death' (*CAD*: 115). Later Matilda dissolves into tears as she is
overwhelmed by a reverie in which pictures of Mary's future
happiness mingle with images of the past (*CAD*: 203).

If 'fictive' images take on the aspect of 'real' ones, real ones in
their turn threaten to dissolve into the illusory. Characters constantly doubt their senses. Alleyn's heart rises as he discovers
Mary's miniature, until his rapt consumption of the picture is
interrupted by 'the reality!' (*CAD*: 193). When Mary abruptly
departs, Alleyn 'almost doubted whether a visionary illusion had
not crossed his sight to blast his only remaining comfort' (*CAD*:
194). After the frightened guard's hasty retreat, Osbert begins to
think his sense impressions were 'the phantoms of a sick imagination' (*CAD*: 161).

We will investigate the phantasmal more fully later on; here it
is enough to note that in addition to the above it produces a
'topographical' mirroring. After his abortive attempt at escape
Osbert finds himself

> conveyed from the tower into a more centrical part of the castle,
> whose Gothic windows, partly excluding light, threw a solemnity
> around, which chilled the heart almost to horror. He heeded not this;
> his heart was occupied with horrors of its own. He was now involved
> in a misery more intricate, and more dreadful, than his imagination
> had yet painted.

> (*CAD*: 115–16)

Malcolm's castle is a gloomy labyrinth, but so, too, is Osbert's
distressed mind. The physical topography of Dunbayne and the
state of Osbert's mind mirror each other. The phantasmal blurring
of real/unreal, life/death also leads to the conflation of inside/
outside.

Earlier I said that Radcliffe helped create a new 'topography of the self', one we retrospectively call Romantic. I spoke of the sensed reciprocity between the rhetoric of the self and the rhetoric of nature, where we find ourselves alluringly figured in the poetics of landscape description. Wordsworth discovered himself in the scenery around Tintern Abbey; we, in turn, do so through his language. But before Wordsworth, Radcliffe too had developed an art of suggesting tantalising yet obscure correspondences between nature's 'archetypes' and her readers' desires for self-becoming. But Radcliffe extends her artful use of the 'pathetic fallacy' – of playing with the obscure boundaries between self and nature – beyond landscapes. We find it too in her use of the phantasmal, although here the correspondences are not between, say, the self's desire for transcendence and lofty mountains, but between fears of entrapment and an imagery of incarceration, death or unreality.

In assessing the origins of Radcliffe's popularity it is important to note the way in which she gratified her readership's desire for the noumenal, in the religious sphere (through the sublime) and in the every day (through the picturesque). But equal note must be given to the way she provided fictions which afforded a contained expression of her readership's anxieties. One such anxiety concerned the mutability of the self: either the fear that the self was fragmented, divided against itself; or, if it was coherent, that it was no more than the sum of mechanical, associative processes. Either possibility led to a feeling of unreality. *The Castles of Athlin and Dunbayne* used the phantasmal to explore this feeling. While much of her art changed after her first romance, the theme of insubstantiality did not.

Of course, insubstantiality was not her only or even primary concern; rather it was the background to more immediate themes, such as, for instance, sexual politics.

2. *A Sicilian Romance*

The perpetuation of property in our families is one of the privileges you most warmly contend for; but it would not be very difficult to prove that the mind must have a very limited range that thus confines its benevolence to such a narrow circle, which, with great propriety, may be included in the sordid calculations of blind self-love.

A brutal attachment to children has appeared most conspicuous in parents who have treated them like slaves, and demanded due homage for all the property they transferred to them, during their lives . . .

Who can recount all the unnatural crimes which the *laudable, interesting* desire of perpetuating a name has produced? The younger children have been sacrificed to the eldest son; sent into exile, or confined in convents, that they might not encroach on what was called, with shameful falsehood, the *family* estate . . .

The same system has an equally pernicious effect on female morals. – Girls are sacrificed to family convenience, or else marry to settle themselves in a superior rank, and coquet without restraint . . .

Whether the glory of Europe is set, I shall not now enquire; but probably the spirit of romance and chivalry is in the wane; and reason will gain by its extinction.

Mary Wollstonecraft, *A Vindication of the Rights of Men, in a Letter to the Right Honourable Edmund Burke. Occasioned by His Reflections on the Revolution in France* (1790: 42–5, 61)

To read *A Sicilian Romance* (1790) after *The Castles of Athlin and Dunbayne* (1789) is to move from a preliminary sketch of the enchanted world of the mature Radcliffe into something like its finished state. Apart from the improved quality of writing, this is due to changes to plot and setting. We now have, not a hero, but a heroine, Julia Mazzini. Whereas Mary in *The Castles of Athlin and Dunbayne* was a passive observer of events – even when abducted – Julia actively takes flight. She criss-crosses the exotic Sicilian landscape, encountering abbeys, pastoral cottages, dungeons, caves, encampments of banditti, sublime and picturesque vistas, even a shipwreck. The more varied scenery – and the more varied plot – helps Radcliffe create a more complex narrative texture. There are still signs of 'immaturity', especially in the breathless pace and ceaseless calamities. *A Sicilian Romance* is a gratifying – if at times unintentionally comic – text.

Unlike her first romance, her second is specific about its temporal setting. The action takes place 'towards the close of the sixteenth century' (*SR*, 3). The narrator later elaborates on the significance of this:

The rude manners, the boisterous passions, the daring ambition, and the gross indulgences which formerly characterized the priest, the

nobleman, and the sovereign, had now begun to yield to learning ...
The dark clouds of prejudice break away before the sun of science,
and gradually dissolving, leave the brightening hemisphere to the
influence of his beams. But through the present scene appeared only
a few scattered rays, which served to shew more forcibly the vast and
heavy masses that concealed the form of truth. Here prejudice, not
reason, suspended the influence of the passions; and scholastic learning,
mysterious philosophy, and crafty sanctity, supplied the place of
wisdom, simplicity, and pure devotion.

(SR, 116–17)

According to the popular historical sense of the period, the late
sixteenth century formed a 'Gothic cusp': it was a transitional
phase, when the Gothic epoch came to an end, and the modern one
began. But as the quotation from Mary Wollstonecraft indicates, by
1790 this historical myth had gained a new meaning, and a new
application.

For the radicals of the period, 1790 marked a new, blissful,
dawning – day breaking, once again, over a 'Gothic' order. As we
saw in the last chapter, Edmund Burke was mainly responsible
for the word's modishness among radicals. His *Reflections* had read
the French Revolution as a kind of chivalrous anti-romance, where
heroes conspicuously fail to rescue the Queen from the mob's
many-headed monster. The radicals seized Burke's conservative
rhetoric, turning it against him. England's old regime was indeed
chivalrous – chivalrous and Gothic. And like the original 'dawn
of the modern', this new revolution would destructively expose
England's Gothic remnants to the breaking light.

Mary Wollstonecraft joined the radical attack. She typifies the
constitution defended by Burke as 'an ancient castle, built in
barbarous ages, of Gothic materials' (Wollstonecraft 1790: 94). She
covers the point from various angles; she refers sarcastically to
Burke's 'gothic notions of beauty' (9), and to his 'Gothic affability'
(31). He has made his 'humanity give place to Gothic gallantry'
(84). Her final parry is meant to devastate: 'Man preys on man;'
and you mourn for the idle tapestry that decorated a gothic
pile, and the dronish bell that summoned the fat priest to prayer'
(144).

The significance of the opening quotation from Wollstonecraft
is that it interprets primogeniture as a key instrument of the old,

Gothic order. To the idol of protecting the survival of the 'family estate', its name and 'house', younger children were readily sacrificed, sentenced to mercenary marriages, 'sent into exile, or confined in convents'. All this, moreover, was an expression of 'blind self-love'.

A Sicilian Romance shares Wollstonecraft's radical sentiments. The time when it is set — the Gothic cusp — supportively echoes the present 'dawning'. In both, an age of feudal or aristocratic privilege gives way to a modern, egalitarian 'enlightened' one. The difference between the epochs are reproduced along both generational and gender lines. 'Ferdinand, fifth marquis of Mazzini . . . was a man of voluptuous and imperious character.' His first wife, by contrast, was a lady 'distinguished for the sweetness of her manners and the gentleness of her disposition' (*SR*, 3). The children, and, with one exception, the women of the romance belong to the new age of dawning sensibility, while the older generation of men belong to the feudal epoch, then in the process of eclipse.

The plot of *A Sicilian Romance* keeps primogeniture in its sights, however it turns. Mazzini has a son, Ferdinand, and two daughters, Julia and Emilia, in their late teens and early twenties as the story opens. On the death of his first wife, some ten years before, Mazzini had remarried a younger woman, Maria de Vellorno. Mazzini sets the plot in motion when he arranges Julia's marriage against her consent. Julia rebels, partly because she has fallen in love with the young, romantic Count de Vereza (Hippolitus), and partly because Mazzini wishes her to marry his 'double', the Duke de Luovo:

> The Duke de Luovo was of a character very similar to that of the marquis. The love of power was his ruling passion; — with him no gentle or generous sentiment meliorated the harshness of authority, or directed it to acts of beneficence. He delighted in simple, undisguised tyranny. He had been twice married, and the unfortunate women subjected to his power, had fallen victims to the slow but corroding hand of sorrow.
>
> (*SR*, 57)

Mazzini chooses Luovo out of self-aggrandisement, even though Luovo is clearly a sociopath. According to the feudal lights of

Mazzini's society, a father has a right to dispose of his daughter as he pleases: she is his property. Mazzini's ultimatum to Julia is marry Luovo or accept banishment.

Instead she and Hippolitus elope, assisted by Ferdinand. They are betrayed. Mazzini confronts them, dealing Hippolitus (or so Julia thinks) a mortal wound. The wedding with Luovo is re-arranged, but Julia escapes with a serving maid, with whose parents she lives, disguised as a peasant girl. The enraged Luovo scours the countryside in pursuit. Madame de Menon, the girls' 'governess', and former friend of their mother, also in flight, stumbles into Julia's retreat. She advises Julia of the danger of Luovo's search party, and they retire to an abbey for protection, only to be discovered by Mazzini's spies. The abbey's 'Padre Abate' extends protection to Julia, but only if she takes the veil. Julia prefers the convent's live burial over marriage to Luovo, but Ferdinand dramatically appears on the eve of Julia's irrevocable decision, informing Julia that Hippolitus yet lives. The news steels Julia's nerves while giving heart to her desire; she 'elopes' once again, this time from the abbey. Julia and Ferdinand travel alone through perilous country.

Hippolitus sets out in search of Julia, having recovered from his wound. On a moonlit night he encounters the extensive ruins of a monastery, now the fortress of a vicious gang of banditti, whom Hippolitus startles mid-murder. Confused, Hippolitus loses himself deeper in the ruin's maze. In its depths he discovers a captive young woman, apparently unconscious: 'Her face was concealed in her robe; and the long auburn tresses which fell in beautiful luxuriance over her bosom, served to veil a part of the glowing beauty which the disorder of her dress would have revealed' (SR, 163). Two 'assassins' fight to the death for the right to enjoy her body. Hippolitus hides in the next room, but rushes to the rescue as the young woman screams in the arms of the victorious bandit, apparently in the act of claiming his prize. Hippolitus 'became fixed like a statue when he beheld his Julia struggling in the grasp of the ruffian' (SR, 164). Hippolitus slays the bandit, but the disoriented couple end up in the monastery's innermost vault, now used by the banditti as their charnel house. The couple are forced to wait among the rotting bodies.

They are rescued by soldiers only to be set upon, the next day,

by the Duke of Luovo. Hippolitus is captured but Julia manages
to escape through a series of obscure caves, mysteriously equipped
with trapdoors; through one of them she discovers an inner chamber, in which a mild-faced woman is held captive. This, we learn,
is Julia's mother.

The full story now emerges. Mazzini, infatuated with Maria de
Vellorno, lost interest in the Marchioness a few years after the
birth of their children. Her poor health – induced by cruelty –
provides Mazzini with an opportunity of entombing his wife in a
dungeon of the castle's south wing, an act cloaked through an
elaborate deception. He attributes her death to a fever, burying
her in effigy. His new wife was 'a woman of infinite art, devoted
to pleasure, and of an unconquerable spirit' (*SR*, 3). Mazzini
'loved her with romantic fondness, which she repaid with seeming
tenderness, and secret perfidy. She allowed herself a free indulgence in the most licentious pleasures' (*SR*, 10). Vellorno is eventually betrayed by one of the servants; Mazzini discovers her in
the arms of one of her young lovers. Mazzini's infatuation leaves
him irresolute. Not so Vellorno, who poisons Mazzini before stab-
bing herself. On his death-bed Mazzini confesses the Marchioness's
whereabouts to Ferdinand, but Ferdinand, checking, discovers no
sign of the Marchioness (or Julia). Hippolitus, escaping from
Luovo, had rescued them; Ferdinand finally catches up with them
as they wait to embark for Italy.

The story-line of *A Sicilian Romance* – with its amazing coincidences, hairbreadth escapes and feverish action – looks back to
the narrative clumsiness of *The Castles of Athlin and Dunbayne*. At
one point, every irascible old count in Sicily seems to be scouring
the countryside for his renegade daughter. But as a counterbalance,
Radcliffe's second romance discovers a cunning use of inset narratives that looks forward to the more sophisticated works to come.
These inset stories amplify on the main themes.

The main themes themselves are enriched by the changes Radcliffe makes to her plot. *A Sicilian Romance* gives us in a developed
form what feminist critics have come to call the 'female Gothic',
a narrative in which a daughter seeks for an absent mother. It is
worth recalling that when Catherine Morland in *Northanger Abbey*
speculates on the crimes of General Tilney she principally draws

upon the horrors of *A Sicilian Romance*: Catherine believes the General has murdered his wife, left her to rot in a dungeon while burying her in effigy, or simply, like the Duke de Luovo, cruelly oppressed her to death. Critics argue over whether Austen's novel endorses Catherine outgrowing the childish vision of Gothic romance, or whether that vision, against the grain of authorial parody, establishes its own truth.[1] The argument boils down to whether the General is, after all, a 'Montoni' (antagonist of *The Mysteries of Udolpho* and Radcliffe's most famous villain). That Catherine should imaginatively resort to the Radcliffe romance in which the plot of the female Gothic is most pronounced – one might even say blatant – suggests that Austen sympathised with Wollstonecraft's concerns, beneath the bluff common sense that would see General Tilney as no more than an upper-class boor.

Northanger Abbey's affinity with *A Sicilian Romance* becomes more apparent when we consider the flip side of the absent mother: a present father. One of the most persistent misconceptions of Radcliffe is that her villains are motivated by sexual desire. Some, like the Duke of Luovo, or the Marquis de Montalt (from *The Romance of the Forest*) clearly are. But her influential villains, such as Montoni or *The Italian*'s Schedoni, are not – at least not principally. It is easy to see where the misconception comes from. Radcliffe's villains have been mediated, first through the 'Byronic hero' and then through Charlotte Brontë's Rochester. In these figures, what is in the background of Radcliffe's later villains – sexual desire – comes to the fore. But what Radcliffe foregrounds is her antagonists' material – not sexual – rapacity; they are ambitious, greedy on a grand scale (Poovey 1979). It is because of their material ambitions that they are ready – like Mazzini – to sacrifice their daughters' happiness, or commit any crime. General Tilney might not be ready to bury alive members of his family, but he is clearly not too bothered about his children's happiness when it comes to Burke's privilege: 'the perpetuation of property in our families' (Wollstonecraft 1790: 42).

The inset tales of *A Sicilian Romance* amplify this poor figure of the 'father', until the figure swells, institutionally, into patri-

---

[1] For a further discussion of – and bibliography for – *Northanger Abbey*'s relation to the Gothic, see my *Gothic Writing: 1750–1820* (1993: 143–59)

archy. The first inset tale – Madame de Menon's history of Louisa, Julia's mother – seems innocuous enough. The Count di Bernini and his daughter Louisa were the last remaining members of a family devastated by an eruption of Mount Etna. Nevertheless, the now relatively impoverished Count 'adopts' two distant, orphaned relations: Madame de Menon and her brother, Orlando. Louisa and Orlando fall in love, but a 'false delicacy' prevents them from marrying, Orlando especially believing that to do so ' "poor as he was ... would be to repay the kindness of the count with ingratitude" ' (SR, 31). He joins the army instead, bringing home on leave the Frenchman Madame de Menon eventually marries. The two men quarrel over a trifle when away, de Menon killing Orlando in a duel. Mazzini had earlier proposed marriage to Louisa, a suit Louisa's father forbore to press when he understood his daughter's inclinations. With Orlando dead the ' "world was now become indifferent to her, and as she had no prospect of happiness for herself, she was unwilling to with-hold it from the father who deserved so much of her" ' (SR. 32). Louisa marries Mazzini, with the disastrous results unfolded in the main narrative.

In effect, the inset tale gives us an 'unhappy pastoral', where the worm is already in the apple. Etna indirectly does the family a favour by destroying its dynastic ambitions along with its property, thus clearing the way for an idyll of sensibility, of love under modest but feeling circumstances. That the provincial idyll comes to a calamitous end is not, in this instance, owing to the father, who is here the soul of benevolence; and yet the children have internalised 'patriarchal' values, hence Orlando's diffidence, and Louisa's deference to her father's happiness, which she restores by marrying him back into a dynastic lineage. In a way that echoes Mary's painful choice in The Castles of Athlin and Dunbayne, Louisa sacrifices herself for her father. The point is underlined by the sequel to Madame de Menon's story. She is reconciled with her husband after the fatal duel, but he eventually perishes from grief. Without proof of her marriage, her French brothers-in-law dispute her entitlement to her husband's estates. Outside the pastoral idyll depicted in Madame de Menon's nostalgic recollections there is a 'real' world ruled by materialism and greed, where women are excluded, except as accessories. This 'outside' is also 'inside'. Invading the domestic and pastoral spheres alike, the real world's ineradicable corruption is the latent poison that ruins the women's happiness.

The theme is continued with the story of Cornelia, the mysterious, languishing nun Julia is unaccountably drawn to in the 'obscure recesses of St. Augustin' (*SR*, 116), where she takes refuge. Cornelia begins her tale by praising the virtues of her ' "noble father. He united in an eminent degree, the mild virtues of social life, with the firm unbending qualities of the noble Romans, his ancestors, from whom he was proud to trace his descent" ' (*SR*, 119). Significantly, the memory of his virtues produces an emotion in her analogous with the sublime: the recollection 'elevates my mind, and fills my heart with a noble pride'. As it happens her father's 'fortune was unsuitable to his rank. That his son might hereafter be enabled to support the dignity of his family, it was necessary for me to assume the veil' (*SR*, 119). Lamentably, she was already in love with Angelo, a poor noble; worse, the Marquis Marinelli, 'illustrious at once in birth and fortune' (*SR*, 120) had solicited her hand despite her aversion to him. Cornelia's father generously gives her the choice of accepting the veil, or marrying Marinelli. Cornelia opts for the veil, but the prospect undermines her health. Her brother (whom we now learn is Julia's lover, Hippolitus), perceiving how matters lie, offers to surrender a portion of his estate in order to enable the marriage of Cornelia and Angelo. The father reluctantly agrees, but then Angelo is reported to have fallen in a foreign engagement. Cornelia takes the veil in despair. Her tragedy is compounded when it transpires Angelo has not died at all. To be near her he becomes a monk, taking her confession. The encounter is too much for Cornelia, who completes the process of dying from grief and disappointed desire.

There is a third inset tale. The Duke de Luovo sees a young couple fleeing, and believes it to be Julia and Hippolitus. He gives chase, finally capturing them. They turn out to be the wrong couple. 'This lady was the youngest daughter of a Sicilian nobleman, whose avarice, or necessities, had devoted her to a convent.' To avoid her fate, she elopes with her lover 'whose only fault, even in the eye of her father, was inferiority of birth' (*SR*, 94).

All three stories ring the changes on a common theme: the readiness of Sicilian fathers to sacrifice their daughters to the needs of primogeniture, to the dynastic demands of the 'house' (where the house is an extension of the father's 'self'). The stories also vary, offering echoes of, and angles on, Julia's fate. I said earlier that the romance divides along generational and gender lines: the males of the older generation are strict 'genealogists' at best, rapacious ones at worst, while the women of the older generation and the young belong to the new age of dawning sensibility. The inset tales appear to conform with these divisions: the stories of Julia's mother and her 'sister-in-law' (Cornelia) are softened versions of her own, as here the fathers' acquisitiveness is blunted by emerging sensibility. Julia's own story, or that of the 'younger daughter of a Sicilian nobleman', involving fathers of the old school, are straightforward tales of feudal oppression. But as the stories echo and amplify each other the divisions begin to blur. The view that sensibility revolutionises feudal patriarchy begins to lose its cogency.

The lesson is enforced by the episode of the Padre Abate. The abbey's architecture is itself significant:

> The abbey of St. Augustin was a large magnificent mass of Gothic architecture, whose gloomy battlements, and majestic towers arose in proud sublimity from amid the darkness of the surrounding shades. It was founded in the twelfth century, and stood a proud monument of monkish superstition and princely magnificence.
>
> (*SR*, 116)

'Proud sublimity' indicates that, unlike the natural, this is not a healthy kind. It is, indeed, a perversion of the 'natural sublime', which ought to bespeak the inscrutable power of the supreme maker; on the contrary, the abbey, Babel-like, mounts a profane challenge. The abbey's sublime profanity is evident in the mixture of the material and religious; the abbey, moreover, is martial, and 'male'.

All these sinister qualities are concentrated in the Abate. Both Madame de Menon and Julia are forced to plead for Julia's safety, for although the abbey ought to be an asylum for the persecuted, such asylum in fact rests on a tyrant's capricious will. The Abate initially shares Mazzini's view that a father has the right to dispose of his daughter as he pleases; he will only grant Julia protection if her father fails to ask for her. When Mazzini does so in threatening and insulting terms, the Abate determines to protect Julia, but only because, intensely jealous of his religious authority, he refuses 'to yield the prerogative of the church to that of the father' (*SR*, 133). Madame de Menon's insufficiently profuse gratitude inflames his malevolence. Caught between vindictiveness and hatred of the Marquis, the Abate sends for Julia in order to indulge a sadistic pleasure: although determined to spite her father, he tells Julia the contrary in order to pleasure himself by watching her abject pleading. Twice the Abate's baser passions conflict: malignity towards the Marquis battles with his pride, piqued by Julia's refusal to grovel; and when the Marquis tries to bribe him, avarice contends with vindictiveness. Forcing Julia to take the veil is simply a further refinement of his malignity, for by devoting her life to religion Julia destroys not just her own, but her father's hopes.

In the end Julia's choice is the same as Cornelia's: an arranged marriage with someone she detests or 'to be immured for life within the walls of a convent' (*SR*, 142). Despite the benevolent pretensions of spiritual or temporal fathers, such a choice appears to be – at bottom – a woman's fate. It is, moreover, an institutionalised fate.

If in Radcliffe men have the power at the expense of women, it comes at a terrible price: their subjectivity. Radcliffe's 'Gothic' fathers do not possess an inner realm distinguished by a set identity, clear choices and an operative will. 'Inside' one discovers a chaos of contending passions. The Abate does not choose his course of actions: his ego is like the feather in *Antony and Cleopatra*; caught between conflicting tides, it eventually inclines one way rather than another, but not of its own volition. The same is also true of the Duke of Luovo and Mazzini.

In comparison with these possessed 'fathers', Radcliffe's heroines enjoy a subjectivity, an inner world of perceived independence and choice. However, the more we observe them the more we see that they, too, are trammelled. Their behaviour eloquently bears witness to the constraints under which their threatened egos labour. They evince a whole series of 'hysterical' symptoms: they faint, fantasise, hallucinate, block out desire, repress anger. Generally, Radcliffe's heroines' threatened subjectivity is represented as a perilous 'threshold', where moving back or forwards involves dangers.

The image of the threshold is introduced at the beginning of
A Sicilian Romance in a way that echoes *The Castles of Athlin and
Dunbayne*, while anticipating the rest of Radcliffe's *oeuvre*: two
young women wait on 'the boundaries of their fathers' domains'
(*SR*, 6), where they gaze wistfully towards the world outside from
which they have been excluded. The heroines – the sisters Emilia
and Julia – prefigure Jane Austen's central characters in *Sense and
Sensibility* (while looking back to Sophia Lee's *The Recess*), except
that Radcliffe's romance tracks the career of sensibility only: the
sensible Emilia fades into the background. This choice is inherent
in Radcliffe's starting point, which is to track the aspiring female
'soul': a spirited young woman of sensibility confronts her destiny.
We first observe Julia trapped within her father's house: here, on
the threshold of life, she dreams in a manner later echoed by
Tennyson in 'The Lady of Shallot'. But whereas Tennyson's 'lady'
dies upon directly viewing her 'prince', Radcliffe's lives. But the
appearance of Hippolitus does materially alter matters: now, without his presence, all is indifferent; what was home, is now prison.

The theme of baffled desire is echoed in the inset tales: without
Angelo, Cornelia's world has become a blank; without Orlando,
Louisa Bernini ceases to live for herself. As a consequence Louisa
surrenders her subjectivity, her inner life, and marries the man of
her father's choice, while Cornelia chooses a convent. Julia's narrative is a romance in the conventional sense of the term, a story
that ends happily in marriage. The inset stories belong to a different narrative register, at once symbolic and 'realistic': they provide
mementoes of life outside romance, where love falters. Their imagery, overwhelmingly, is of live burial, of the death of subjectivity,
of the inner, questing life.

Or rather, Cornelia's and Louisa's stories sketch in a neither/
nor, one setting the boundaries of female subjectivity: neither spin-
sterhood nor marriage. If the threshold is Radcliffe's recurring
image, her recurring theme is women's subjection to 'impossible'
choices: Mary must wed Malcolm or witness her brother's death;
Adeline must give herself to her uncle or elope with Theodore;
Emily must sign away her estates or suffer Montoni's cruel whims;
Ellena must take the veil or marry as the Marchesa dictates. There
is a general connection between image and theme, for it is when
they are incarcerated that they are subjected to these impossible

choices; stuck between alternatives, they gaze out from their turret windows.

The 'neither/nor' of each romance explores a different aspect of male power and female resistance. In *A Sicilian Romance* the dread alternatives are figured through the life stories of the women who surround Julia, who is indeed caught on a threshold; here she dreams, is prone to reverie, to the delights provided by the feeling heart, where imagination and sensibility are at one. To stay where she is, to retreat deeper into herself, to remain fast within her father's house, is to risk Cornelia's fate. Within the patriarchal institution of the abbey (for the convent is subsumed within it) Cornelia is allowed to dream, to enjoy unhindered the ambiguous fruits of sensibility, but without the beloved other – without objects of desire – this inner world petrifies. The opposite choice – given the *realpolitik* of the marriage market – is a dynastic marriage: the woman, treated as a commodity, assumes the inner life of a commodity. To acquiesce to the demands of alliance, as Louisa does, is to risk the death of subjectivity.

The 'threshold', then, is a recurring structure in Radcliffe, and can be schematised in the following way. First and foremost, the threshold is a literal part of a patriarchal structure, be it a window in the family 'house' or a turret in a convent (where convents invariably turn out to be adjuncts to abbeys). Within this structure the heroine is tempted to regress inwardly towards the delights of sensibility, to melancholy, reveries and dream, while simultaneously being drawn outward towards the proscribed beloved. The threshold dramatises two unsatisfactory choices: renunciation of desire unsatisfactorily compensated for by maternal sensibility, or desire 'gratified' but within the unwelcome terms of a paternal will. The threshold also has a figurative dimension, in that the neither/nor it dramatises remains true of the heroine's fate up to (and even, possibly, including) the final resolution. While caught within her threshold the heroine is never truly well.

The supernatural is used to underline this lack of health. The mysterious noises emanating from the south wing of Mazzini's house, where Louisa is buried alive, usurp the girls' (and Ferdinand's) reason. Overcome by superstitious fears, they literally lose control of their thoughts: their subjectivity – their independence of mind – comes under threat. But the greatest challenge is figurative, and as such only the reader can pick it out. The source of the noise, the 'entombed mother', is a figure for male power: as a metaphor it brings together Cornelia in her convent, and Louisa in her marriage. It also draws an uncomfortable parallel between Julia dreaming at her threshold and her mother buried alive within the same paternal structure.

The identification of marriage with the death of subjectivity is particularly evident in the stories of Mazzini's two 'wives', Maria de Vellorno and Louisa (as the 'entombed mother'). Maria de Vellorno is, in a sense, a double of the romance's Gothic fathers: like them, she has lost control of her passions, has become a creature of impulse. In the associative chaos that is her inner self, desires triumph, as they will. In Wollstonecraft's terms, she has taken the other life path available to women: to 'marry to settle themselves in a superior rank' in order to 'coquet without restraint'. Louisa loses her subjectivity for quite different reasons. Imprisonment has deprived her of her children. Her nurturing 'instinct', frustrated, now domineers her mind. Within the realm of the romance's figurative meanings the causality reverses itself: to nurture to the exclusion of all else is tantamount to live burial.

A complex 'feminist' critique thus begins to emerge from *A Sicilian Romance*. The narrative associates Julia's 'sensibility' with female subjectivity, identifying it as the natural language of feminine self-expression. The temporal setting links a Gothic, feudal past with repressive, patriarchal institutions. Sensibility in this context amounts to the dawning of a revolutionary age of female freedom and independence, one which will see the death of primogeniture, the chief instrument of patriarchy, the old order.

But the effect of the inset stories is to shade this simple picture. According to the lights of these narratives, Julia's sensibility evades patriarchal authority with suspicious ease. Sensibility itself now appears somewhat uncertain. At best it emerges as no more than a 'stopgap', a half-way house between equally unpleasant alternatives: of a deadening retreat into the self, or an equally calamitous move forward into 'patriarchal' marriage; of surrendering oneself to pleasure – at the cost of selfhood – or accepting the equally limiting reality of conventional gender roles, of 'nurturer'. At worst, sensibility looks like part of the problem, like another 'partriarchal' symptom.

Despite *A Sicilian Romance*'s greater sophistication, it does not move beyond the subtextual hinting which tentatively identifies sensibility as a stopgap; and that is because it is still overly wedded to the literal.

This is especially true of its depiction of violence. When Nathan Drake praised Radcliffe for her artful mastery of the 'material sublime' – of presenting physical terror in a tactful way – he could not have had *A Sicilian Romance* in mind. Certainly the work is the one with the most explicit scenes of violence in Radcliffe's *oeuvre*. When Hippolitus encounters the banditti he observes them rifling the pockets of a dying man they have just 'murdered'; when they rip from his neck 'a miniature picture' (*SR*, 161), the man raises himself in protest. A final blow leaves him weltering in his blood.

Two things intensify the shock of the violence. Earlier we observe Julia and Emilia fondly regarding their mother's miniature. It is not just that it is a valuable object for them; in their mother's absence, it is, in an obscure but definite way, an aspect of their identity. That the banditti snatch the dying man's miniature – after which he desperately lunges – visually intensifies the manner in which the victim has been divested of his humanity. Secondly, we are led to believe that the victim is Ferdinand, so our emotions are engaged.

The same shockingly overt presentation of violence is evident in the depiction of the attempted rape of Julia, which we see through Hippolitus's horrified eyes. Although this cunningly places the reader in a compromised position – the partially stripped Julia presenting an ambiguously attractive tableau of virtue in distress – it is, nevertheless, unhelpfully literal. In her later works Radcliffe will use the disfigured female body as her most potent image for the power that keeps Julia stuck in the stopgap of sensibility. But this 'disfigurement' is not literal, but 'figurative'. Radcliffe's heroines repeatedly encounter limits that threaten their subjectivity. We have to wait until the *Romance of the Forest* before the full extent of these limits becomes apparent, and it only becomes apparent through the figurative.

6

In the realm of the figural:
The Romance of the Forest

She only wrote as she felt, it is true, but as she felt, few of those who
had sat down to write a story had felt before her. For in what novels
and romances, till she took up a pen, shall we find places and scenery
substituted for the human interest?

The taste for landscape is, like the landscape painting, comparatively modern . . . there were minds, an increasing multitude, whom
landscape haunted to a sort of pain, while human passions and sorrows
left them almost unmoved and cold.

Such a mind was Mrs. Radcliffe's . . . She did not paint the nature
we behold daily, though she knew it in all its changes, but that we
dream of in languid, summer mood. Hence her wonderful hold over
memory, for, if details charm as we read, it is general impressions we
remember.

A French critic has said . . . that no one knew better than Mrs.
Radcliffe how to appeal to the secret superstition innate in the human
heart. We think we may add that in making the forest the home of
her characters she appealed to a feeling as subtle, as mysterious, and
as deep as superstition: man's secret desire to be alone. It is the passion
of childhood and of youth, of that season of life when the heart is all
ardour and the mind all wealth; when solitude is not the dreary void
it becomes later, but a world peopled with images lovely and rare . . .
But solitude is not merely dear to our imaginative faculties; it is
irresistibly alluring to a natural, though not amiable, feature in every
heart — selfishness.

Julia Kavanagh (1863: 258–81)

It is in *The Romance of the Forest* that Radcliffe's art fully enters
the realm of the figural. This statement – as it stands – is decep-
tively simple. To begin with, narrative is inherently figurative. For
instance, a gate in a field is only a gate, but a gate in a field in a
story is (possibly) a symbol of transition or passage. Even in naïve

Gothic romances this figurative tendency is heightened by the genre's characteristic props: its typical motifs – such as the castle or live burial or parental secrets – teem with latent meanings. So when I say that in *The Romance of the Forest* Radcliffe's art fully enters into the realm of the figural I mean something more than what is inherent within romance narrative.

I have in mind two developments that set *The Romance of the Forest* apart, not just from Radcliffe's previous novels, but from previous romances. The first is the consolidation of the plot of the female Gothic, where we encounter a heroine simultaneously in search of an absent mother and in flight from a 'patriarchal' father. This is significant because the plot has a mythic aspect. I want to use 'mythic' carefully here. I do not intend a structure with a universal meaning. I mean a 'myth' which, having fallen into history, has meanings localised in time and place. *The Romance of the Forest* vibrates with a new figurative intensity to the degree that it finds itself in tune with a mythic deep structure underlying the plot of the female Gothic.

The second development is one of narrative sophistication. *The Romance of the Forest* shows itself to be self-aware of its figural vocation, which it does by setting out the figural as problematic. This is especially true of its sensitivity towards the complexity of the relationship between the literal and the figurative, an awareness further manifest in a new-found adeptness in playing off (in the terms of narratology) 'plot' against 'history'.

When I said in the first chapter that Radcliffe was involved in the creation of a new topography of the self, I mainly had in mind the figural sophistication of her texts from *The Romance of the Forest* on. In this chapter I have two main aims: to show how *The Romance of the Forest* develops the figural, and, secondly, to suggest how the figural dovetails with the 'mythic' (in my qualified sense).

In so far as the figural involves textual features, explication is unproblematic. The 'mythic dimension of the female Gothic' is, on the contrary, problematic in the extreme, for here we are dealing with matters which are, to an extent, extra-textual. To explore what it was that made Radcliffe's art so potent – what it was that helped her to succeed as the 'Great Enchantress' – ineluctably leads us to consider the intangible aspects of Radcliffe's art. In order to at least gesture in the direction of the 'mythic' I have enlisted the aid of Elisabeth Bronfen, who has, in *Over Her Dead Body: Death, Femininity and the Aesthetic*, analysed at length the extra-textual meanings of the figure of the missing or dead mother so central to the female Gothic. In particular, I will look at Bronfen's discussion of Freud's late essay, 'Beyond the Pleasure Principle', and at Jacques Lacan's commentary on it. Given the complex nature of the material I shall first rehearse the relevant substance of Freud's essay, before turning to Lacan's commentary and Brofen's discussion. In doing so I hope to erect a theoretical framework for understanding the mythic dimension of Radcliffe's 'female Gothic' plots.

As Freud himself tells us, 'Beyond the Pleasure Principle' is one of his strangest, most speculative texts. The essay conducts us into a realm of primeval forces, bizarre compulsions, of dreams beyond the explanatory ken of conventional psychoanalytical theory. We encounter the most alien of Freud's drives, the 'death instinct', which is not so much a drive as a kind of biological inertia in which all living matter strives to relapse into non-being, into inorganic nullity.

Freud was led into this dark realm through a consideration of repetition, formerly a fundamental and unproblematic aspect of psychoanalytic thought. Freud had believed that the repetitive acts of neurotics were designed to restore a pleasurable equilibrium to the mind. This cosy view was subsequently shattered by Freud's encounter with several kinds of repetition where the pleasure principle – the instinct to maintain the mind in a state of un-pain – was not apparently operative (hence the title of his essay).

The 'fort-da' game was one such instance. Freud had noticed how his grandson obsessively played a game with several variants: the boy threw away his toys, uttering 'o-o-o'; or he tossed a kind of 'yo-yo' into his crib, making the customary 'o-o-o' noise when it was out of sight, before joyfully greeting it with 'da' as he reeled it back in; or he said 'Baby o-o-o' when he ducked out of sight of a mirror. 'Da' means 'there', so Freud surmised that 'o-o-o' must be the baby's version of 'fort', meaning 'gone'. The child's game rehearsed disappearance and retrieval, of 'gone-there'.

Freud interprets the game by relating its content to the mother's repeated absences, to the loss of the maternal body. The game has a symbolic meaning: the child's toys (his 'love objects') are substitutes for his mother. The game provides the child with several benefits: the return of the symbolic object affords the child joy; by staging the disappearance and return of his objects the child attains a vicarious sense of mastery; while the first stage of the game – throwing the objects away – appeases his aggression against his mother for her betrayal in leaving him.

But beneath – or beyond – these 'rational' compensations Freud discerned an irrational motivation at work, which he designates primary narcissism. We are to understand the child initially under the sway of the primary processes (which are pre-verbal, sensory and pleasure-directed). Here, an infant has to do no more than hallucinate a desire to experience it; if the child desires milk, it is as if the milk is really there. As a consequence the primary processes constitute a self-enclosed world of presence, plenitude and pleasure. But shortly the reality principle comes into play. This principle is distinguished by reality-adaptive devices, such as language. Here the child is thrown into a world of substitutions, in terms of the 'fort-da' game, of symbolic toys rather than the mother for which they stand. This cleaving to the reality principle leaves a 'narcissistic scar'. The new world of substitutions – and language – is a world of absence, of deferred gratification. A gap is left in the ego.

The child's 'fort-da' game – of obsessively throwing away his toys – is an instance of this primary narcissism, as through his game the child attends to the wound it has recently suffered through the absence of the mother, through both her literal absence and her absence at a symbolic level. Indeed, the acquisition of language itself, insofar as it is a system of substitution, encodes the very absence (or lack) from which the child now suffers. Freud was untroubled by the child's experiences of primary narcissism; it was when he discovered adult patients recurring to the scene of loss inherent in primary narcissism without any compensating pleasure that he began to feel that there was some other, dimly understood drive at work in the unconscious. Neurotic repetition – no matter how bizarre – discloses some secret logic; but this newly discovered form of repetition revealed no logic at all. Rather, it was as if some destructive alien force inhered within our own cells.

I now want to turn to Jacques Lacan's interpretation of the game. Lacan's account is filtered through his theories of the Imaginary and the Symbolic, which hold roughly the same position in his system as the primary and secondary processes do in Freud's. Like the primary processes, the Imaginary is a world of presence, plenitude and immediate gratification. The Symbolic order, by contrast, is a state of lack, of language, of substitution and deferred pleasure. It is also an order of sexual and social difference. The child's narcissistic wound is delivered with the splitting of the Imaginary, with the child's separation from the maternal body, with a sudden plunging into a world of difference and endlessly deferred pleasure. In the Symbolic presence is always somewhere else, just as, in language, meaning is circular and regressive: one definition (one substitution) merely refers to another, and so on, *ad infinitum*. In Lacan's system, this process of endless deferral is what 'desire' is. This process begins with the Oedipal advent of the father, whose 'law' (the incest taboo) splits the child from the maternal body. In the world of difference that is simultaneously language and the Symbolic order the 'phallus' comes to represent, not just the delivery of the narcissistic wound, but representation itself, the socialised order of substitution, difference and deferral.

Lacan calls the key moment of transition from the Imaginary to the Symbolic 'the mirror stage'. The child's image of himself in the mirror as a unified 'subject' is a delusive one: he misrecognises himself as a 'whole'. Insofar as the mirror produces 'reflections' – rather than the thing-in-itself – it is axiomatically part of the substitutive, Symbolic order. The mirror stage, so to speak, looks both ways. The child's image as a 'whole' recalls the state of plenitude from which he has become separated, even as his captivation by a delusive image announces his entry into the Symbolic.

In his reading of the 'fort-da' game, Lacan concentrates on the emergence of the difference that makes language possible; in his view, the symbolic game of loss and recuperation is significant not because of what is lost and regained (the mother's body): its importance lies with the fact that it is symbolic, a game of substitutions, of linguistic difference (as between the phonemes 'o-o-o' and 'a'). The game announces the child in the process of entering the Symbolic.

Elisabeth Bronfen approaches this material by foregrounding two of Freud's marginal comments. Freud had added an anecdote to his essay confirming that the child's throwing is a symbolic act of ridding. After a year the boy modifies his game: in throwing he now says 'Go to the fwont!'. The child's father was then, indeed, at the front (during the First World War). Here, the hostile impulse is directed, not towards the mother, but the father: the child, says Freud, 'had no desire to be disturbed in his sole possession of his mother' (Freud 1984: 286). Freud inserts the Oedpius complex into his account.

The second comment is a footnote. 'When this child was five and three-quarters, his mother died. Now that she was really "gone" ("o-o-o"), the little boy showed no signs of grief' (Freud 1984: 286). The 'mother' was also Freud's daughter: if the son was not affected, the father was. As Freud pursues his dismal meditation on what lies beyond the pleasure principle, on the primordial inertia dragging us back into non-being, it is hard not to catch accents of his own displaced mourning, of anger and bafflement finding expression in his outlandish speculation (his own characterisation) on an absurd biological order. In Bronfen's view, Freud's bafflement is presided over by an 'imago' of the 'maternal' body, by the haunting memory of his dead daughter.

Elisabeth Brofen indicates the significance all this has for the female Gothic. She is commenting on Freud's insertion of the Oedipus complex into his discussion of the 'fort-da' game:

> By suggesting that the child equates the pleasure gained from throwing a toy with that of the father's absence due to war, Freud attempts rhetorically to move away from a theory about symbolization and its relation to the disruption of the mother/infant dyad caused by loss, toward one that links symbolization with anxiety about the father's intervention. This suggests that the mother's death can be acknowledged in Freud's text only at the exact moment when her structural position as ground of the child's ego construction is being effaced by that of the father.

> (Bronfen 1992: 28)

In the construction of the ego, the father, not the mother, is
allocated the pivotal role. The obverse of the Oedipus complex's
privileging of the father is the marginalisation of the mother. In
Bronfen's view, the displacement of the mother from the scene
of interpretation (typified in both Freud's and Lacan's accounts)
simultaneously aestheticises the feminine body as an image of
death, while charging it with anxiety (precisely because it is
displaced). The mother's body is the 'natural' image of loss, and
therefore death: shunted to the margins of interpretation, it's meanings come back to haunt the 'critic', just as, one may say, the
displaced image of Sophie Freud's body haunts the language of
'Beyond the Pleasure Principle'.

These issues interweave with the female Gothic on several levels.
Our earlier description of the typical plot of the female Gothic –
a daughter's search for an absent mother – curiously chimes with
Freud's theory of the 'fort-da' game. Here, too, loss of the maternal
body appears to be connected to a 'primary narcissism', to a primal
wound at the core of the daughter's identity, which – in her quest
– she can never completely repair. But in addition, the daughter
is frequently in flight from the 'father', or his substitutes, often
with incestuous entanglements and overtones.

Equally, just as (as Bronfen notes), Freud and Lacan introduce
the 'Oedipus complex' as the pivotal event into the child's acquisition of, or entry into, the reality principle or the Symbolic,
thereby displacing the role of maternal body, so psychoanalytic
critics of the Gothic have traditionally focused on the Oedipus
complex as its primary determinant. It was to redress this exclusion
of the 'maternal' that feminist critics coined the phrase 'female
Gothic' (Moers 1977; Fleenor 1983; Kahane 1985).

Radcliffe's work dramatises – and anticipates – the debate.
For Radcliffe's female characters, the absent maternal body is the
ground of their being. Julia's obsessive interest in *A Sicilian
Romance* in her miniature of her 'dead' mother figures the loss of
the maternal body. The mother herself is characterised by 'sensibility', by a feeling heart and a receptive imagination. Julia on
the threshold stands for those other Radcliffe heroines who find
themselves at a window, staring out, caught in a 'neither/nor' of
two unsatisfactory choices (as analysed in the last chapter). There

is the impulse to revolve inwards into the self, into 'maternal' sensibility, into reverie and dream. But without the beloved other (the prohibited suitor) this proves a regressive world, one stripped of desire and hence meaning. The former state of childish pleni-tude is no longer a possibility.

In this respect an analogy arises between Radcliffe's figure of the heroine on a threshold and Lacan's mirror stage. For both, to move 'forward' is to enter a state of 'desire', of endlessly deferred presence. We saw how in *The Castles of Athlin and Dunbayne* the real and the illusory constantly fade, one into the other: illusory images take on the force of reality, while real ones appear illusive. In Radcliffe, this is the typical state of being 'beyond' the threshold, one of deferred presence. Moreover, this deferral is linked to the 'law' of the father, to his peremptory commands banishing the preferred lover and enforcing his despised substitute. With the absence of the preferred lover, the world turns into a blank. Radcliffe's heroine on a threshold looks both ways, inwards towards 'maternal' sensibility with its delusive image of subjective wholeness (delusive, because the heroine is still caught within a patriarchal structure, the family 'house' or abbey), and outwards towards a patriarchal order of repression and deferral.

Rather than moving towards the advent of the father as the decisive event in the formation of her heroines' identities, Radclif-fe's plots balance the maternal against the patriarchal, the one linked to a unity her heroines have lost and cannot recover, the other associated with prohibition, division and deferral. Freud's analysis of the 'fort-da' game re-attributes the formative role from the absence of the maternal body to the advent of the castrating father; but in Radcliffe these two figures exist simultaneously, the one blocking a route back, the other inhibiting a move forward; the one delusive, the other violent.

In digressing at length on psychoanalysis I do not mean to suggest that psychoanalysis explains Radcliffe, or even (as some argue) vice versa (cf. Thorslev jr 1981). It is rather that the Gothic and psychoanalysis invite a dialogue with each other, in which their voices, similar but different, ramify into something else, for good historical reasons. I want to complete my 'frame' by briefly glancing at some suggestions as to what these historical reasons might be.

To begin with, as narratives, psychoanalysis and the Gothic are coeval. They both begin to take shape around the end of the eighteenth century and both break narrative precedents (Foucault 1979). Conventional novels before the Gothic romance drew a link between providence and plot, with God's purpose finally untying the complications. In Gothic novels, shaping forces are once again dimly discerned, but the suspicion now becomes that they are neither benevolent nor meaningful (Thorslev jr 1981; Brooks 1973). In psychoanalysis, previous narratives of subjective, and therefore moral, autonomy are also replaced by suspicions of latent and indifferent drives. As narratives, both the Gothic and psychoanalysis emerge out of the historical wreckage of older paradigms of thought and belief that had formerly 'explained', or given shape to, notions of identity and destiny.

As Elisabeth Bronfen argues, these issues take on a pointed character when he come to consider changing attitudes towards death. As regards Radcliffe and the Gothic, the most stimulating work has been done by Terry Castle, using the French historian Philippe Ariès' *The Hour of Our Death* (Castle 1987). Castle begins with the feature we noticed in *The Castles of Athlin and Dunbayne*, the tendency of the illusive to seem real, and the real to seem illusive. Not just the absent, but the dead come alive in the minds of the living, while the living fade into the 'dead', becoming illusively present, in the manner of spectres. Castle links this 'spectralization' to a repressed fear of death, which Ariès argues comes into being during the late eighteenth century. Whereas death had its place in the rhythms of traditional life, new taboos and customs surround it in the 'modern' world. No longer understood as a phase of a rational order, death now comes to figure the irrational itself, with the result that new strategies arise to hide, displace, or disguise death. Castle reads *The Mysteries of Udolpho* as an instance of this new, modern sensibility, one offering consolations to the reader, for spectralisation – by blurring the boundaries between the dead and the living – effectively negates the reality of death.

Ariès' historical perspective on death contextualises Freud's 'Beyond the Pleasure Principle'. Freud's early work – based on the pleasure principle – bears some similarity to Radcliffe's 'explained supernatural': manifest absurdities (such as dreams or 'slips of the tongue') turn out to have a rational explanation, or 'latent meaning'. But when Freud comes to analyse the 'death' instinct his language turns Gothic: we are now in a realm of the inexplicable and primitive. We hear of 'primaeval experiences not present in a bound state'; of elixirs of life; of subjects radically fragmented along an Eros/Thanatos fault line; of the need for figurative language to even hint at these dim regions. Freud's discourse experiences the return of the supernatural, of natural ministries beyond our ken. Given that the essay was written in the shadow of Sophie Freud's death, the suggestion arises that Freud's 'speculations' are a displaced attempt to cope with death; that without either a paradigm that would explain it, or social customs to 'naturalise' it, Freud takes refuge in a narrative capable of 'containing' mortality. The narrative form that comes most readily to hand is the Gothic, with its dimly understood agencies, its images of division and entrapment, of deep, inner, self-betrayal. And the reason Gothic comes to hand is that, historically, it is the first literary form to come into being as a response to modern ways of dying.

Juxtaposing Radcliffe and Freud brings out the 'mythic' aspects of the female Gothic. It helps us see the absent maternal body in Radcliffe as an image of loss, but also of death, with the maternal body, in its idealised imagery, simultaneously a denial and an admission of 'unbound' terror. In this respect the spectral realm of the absent mother is analogous to Freud's speculations on a 'supernatural' death instinct, where death cannot be accommodated, except in narrative itself, the transformation into story offering the only compensations.

But the world of the father in both Radcliffe and Freud is more immediate. In Freud's system, the Oedipus complex represents the sharp end of socialisation, where particular social values – such as patriarchy – are inscribed within the individual. In Radcliffe the figure of the father is equally socially and ideologically determined.

Splitting Radcliffe's female Gothic plot into its principal parts – absent mother and present father – invites two complementary accounts. Psychoanalytically, the mother is the 'natural' figure for loss for the simple reason that she is initially the child's experience of 'presence'. Ariès' views on death and the late eighteenth century would tend to cement this association of the maternal body with unaccommodated loss. Conversely, in the late eighteenth century the father is the 'natural' image for 'repression', if for a somewhat paradoxical reason. Patriarchy should not be understood simply as the institutionalisation of male power. It is, in addition, an order of signification. Radcliffe's unsavoury father-figures may be construed as an assault on patriarchy, but this did not arise because 'patriarchy' was then strong; it arose because it was 'weak', and under attack (Stone 1979). In the late eighteenth century the power struggle between 'things as they are' and those on the political margins intensified. This struggle had many 'sites', including 'individualism' and the condition of women. Radcliffe's assaults on the prestige of the 'father' may be seen as part of this process, and because the figure of the father stood at the centre of an order of socialised meanings, the assault had extensive reverberations.

My suggestion, then, is that we should understand the hold the Great Enchantress had over her public as springing from the mythic power of her narratives. Her genius lay in her ability to tap into the social, cultural and psychological meanings of the female Gothic, a plot structure that was, in turn, in phase with some of the period's deep historical shifts. This mythic burden was one aspect of the figural quality of her mature work; however, it would not have been so potent if it had not been so artful, and so it is to the artfulness of *The Romance of the Forest* that I now want to turn.

I want to approach *The Romance of the Forest*'s artfulness through plot. All of Radcliffe's romantic plots hinge on a moment of recognition, on the discovery of true identities. Mary cannot wed Alleyn until his true identity is disclosed, nor can Julia marry Hippolitus until the discovery of Julia's mother. But in terms of complexity the two plots are quite different. In the first, one thing leads directly to another – disclosing Alleyn's noble birth unties the complications – whereas the 'causality' of the second forces us to probe deeper. Why must Julia discover her mother before she can marry? There is an incidental cause and effect: finding the mother betrays the father, the primary obstacle. But beyond that the reader is forced to conjecture. My own is that the imprisoned mother represents an aspect of Julia's cultural fate, is in fact a 'figure' for the social destiny of late eighteenth-century women (as this destiny was generally repressed it appears exaggerated in its returned, figurative form: dull or oppressive marriage becomes entombment). The confrontation with this figure is somehow necessary for the resolution of Julia's identity, a resolution that must – at the level of plot, at least – precede marriage. A curious paradox of Radcliffe's reception is that, despite the fact that her romances are structured on the love interest, very little of the criticism actually dwells on her handling of actual 'romance'. This is partly because – with the possible exception of Vivaldi from *The Italian* – her heroes are identikit figures without personalities of their own, and partly because the thematic interest centres on what it is that enables Radcliffe's heroines to marry, what it is that frees them from their thresholds; and, generally speaking, the matter relates to discoveries connected in some way to the heroine's identity.

The Romance of the Forest's treatment of the relationship between discovery and identity represents another step up in narrative sophistication. In purely technical terms, *The Romance of the Forest* carries on from where *A Sicilian Romance* left off. In comparison with her first text, *A Sicilian Romance* introduced four complicating innovations or improvements. It has a framing narrative (the story is ostensibly told to the narrator/traveller); the explanations for the supernatural appearances are delayed, thus stimulating conjecture; its inset tales are interpolated with greater finesse; and, as we have just witnessed, its recognition scene is handled in a thematically teasing way.

With one exception, *The Romance of the Forest* is more 'naturalistic' in its devices. The story begins in mid-action; Adeline's early history is subsequently told in her own words, and because they are her own words they are more open to interpretation (we are invited to speculate why it is that she tells her story in the way that she does), and there is more 'subtext', more information about Adeline that is left unspoken. The exception is the inset narrative (the elliptical manuscript discovered by Adeline in the abbey's dungeon). Its hackneyed character strains credibility, as Jane Austen was quick to point out through her lampoon of the laundry bill in *Northanger Abbey*, which is based on this episode. Moreover (and it is here that naturalism is most transgressed), the discovery of the manuscript is attended by the only instance of the unexplained supernatural before *Gaston de Blondeville* – the mysterious voice that leads Adeline on.

But it is the very uncertainty as to the status of the discovered manuscript that increases the complexity, and hence meaning, of the narrative of *The Romance of the Forest*. When Adeline shows the manuscript to La Motte he dismisses it as a ' "strange romantic story" ', adding ' "I do not wonder, that after you had suffered its terrors to impress your imagination, you fancied you saw spectres, and heard wondrous noises" ' (*RF*, 144). There is an obvious analogy between Adeline's situation and that of the female writer of romance. Both must contend with dismissive male audiences, with having the products of their imaginations labelled the effusions of a weak, feminine fancy. Adeline's secret, isolated burrowing into the depths of the abbey, and its fruits, the manuscript of mysterious provenance, serve as a kind of symbolic redaction of Radcliffe's own writing career. For the 'proper lady' writing is a furtive act, one that takes place behind the arras. ' "A mystery seems to hang over these chambers ... which it is, perhaps, my lot to develop ..." ' (*RF*, 115) The sense of privacy enforced on the woman writer may seem acquiesence in self-denial, but as with Adeline's breathless acceptance of her mission, the private act of writing/searching itself becomes a subtle form of self-assertion. Just as Radcliffe's writings meditate – in their figurative way – on 'femine' identity, so Adeline's fantasies reflect on her personal one. For the heroine on the threshold the way out is to burrow within. Superstition, fancy and dream offer themselves as 'inner' windows on the self.

So the question becomes: is the discovered manuscript to be taken on a literal, or a figurative level? Ostensibly it is the prison literature of Adeline's father, the narrative of his murder. But insofar as the manuscript holds the keys to Adeline's psychological – as well as her social – identity, it may be regarded as a product of fantasy, of romance; as, so to speak, the text of Adeline's reveries, the transcript of her inward searches. Such an interpenetration of the literal and the figurative has the further consequence of blurring the distinction between real and unreal, a tendency the text, in its self-conscious way, highlights from the very beginning.

The sight of the elegant Adeline amidst the desolation of the banditti's house seemed to La Motte 'like a romance of imagination, rather than an occurence of real life' (*RF*, 7).

The point sharpens when we consider the vicissitudes of the plot of the *Romance of the Forest*. At the most basic level the plot is a variant of the 'family romance', itself a common story line in fairy-tales. The classic version of the family romance is a child's discovery of her adoption, her true family being the posh one up the road rather than the nasty and/or poor one she has grown up with. Jane Eyre's swopping of the Rivers for the Reeds would be an example. Here, various unsavoury possibilities are exchanged for the murdered noble, Henry de Montalt. The important point to note is that the convention of the family romance allows – indeed, invites the reader to surmise – that any of Adeline's 'adopted' families may prove to be her true one. We are always only a coincidence away from the final revelation. Thus, in the course of the story, we encounter a bewildering set of parental possibilities for Adeline. We are first made to understand, by Adeline herself, that her father is Louis de St Pierre, 'A chevalier of reputable family, but of small fortune' (*RF*, 35), and that since the death of her mother she has been confined to a convent, until the recent mysterious happenings. The La Mottes become her adopted parents; La Lac, her 'father'. We next discover that Louis St Pierre is the bandit Jean d'Aunoy and that Adeline's real father is her persecutor, the Marquis de Montalt, and that he desires her death in order to protect her mother, who is a nun (and who would be executed on the disclure of proofs of her fornication). It is here that La Motte shudders at the recollection of how close Montalt came to commiting incest, and at his own role as pander to what would have been the incestuous debauch of his 'step-daughter'. Finally we learn that Adeline's true father is Montalt's half-brother, Henry, and that Montalt had murdered him in order to secure the wealth that had come via Henry's wife.

The 'passions which had stimulated [Montalt] to so monstrous a deed were ambition, and the love of pleasure' (*RF*, 342). By contrast, 'Henry was benevolent, mild, contemplative. In his heart reigned the love of virtue; in his manners the strictness of justice was tempered, not weakened, by mercy; his mind was enlarged by science, and adorned by elegant literature' (*RF*, 343). To read the book literally is to opt for a straightforward closure. The temporal setting is once more the 'Gothic cusp', the mid-seventeenth century, where the medieval is on the wane, and the Enlightenment begins to wax. In fleeing Montalt, Adeline is in a sense in flight from the Middle Ages; in the end the modern state, with its disinterested legal apparatus, triumphs over Montalt and his fedual prerogatives and privileges. Here Adeline and her 'father' are doubles in that both attest to the historical victory of eighteenth-century, 'bourgeois' sensibility with its pronounced sense of civil virtues.

The very conspicuousness of the exchange of a benevolent for an evil 'father' foregrounds the device of the family romance. This foregrounding in turn induces scepticism as to the veracity of the manuscript, with its testaments to an ideal father, a scepticism reinforced by the phantasmal air of mystery surrounding its discovery. As we begin to question the authority of the lost manuscript, so the sentimental closure invited by the family romance begins to unravel.

Is the discovered manuscript to be taken literally, or figuratively? In my view the answer is not one or the other but both: balancing the two readings enriches the text. The literal level encourages the view that Adeline has successfully escaped the power of the feudal, but the figurative suggests that the 'benevolent' father is merely a form of compensation for the irremediable reality of his opposite. At the literal level the discovery of the manuscript is connected to the restoration of Adeline's social identity, of her lands, wealth and titles. But figuratively a more complicated chain of reasoning suggests itself, for we are invited to ask: what is it that impels Adeline to fantasise about her 'ideal' father, and what clues does this compulsion give us regarding her identity (now in the deeper sense of a psychological entity)? To reduce the matter to a phrase: read literally the book offers a critique of feudal, aristocratic power; read figuratively, it critiques patriarchy.

The matter conveniently takes the shape of a chiasmus: romance of origins, origins of romance.[1] Adeline's discovery of the story of her murdered father is a romance of origins: the foundling 'fantas-

---

[1] I am indebted to Elisabeth Bronfen for the chiasmus 'romance of origins: origins of romance'.

izes' that she has a noble lineage. This in turn is bound up with the deeper issue of the origin of 'romance'. Adeline's discovery of the manuscript is a 'figure' for this origin. Conventionally, there are numerous ways for murder to out: material objects may supply the tell-tale clues, such as weapons or bodily remains, or the injured spectre may take the direct approach, as in *Hamlet*, and spill the beans himself. Discovered manuscripts are also a conventional means of disclosure in romances: what the *Romance of the Forest* does is find a way of defamiliarising the device, of making the choice significant, thereby giving it new thematic meaning. This is first of all evident in the anomalous fact that the discovery of the manuscript is not the incident on which the plot turns. Indeed, the manuscript is quite incidental to the resolution of the plot: everything that needs to be known emerges in court independent of the testimony offered by Adeline's elliptical script. The manuscript's significance, rather, is metonymic: it stands for 'romance', for writing by women, for the secretive process whereby women romancers produce their ambiguous, multivalent texts.

As we pursue this line of enquiry we begin to see that diametrically opposite things are hinged round the chiasmus. The romance of origins idealises the father, whereas the origins of romance indict him. The father is now a tyrannical figure whose guarded secrets enforce the subterfuge of coded writing. To put the matter in our earlier terms, the literal level with its 'sentimental' closure may appease the 'gentlewoman's sense of propriety, but the figurative offers concealed scope for the 'woman writer' (a secretiveness encoded in Adeline's private discovery/production of the manuscript/romance). Reading the work literally means taking the 'conservative' vision of the 'romance of origins' at face value. Conversely, the 'origins of romance', which begins to emerge when we read figuratively, subversively locates itself in the very structures of social power which force the woman writer to secrecy, to figurative writing, to 'romance'.

I do not mean to suggest that we are to take Radcliffe as a cryptic radical intent on smuggling in a subversive tract under the noses of censorious male readers. What I want to draw attention to, rather, is the way the text undermines – indeed, constantly makes an issue of – what it is we are to understand as 'real', with the consequence that the differences between the literal and the figurative begin to blur. What is consequently disclosed is not to be read as a simple allegory of an encrypted, radical truth: it is through the by-play of the figurative and literal that the complex, critical, social vision emerges.

For example, on two occasions Adeline experiences supernatural terror upon looking into mirrors. The first occurs during her captivity by her 'father', who is about to release her into the custody of La Motte. Unable to sleep properly, Adeline tells us that she fell into

> a sort of waking dream: I thought that I was in a lonely forest with my father; his looks were severe, and his gestures menacing: he upbraided me for leaving the convent, and while he spoke, drew from his pocket a mirror, which he held before my face: I looked in it and saw, (my blood now thrills as I repeat it) I saw myself wounded, and bleeding profusely. Then I thought myself in the house again; and suddenly heard these words, in accents so distinct, that for some time after I awoke, I could scarcely believe them ideal, 'Depart this house, destruction hovers here'.
>
> (*RF*, 41)

In the second, she reposes after reading the tale of suffering related in the manuscript. Her 'fancy, which now wandered in the regions of terror, gradually subdued reason. There was a glass before her upon the table, and she feared to raise her looks towards it, lest some other face than her own should meet her eyes ... A hollow sigh seemed to pass near by' (*RF*, 134). As motifs of supernatural terror these passages are conventional enough: their originality depends on their context.

The relevant context is the discourse of modesty which was instrumental in the late eighteenth-century construction of the 'feminine'. Jean-Jacques Rousseau's *Emile* offers a typical, influential example. Rousseau advances the argument that women are natural coquettes. They take to artifice instinctively. A modest woman is incapable of lying, even when she tells 'artful' untruths:

> Why do you consult their words when it is not their mouths that speak? Consult their eyes, their colour, their breathing, their timid manner, their slight resistance, that is the language nature gave them for your answer. The lips always say 'No', and rightly so; but the tone is not always the same, and that cannot lie. Has not a woman the same needs as a man, but without the same right to make them

known? Her fate would be too cruel if she had no language in which to express her legitimate desires except the words which she dare not utter.

(Rousseau 1974: 348)

The passage identifies desire with language. For men, desire and language are connected without complications. But for women the matter is different. They are forbidden to express their desire in words: their natural language for the expression of desire is the semiology of the body. It is through its 'artful' means that they find their 'natural' tongue.

Rousseau himself approvingly points to where this construction of the feminine leads: 'A young and beautiful girl will never despise her body ... she will never lament earnestly in the sight of God that she is an object of desire ...' (Rousseau 1974: 355). It was this sensual objectification of women – together with Rousseau's celebration of it – that particularly scandalised Mary Wollstonecraft.

However, Rousseau's 'modesty' did more than construe women as objects of desire. By insisting that woman's natural language was the body Rousseau figured women as doubly monstrous. Lacking language, *per se*, is one definition of the monstrous, of misshapen humanity, while to insist that women's 'language' is always cunning and indirect – a matter of coquetry – is to make a dehumanising comparison with men. According to Rousseau, man, deep down, is a creature of nature; woman, of artifice.

Rousseau's formulation also re-works the double-sidedness of sensibility investigated earlier. As a representation of modesty, woman has a potent ability to stir chaste desire within the male observer, but as this representation simultaneously disbars woman from language (in the conventional sense) her power to act is severely limited. Instead she must passively await the effects of her visual presence; her paradoxical lot is to become a speaking picture, a dumb object that tells.

A recurring figure for this aspect of the construction of the feminine was 'virtue in distress' (Brissenden 1974), the stock situation of a young woman in peril of a fate worse than death. As a spectacle virtue in distress was meant to awaken sympathy within the male viewer, moving him to benevolent feelings and noble deeds. But while the spectacle was calculated to accentuate his humanity, the representation itself denied hers: her role was to be no more than a visually affecting object.

In *The Castles of Athlin and Dunbayne* Radcliffe reproduces the conventional construction of the feminine implicit within the discourse of modesty. Alleyn receives from Mary not a declaration of her feelings but 'a blush which spoke more than her tongue could utter' (*CAD*: 72). Laura 'wished to speak her gratitude, yet feared to tell her love; but the soft timidity of her eye, and the tender glow of her cheek, revealed the secret that trembled on her lips' (*CAD*: 167). But for Mary, especially, the inability to employ language to express her desire – to connect feeling with self-expression – has considerable costs. Mary endeavours to control her 'weakness', her love for Alleyn: she 'closed her lips in silence. Her health gradually declined under the secret agitation of her mind; her physician knew her disorder to originate in suppressed sorrow, and advised, as the best cordial, a confidential friend' (*CAD*: 89). Except the physician does not know the origins of her 'suppressed sorrow', nor is 'a confidential friend' any help, for her desires are – for the modest female – beyond language, and therefore 'confidence'. This secret love 'corroded her heart' (*CAD*: 225).

As Radcliffe's career goes on she finds increasingly subtle and profound ways of mounting a critique against the construction of the feminine found in Rousseau. In *A Sicilian Romance*, although Julia has, like Mary, a speaking body, she is also more decisive, more ready to voice and act upon her desire. More significantly, perhaps, the representation of the attempted rape of Julia catches the reader out in discomfiting voyeurism.

But in *A Romance of the Forest* Radcliffe's critique takes on a new order of complexity. Adeline's initial introduction conforms with the conventional iconography of virtue in distress. As La Motte waits in the mysterious house a door opens, admitting a man 'forcibly dragging along, a beautiful girl, who appeared to be about eighteen. Her features were bathed in tears, and she seemed to suffer the utmost distress . . . She sunk at [La Motte's] feet, and with supplicating eyes, that streamed with tears, implored him to have pity on her' (*RF*, 5). La Motte is appropriately moved. This is partly because Adeline conforms to virtue's dress code: 'A habit of grey camlet ... shewed, but did not adorn, her figure: it was thrown open at the bosom, upon which part of her hair had fallen in disorder, while the light veil hastily thrown on, had, in her confusion, been suffered to fall back' (*RF*, 7). Rousseau discourses on this dress code apropos his ideal Sophy: 'no article is selected at random, and yet there is no trace of artificiality. Her dress is very modest in appearance and very coquettish in reality; she does not display her charms, she conceals them, but in such a way as to enhance them' (Rousseau, 1974: 356). Adeline's dress is a model of this simple elegance, of instinctive coquetry, of the artificiality that disguises itself.

In introducing Adeline in this way Radcliffe appears to fix her identity within the conventions of the modest female, of virtue in distress: we see her caught – and defined – within the male gaze. She is presented to us as one of Rousseau's 'monsters'.

However, that we also see her so caught and defined by the gaze of La Motte ought to give us pause, once we recollect his dubious standing. But more significantly we observe in Adeline's own story, and especially in her own account of her story, the effective destabilisation of this construction of the feminine.

Adeline's waking dream has three main components. She is alone in the forest with her angry father; he holds up a mirror in which she sees herself wounded and bleeding; a supernatural voice urges her to fly. A first reading will differ from a retrospective one. Initially the dream appears to be contradictory: the father is both angry and (through his projected voice) solicitous of her safety. Retrospectively the contradiction disappears. The 'father' is not Louis de St. Pierre but Montalt (subsequent to the dream it is Montalt who has her abducted in the forest), while the voice is not Montalt's but that of Henry, Adeline's 'true' father, who guards her by preternatural means.

In the supernatural realm of romance, mirrors signify things as they are, but also as they will be. The image reflected in the mirror held up by 'Montalt' represents a prognostication circumvented by the warning of the mysterious voice. But mirrors, signifying things as they are, also reflect identities. In the phantasmal moment of her waking dream (itself 'romance' in microcosm) Adeline has her 'identity' reflected back to her by a paternal image: it is one of bodily disfigurement. In a first reading this violent image is mysteriously associated with the ambiguous father (simultaneously malign and benevolent). Retrospectively matters appear to clarify, for the violence is now associated with the malign 'father', with her uncle Montalt.

The second incident maintains the conjunction of mirror and voice. Adeline has just been reading the secret manuscript – the prison writings – of her murdered father. Her expressions of pity are answered by a preternatural sigh. Just previous to this she fears to look into her mirror lest some face 'other than her own should meet her eyes' (*RF*, 134).

To an extent this is conventional enough. Strange faces staring back from mirrors are a familiar expression of the uncanny (Freud 1958), and at this point Radcliffe clearly wants to heighten the eerie tension. But thematically the threat of non-recognition is highly significant, for it suggests that Adeline's fantasy of an ideal father (the romance of origins) blocks her 'identity'.

I earlier mentioned that *A Sicilian Romance* advanced Radcliffe's art of keeping her readership guessing by delaying the moment when the supernatural was explained. By the same token – and this is a method she perfects in *The Mysteries of Udolpho* – closure is deferred. Closure witnesses the imposition of conservative 'common sense'. The supernatural, by contrast, opens up radical meanings. On a first reading such meanings proliferate, ones curtailed in a retrospective reading where all has been safely 'explained'.

So it is here. A first reading suggests that the benevolent and malign fathers are of a piece, are different sides of the same, contradictory coin. We first see Adeline constructed as a 'modest' woman via the narrator's 'benevolent' male gaze (for it envisages her as an embodiment of virtue in distress); we next see her through the medium of the malign father's mirror, where she appears violated and disfigured. Just as the father's dual aspects are different sides of the same coin, so are these representations of Adeline: the flip side of Rousseau's discourse of modesty is the violence implicit in his reductive idealisation of the feminine. And for Adeline, neither image is a sound basis for 'identity'.

These episodes with mirrors present us with an intriguing 'fit' between Lacan's theory and Radcliffe's text. For Lacan, the 'mirror stage' is that moment when the child misrecognises herself as a coherent identity. Adeline's fear of looking into the mirror may be construed as her antipathy to entering the 'Symbolic', the realm of patriarchal discourse which will construct her differently than she feels herself to be (that is, a socially constructed identity). Conversely, in the first instance, the image reflected back to Adeline in the paternal mirror is one of bodily mutilation.

There are two complementary ways of understanding this. First, the Symbolic order 'mutilates' the subject's 'true' image; secondly, the mirror 'reflects' back the way the Symbolic order constructs the subject's identity – here, as the violation implicit in the discursive structure 'virtue in distress'. In Radcliffe's own terms, both episodes reflect the heroine's typical anxiety that in leaving the threshold for an order defined by the father's choices she will lose her 'sensibility', and hence her identity. And yet sensibility – with its incorporation of 'virtue in distress' – belongs to the very order that confines her. (When in the last chapter I said that *A Sicilian Romance* did not go beyond hinting at the 'stopgap' nature of sensibility, I meant that it was relatively inarticulate about the disadvantages sensibility held for the Radcliffe heroine caught on her threshold. *The Romance of the Forest* is articulate in that it brings out sensibility's discursive or Symbolic hazards.)

I am not sure what to make of this ready 'fit' between Lacan and Radcliffe other than to reiterate my earlier point that for good historical reasons Gothic writing and psychoanalysis are often to be found in conversation with each other. There is one point I am sure about, though, and that is that it is owing to their artfulness that Radcliffe's texts are to be found in such conversation. There are many Gothic novels of the period without *The Romance of the Forest*'s teasing complexity. That it does tease owes much to the skill with which the literal and figurative are held in equipoise.

At this point I want to take a further look at Radcliffe's representation of landscape, a discussion that looks back to what I said on the matter in Chapter 5 but also forward to Radcliffe's remaining texts. I introduce it here because I now want to bring out the figurative aspect of Radcliffe's landscape art, which also falls in with the textual rhythms we have been looking at, of deprivation and replenishment, of maternal promise and patriarchal threat. In terms of scenery these alternating rhythms are most evident in the sublime and the picturesque.

In terms of pictorial references Radcliffe's contemporaries understood this rhythm as the complementary art of Claude Lorrain and Salvator Rosa. In the eighteenth century these painters were fashionable and widely known. It was a mark of the esteem in which Radcliffe was held that she was considered to possess a unique prowess to create verbal equivalents of their visual landscapes. Indeed, so habitual was the identification of Radcliffe with 'Claude and Salvator' that William Hazlitt felt compelled to point out that her 'descriptions of scenery' were nothing like theirs (Hazlitt 1907: 165). As a critic passionately fond of Claude and Salvator Rosa, Hazlitt was being something of a stickler. He did not dispute the general point regarding Radcliffe's visualising powers, but the comparison needled him.

That was in 1818, long after the association with Claude and Salvator Rosa had become fixed. It was an association Radcliffe herself had sought. Her references to them guaranteed her writing aesthetic kudos, while underpinning her 'naturalism'. Both painters were active in the seventeenth century. Radcliffe's trick was to validate the romanticism of these artists' representations by situating her narratives in the same period, and often in the same environments, as they did. Her verbal depictions re-enforced their visual ones. This meant that her readers often had visual references to draw on. More subtly, Radcliffe's working assumption was that Rosa and Claude were faithful copyists of their seventeenth-century Mediterranean world. Her art validated theirs; but so, by the same token, did theirs hers.

To the extent that Claude was associated with a pastoral subject-matter he was thought of as a painter of the 'picturesque'. Less dramatic than Rosa, he was particularly famous for his ability to recreate the southern Italian light. At once crystalline yet textured, Claude's 'light' gave his pictures – often of the Roman Campagna – a 'timeless' feel, at once displaced, as if of an irrecoverable past, and yet contemporary, as if it were a recent past. For the eighteenth-century viewer, it caught the very texture of nostalgia. Claude's landscapes were both ideal and naturalistic, imaginary, and yet convincingly detailed.

By contrast, Salvator Rosa was viewed as the painter of the

sublime. Both his natural and human subject-matter tended to the wild, to nature beyond the fence. The subject-matter with which he was most often associated was mountain scenery populated by half-savage banditti. Whereas Claude favoured a semi-luminous light suffusing the entire canvas, Rosa preferred a heavier use of chiaroscuro, the resulting obscurity reinforcing the sublime effects of his paintings. In both, scenery tended to dwarf the immediate human interest, the figures in the foreground.

Radcliffe's scenic descriptions oscillate between the picturesque and the sublime, Claude and Rosa. The predominant mood of the picturesque is melancholy over the inevitability of passing time. Although Radcliffe's picturesque appears to turn on absence – the melancholy viewer is filled with a poignant yearning for something that forever eludes her – it is actually a moment of plenitude, one associated with maternal nurturing. This is because the picturesque moment is for the heroine an instance of artistic self-fulfilment. The pre-Romantic values associated with the picturesque – sensibility, melancholy, isolation, a heightened sense of mortality – form a contemporary 'iconography' of the creative, what one might call genius in its various moods. When the heroine retires to a picturesque glade, when she revolves inwardly, in poetic reverie, she puts herself in touch with the sensibility which was then understood as the quick of modern poetry. She finds her inner self nurtured by ambient nature: only in this aesthetically fecund isolation can her inner, Romantic self find fulfilment. Music is often used by Radcliffe to symbolise this synaesthesia of creative isolation, the ravishing of the senses.

As an example, take the moment when Adeline feels she has lost the love of Madame La Motte, her surrogate mother. In immediate compensation Adeline finds a substitute for this maternal love in nature's picturesque beauty:

> She wandered on without noticing the distance, and, following the windings of the river, came to a dewy glade, whose woods, sweeping down to the very edge of the water, formed a scene so sweetly romantic, that she seated herself at the foot of a tree, to contemplate its beauty. These images insensibly soothed her sorrow, and inspired her with that soft and pleasing melancholy, so dear to the feeling mind. For some time she sat lost in a reverie, while the flowers that

grew on the banks beside her seemed to smile in new life, and drew
from her a comparison with her own condition.

(RF, 75)

Nature's romantic images 'soothe her sorrow' before 'inspiring'
her melancholy. This moment of creative plenitude, where nature
mirrors her moods, results in Adeline singing a sonnet in which
she sketches out her condition through the figure of the co-respon-
sive lily. When Adeline stops, she catches her first glimpse of
Theodore, who, enraptured, replies in kind.

Several things come together in this passage. 'Picturesque'
nature nurtures the heroine; this nurture is a substitute for the
maternal; and both the heroine's creativity and her identity are
strengthened by it. As we have seen before, the love interest is
introduced only when the heroine's sense of identity is at its most
robust. Radcliffe's heroines do not discover their identity through
love; rather 'love' or marriage is the consequence of their self-
assertion, their self-discovery and creation. So it is here: desire and
its object (Theodore) enter the scene as a consequence of Adeline's
creative self-fashioning.

To an extent Radcliffe's sublime works in a manner antithetical
to her picturesque. The picturesque appears to turn on self-abasement. In accepting the melancholy truth of the mortality of all
things, the heroine allows herself to blend in with the mass.
But insofar as the picturesque scene affords a moment of self-
communion it is also, paradoxically, an instance of self-assertion.
In Radcliffe's sublime the order is reversed. Ostensibly God's presence is momentarily glimpsed through his natural works. As a
transcendent experience, one's place in the divine order ought to
be revealed during this glimpse; moreover, the moment ought
to be a founding moment of identity (as it is, for instance, in
Wordsworth's scheme of things). But in Radcliffe the sublime does
not work in quite such an unambiguous way.

The most clear-cut example of Radcliffe's natural sublime occurs
in *The Italian*. The heroine, Ellena de Rosalba, regards the mountain scenery beyond her 'threshold', in this case a convent turret
where she is kept prisoner:

> Hither she could come, and her soul, refreshed by the views it
> afforded, would acquire strength to bear her, with equanimity, thro'

the persecutions that might await her. Here, gazing upon the stupendous imagery around her, looking, as it were, beyond the awful veil which obscures the features of the Deity, and conceals Him from the eyes of his creatures, dwelling as with a present God in the midst of his sublime works; with a mind thus elevated, how insignificant would appear to her the transactions, and the sufferings of this world!

(*I*, 90–1)

Eighteenth-century aesthetics distinguished between the natural and the rhetorical sublimes (Monk 1960). Common to both was the notion that divine order lay behind the jumble of appearances (Price 1969). The divine order was not directly perceivable, hence the special prestige enjoyed by the sublime, which was thought of as the aesthetic experience in which the indirect apprehension of the supernal was at its most intense (Hamilton 1983: 50–7). Radcliffe's subjunctive 'as it were' registers the tenuous nature of the sublime glimpse: it is only *as if* one beheld God's face behind the veil. The metaphors signalled by the subjunctive ('veil' and 'dwell') indicate that in the realm of the divine we are restricted by the crude approximations of language.

In La Luc's succinct definition of it, the natural sublime occurs when we are led to contemplate (indirectly) 'the sublimity of [God's] nature in the grandeur of his works' (*I*, 265). The rhetorical sublime was understood as the expression of a sense of the divine power through the grandeur of words. The classical example was the *fiat lux* described in *Genesis*.

If we extend the rhetorical sublime to include statements made through other media, such as architecture, then it becomes clear that Radcliffe's texts construe the rhetorical sublime as something extremely sinister. The monuments of nature glorify the hand of the divine maker; human monuments profanely glorify human makers. The sublime castles of Radcliffe's villains parody the Christian vision of God in his celestial city. Feudal barons, with the power of life and death over their subjects, lord it over their vassals, masters of all they survey. The mismatch between the divine ideal and the profane reality foregrounds the mendacity of Radcliffe's Gothic villains.

However, it is in the nature of the Gothic genre for parodies to cut both ways. For instance, in Mary Shelley's *Frankenstein*, the monster's maker is incompetent, vacillating and selfish. Comparison with the divine maker highlights Frankenstein's shortcomings. But by the same token the reader is free to interpret Frankenstein as a commentary on God; that is, the Doctor's representation invites us to consider the view that God himself is a bumbling (male) incompetent who flees his responsibilities (Cantor 1984).

In Radcliffe's Gothic, the natural and rhetorical sublimes are mutually destabilising. The heroine's experience of the 'rhetorical' sublime – that is to say, the terror she undergoes in the presence of the villain's castle – fixes her in her conventional femininity: we see her as 'virtue in distress'. In terms of plot, she is persecuted by her father or a father substitute, who generally wishes to sacrifice her to the gods of primogeniture. Such fathers are expressly 'feudal' in comparison with the modern world of sensibility the heroine wishes to escape into. The same contrast foregrounds their roles as figures of patriarchy. Radcliffe's plots have a residual romance element, as we have seen when considering the issue of identity. In conventional romance the complications of the plot are untied when identity is established in social or class terms: the foundling is really a prince or princess, and all obstacles to marriage are removed. But Radcliffe's plots also have a modern element: here we encounter the problematics of Romantic identity, the sense that each individual is somehow unique, and uniquely gifted. Here identity goes beyond the definitions of class.

With this in mind we can see that Radcliffe's rhetorical sublime is an instrument of patriarchy in that it arrests the heroine's identity within the frame of cultural definition. It is part of what the heroine – in seeking out the modern – is in flight from. But in this respect the 'natural sublime' is suspiciously similar in that it too imposes a hierarchical structure of self-abasement. This structure is only latent, and we seem to have good reason for discounting it. After all, the sublime appears to belong to the same family of pre-Romantic values so warmly endorsed by the picturesque. And yet there appears to be a pattern: the heroine on her threshold has the 'choice' of revolving inwards, into an illusive world of reverie, sensibility, and the picturesque; or she can move outwards into a world conditioned by the 'transcendental signifier' of the natural sublime. The one is nurturing and maternal, but also limiting, because inward, and always contained within the incarcerating paternal; the other is the world of desire – it is, after all, the world of the beloved – but is also one where the heroine is continually blocked by the power of the father (in both his 'rhetorical' and 'natural') guises. In this respect the picturesque and the sublime are landscape versions of Radcliffe's recurring 'neither/nor'.

I began this chapter with a lengthy quotation from Julia Kavanagh. Kavanagh's close historical proximity to Radcliffe (and to the sensibility of her first readership) gives Kavanagh's writing an authority modern criticism does well to respect. This chapter is, in many respects, a lengthy gloss on Kavanagh's brief, but acute commentary.

Kavanagh makes several teasingly profound points. Firstly, that Radcliffe's representations of landscape are historically new, and secondly, that *The Romance of the Forest*'s appeal is based on 'man's secret desire to be alone'. Kavanagh furthermore suggests that these developments are a response to a general, historical dislocation in the sensibility of Radcliffe's readership. For this readership, landscape has become spectral (their minds are 'haunted' by it); moreover, their readerly dreams are fed, not by fantasies of connection, of romantic love and the social, but by reveries of isolation.

My suggestion in this chapter has been that Radcliffe's figure of the threshold and her development of the female Gothic plot dovetail with her readership's imaginative needs. The rhythms of the female Gothic are those of presence and absence, of the maternal and patriarchal, rhythms intensified by the sympathetic subject-position of the 'threshold', where the heroine hovers between an inward regression in pursuit of an absent (yet once present) maternal plenitude, and an outward turning towards desire threatened by patriarchal prohibition. These rhythms are reproduced through spectralisation, through the pulsations of plot, through the text's self-reflexive meditations on the origins of romance, and through landscape representation.

In this chapter I have argued that one has to be sensitive to the figurative aspect of Radcliffe's art if one is to understand its complexity or its appeal. The figurative informs her enchantment.

I now want to turn to *The Mysteries of Udolpho*, which itself instructs us in how to read the figural in her art.

7
The hermeneutics of reading:
The Mysteries of Udolpho

A principal characteristic of Mrs. Radcliffe's romances, is the rule which the author imposed upon herself, that all the circumstances of her narrative, however mysterious, and apparently superhuman, were to be accounted for on natural principles, at the winding up of the story. It must be allowed, that this is has not been done with uniform success . . .

Sir Walter Scott, 1824 (Sage 1990: 60)

A novel, if at all useful, ought to be a representation of human life and manners, with a view to direct the conduct in the important duties of life, and to correct its follies. But what instruction is to be reaped from the distorted ideas of lunatics, I am at a loss to conceive.
'Terrorist Novel Writing', *The Spirit of The Public Journals*, I (1797: 228)

the same mysterious terrors are continually exciting in the mind the idea of a supernatural appearance, keeping us, as it were, upon the very edge and confines of the world of spirits, and yet are ingeniously explained by familiar causes . . .
S. T. Coleridge, *The Critical Review*, August 1794 (Raysor 1936: 356)

For the reader devouring Radcliffe's romances in chronological order perhaps the most glaring difference of the *The Mysteries of Udolpho* is its sudden, spectacular use of the 'explained supernatural'. Although *A Sicilian Romance* employed the device, it was apropos a single situation: the 'buried' Louisa, whose bangings and shouts were taken for preternatural utterances. *The Romance of the Forest* not only employed the explained supernatural sparingly, but arguably, on the central occasion, not at all, for it is never made entirely clear whether the voice attendant upon Emily's discovery of the manuscript is an hallucination or spectral speech.

But in *The Mysteries of Udolpho* the explained supernatural abounds. A mysterious singer and sonnet writer haunts La Vallée, and then Udolpho itself: it turns out to be the unfortunate love-sick Du Pont, ever on the margins, but never in view. Disembodied injunctions interrupt Montoni's counsels: it is the hidden Du Pont. Another disembodied voice – this time a woman's – is heard singing within the environs of the Chateau-le-Blanc, first as an awful prelude to St Aubert's death, then as a counterpoint to the supernatural events within the chateau. A face inexplicably appears in a mirror as Dorothée and Emily penetrate the awful gloom of the Marchioness de Villeroi's death chamber. Later, Ludovico disappears from the same wing as he sits out the night, to prove the servants' fears of ghosts groundless. The singer is the sister Agnes, erstwhile Laurentini, who had earlier mysteriously van-ished from Udolpho. The face in the mirror and Ludovico's disap-pearance are in both cases tricks of banditti, who exploit the superstitiousness of the locals to keep interlopers at a distance from their base in the grotto under the chateau.

And yet, although all of the spectral appearances within the novel have material causes, Emily repeatedly fails to maintain mental discipline. Her rationality is continually overthrown by her fearful, racing mind. The 'contagion' of superstition (*MU*, 490) inexorably sweeps away the precautionary measures she leagues against it. The issue pointedly recurs throughout the text. On several occasions Emily smiles indulgently at the credulity of serv-ants, at the fears of the verbally incontinent Annette or at Doro-thée's old-fashioned superstitions. Almost immediately another supernatural appearance will occur, sweeping away Emily's com-placent resolutions to be rational.

Thematically, Emily's weakness links back to St Aubert's death-bed warnings to beware excessive passion in all its forms, including its most beguiling shape: sensibility. Disillusioned and fearful of society, St Aubert wishes to leave his daughter with a surrogate guardian, a developed 'reason'. This, he believes, will provide her with autonomy, the ability to steer a clear course through life's perils. His death-bed warnings are later echoed by Laurentini, now a nun, but once the Marquis de Villeroi's adulterous lover and co-murderer of St Aubert's sister. She cautions Emily:

'Sister, beware of the first indulgence of the passions; beware of the first! Their course, if not checked then, is rapid – their force is uncontrollable – they lead us we know not whither – they lead us perhaps to the commission of crimes, for which whole years of prayer and penitence cannot atone.'

(*MU*, 646)

Aubert's generalised warnings and the particularised example of Laurentini (where fornication proves the first step to murder) establish a worrying framework for Emily's weakness: thematically, 'letting her mind go' has sinister overtones, for once reason has skipped its traces, the passions uncontrollably follow.

Laurentini's view that female adolescents' unfettered passions held mortal danger had a strong contemporary resonance. Captain Thomas Morris's amusing bagatelle *The Polished Grisette* provides a good example. Morris is especially concerned about the lower orders:

Mothers, however trade improve your store,
Make your girls housewifes, and they need no more;
Their best accomplishments are household arts;
Novels and tricks at school make vicious hearts.
As oft a spark unheeded, cities fires,
So horrors rise from youth's uncheck'd desires . . .
The Spirit of the Public Journals (1798: 189–90)

As a final proof Morris adduces the history of Madame la Marquise de Brinvillier. The Marquise lost her virginity at seven. Soon after she became France's 'greatest monster' (she poisoned her patients in the hospital where she masqueraded as a nun, before setting fire to her parents). For Captain Morris moral monstrosity is the natural result of pre-pubescent sex. In the Captain's moral *mise-en-scène*, Brinvillier's violator is nowhere in view. The poem's lesson appears in the pointed contrast between Brinvillier and the prim young miss who refuses to read novels. For the Captain, there is not much to choose, morally, between schoolgirls who debauch themselves with paedophiles and those who open romances.

Although Morris's poem is crude satire, a number of associations naturally – and tellingly – fall into place. Novel reading, sexual desire and criminality (themselves of a piece) are in direct opposition to feminine propriety and domestic happiness. This is the cultural subtext of the explained supernatural in *The Mysteries of Udolpho*. The contagion of superstition amounts to a loss of self-control. In Emily's case this primarily means a runaway imagination of the kind that might be induced by too much novel reading (in the manner of Catherine Morland); but in the examples she has before her (but primarily that of Laurentini) this lack of self-control is linked to sexual desire and criminality. Superstition – the belief in the supernatural – is thus implicitly transgressive. The text's 'explanations' return Emily, not just to 'reason', but to cultural and gender norms.

This thematic aspect of the explained supernatural – with its cultural resonances – was not initially appreciated by Radcliffe's contemporary critics. Walter Scott's approach is typically narrow. For Scott, the explained supernatural was an imperfect solution to a technical problem: 'Romantic narrative is of two kinds, – that which, being in itself possible, may be a matter of belief at any period; and that which, though held impossible by more enlightened ages, was yet consonant with the faith of earlier times' (Williams 1968: 89). Horace Walpole chose the latter, unproblematic option. For Radcliffe, who situated her romances on the 'Gothic cusp', where there were believers and non-believers in equal measure, ancients and moderns, such a solution was not feasible. Instead she tried to effect a compromise through the explained supernatural. Scott objected that the reader feels indignant at being cheated into terror by trivial causes, that in a professed work of fiction assurances of rationality are as misplaced as Bottom's in *A Midsummer Night's Dream*, and that, anyway, the explanations are as improbable as the machinery they explain away. As Coleridge put it, the 'trite and the extravagant are the Scylla and Charybdis of writers who deal in fiction' (Raysor 1936: 356).

Scott's commonsensical assessment misses the point, which is that Radcliffe's concerns stretch beyond raising the hairs of her readers without incurring the charge of endorsing a preternatural order. The concept of 'superstition' or the irrational was central to her thematic purposes. It was important for her characters to return to the 'daylight', rational world of the dawning Enlightenment, but only after an irrational interregnum, when the mind was allowed to wander, to believe, and conjecture, as it would. Scott's second option – where the supernatural was 'consonant with the faith of earlier times' – did not provide the contrast between the rational and irrational. The explained supernatural did.

To put Radcliffe's artfulness into perspective here it helps to draw an analogy with Freudian theory. For Freud, slips of the tongue, neurotic symptoms, or dreams were only apparently irrational. Behind superficially random thought processes one eventually encountered a repressed thought or wish. For the unconscious to evade the mind's censor, these repressed thoughts needed to be disguised (as metaphors, contiguous associations, or verbal and visual puns).

Similarly, the superstitious beliefs of Radcliffe's heroines often express otherwise impermissible thoughts, conjectures, wishes or fears. As ostensibly irrational beliefs they are, as it were, licensed. At the same time, ideas which would ordinarily be censored by the reigning sense of daylight propriety enter into the arena of the novel's discussions. The text does return us to the rational order of the explained supernatural, just as Shakespeare's *A Midsummer Night's Dream* returns its audience to Theseus's common-sensical Athens. But just as the crepuscular events of the forest are as much a part of the *Dream*'s reality as the Athenian festivities, so Emily's florid, superstitious fantasies are as much a part of *Udolpho*'s text as the rational explanations that apparently supercede them.

Indeed, Emily's superstitious fantasies are as important to the reader puzzling out *Udolpho*'s mysteries as dreams are to Freudians unravelling the text of their patients' symptoms. Moreover, once we realise that the conjectures prompted by textual mysteries are as important as the explanations, it becomes apparent that the device encompasses more than seeming instances of the preternatural. Coleridge is once again extremely helpful. In reading *Udolpho*

curiosity is kept upon the stretch from page to page, and from volume to volume, and the secret, which the reader thinks himself every instant on the point of penetrating, flies like a phantom before him, and eludes his eagerness till the very last moment of protracted expectation. This art of escaping the guesses of the reader has been improved and brought to perfection along with the reader's sagacity . . .

(Raysor 1936: 356)

Coleridge has the explained supernatural uppermost in mind when he refers to the 'art of escaping the guesses of the reader', but *Udolpho* presents us with additional mysteries, such as, for instance, the object behind the veil, the sight of which nearly deprives Emily of her reason. Until the very end the object's identity is a blank the reader is invited to fill in; in filling it in she is led up the garden path, sometimes through a delusive patterning of evidence, sometimes through the mistaken suppositions of Emily or others. The final revelations dissipate these conjectures. And yet the shadowy presence of exploded guesses are as much a part of the text – as much a part of what the reader has to interpret and consider – as what is finally disclosed as the 'truth'.

When I said in Chapter 1 that Radcliffe's texts ushered in a new hermeneutics of reading I meant this 'art of escaping the guesses of the reader'. One upshot of this new 'readerly hermeneutics' was the production of texts that readily lend themselves to the interpretative procedures of reader-response theory (Richter 1989). In Radcliffe's mature work, the order in which information is delivered is crucial. The text's meaning must not be confused with the synoptic view of events disclosed at the end with the explanation of the novel's mysteries. The guesses the reader is encouraged to make, and the order in which she is encouraged to make them, must also enter the reckoning. Another way of putting this new hermeneutics of reading is that it breaks the old 'contract' between author and reader (cf. Kermode 1983: 108): in place of the customary agreement between author and reader that a final meaning or order will be revealed, one now discovers that much of the burden of construing the meaning of the text has been shifted onto the reader. The reader must sharpen her sagacity, must enter into the process of guessing. And this is not simply because the reader is invited to surmise who or what is doing the singing, or kidnapping, or voice projection. More profoundly, there are 'gaps' left in the text. The foundations on which interpretation rests are riddled with lacunae the reader is both free – and obliged – to fill in. In this pursuit, the figural dimension, analysed in the last chapter, obviously comes into play.

Udolpho itself clearly distinguishes between the 'explained supernatural' and these deeper mysteries, these 'gaps'. As Blanche and

Emily survey the environs of Chateau-Le-Blanc the mysterious singer is heard once again. Dorothée believes it to be a spirit:

> Emily smiled, and, remembering how lately she had suffered herself to be led away by superstition, determined now to resist its contagion; yet in spight of her efforts, she felt awe mingle with her curiosity, on this subject; and Blanche, who had hitherto listened in silence, now enquired what this music was, and how long it had been heard.

(MU, 490)

The supernatural music is eventually explained: it is Sister Agnes, formerly Laurentini, who has taken to wandering in the woods, singing in fruitless expiation of her criminal participation in the murder of Emily's aunt, the Marchioness de Villeroi. But then the text explicitly refers to its own celebrated device, double-guessing the reader in the process. Dorothée intimates the chateau is haunted, whereupon Emily, smiling, responds that she has recently come from a ' "place of wonders" ' (Udolpho) and has unfortunately ' "heard almost all of them explained" ':

> Blanche was silent: Dorothée looked grave, and sighed; and Emily felt herself still inclined to believe more of the wonderful, than she chose to acknowledge. Just then, she remembered the spectacle she had witnessed in a chamber of Udolpho, and, by an odd kind of coincidence, the alarming words, that had accidentally met her eye in the MS papers, which she had destroyed, in obedience to the command of her father; and she shuddered at the meaning they seemed to impart, almost as much as at the horrible appearance, disclosed by the black veil.

(MU, 491)

It emerges that over and above supernatural appearances, which may be explained, there are other mysteries of a sublunary character which are yet more intractable, less easy to trace, because seated in the obscure recesses of consciousness. Emily's mind here wanders over the two puzzles which most tax her and the reader's sagacity: what lies behind the black veil? And what horrors are confessed in St Aubert's secret manuscript, which Emily had inadvertently and transgressively glimpsed? That Emily now links them in her mind deepens the mystery.

The context in which the linkage takes place compounds it. As Emily gazes out past the casements of Blanche's favourite turret in the Chateau-le-Blanc she suddenly realises that much of the scenery is familiar. It dawns on her that she is in the mysterious chateau near the cottage in which St Aubert died, the one he had regarded with such startled emotion. Emily is 'shocked by this discovery' (*MU*, 490). The phrase reinforces the natural line of suspicion. At the beginning of the romance, Emily, stealing in upon her father, witnesses him reading papers with a ghastly expression, then sighing over and kissing a portrait 'of a lady, but not of her mother' (*MU*, 26). In coming upon the Chateau-le-Blanc he confesses that he knew the unfortunate woman who lived there (the Marchioness de Villeroi), while Dorothée, the Marchioness's ancient serving maid, now evinces a profound curiosity in Emily's looks, which, she says, strangely resemble those of her former mistress. The reader is invited to surmise that Emily is the Marchioness de Villeroi's illegitimate daughter, the fruit of a liaison with St Aubert (a view later emphatically endorsed by the dying Laurentini). The 'alarming words, that had accidentally met her eye in the MS papers' apparently allude to her father's secret, adulterous affair.

But why should these words be recalled by Emily's recollection of the 'spectacle she had *witnessed* in a chamber of Udolpho' (my italics), when she had lifted the veil on the picture which, we are told, was not a 'picture'? The obvious similarity is that both are acts of partial disclosure, of lifting the veil on awful mysteries, figuratively so in one case, literally so in the other. There is also a natural train of thought. Unlike the supernatural appearances at Udolpho – the 'place of wonders' from which Emily has just come – these revelations remain 'unexplained': thinking about the mysteries that have been cleared up naturally reminds Emily of the ones that yet remain obscure.

But as the verb *witnessed* suggests, at a deeper level this disclosure is transgressive. The verb is nicely poised, for the transgression is either Emily's (intruding upon things she should not see) or other people's (Emily is witness to a crime). In sounding the mystery of the 'horrible appearance, disclosed by the black veil', the reader is invited to believe that the concealed object is Laurentini's body, pegged to the wall by Montoni (this is the conclusion to which Catherine Morland, half-way through *Udolpho*, jumps [Austen 1972: 601]). Annette has told Emily that Laurentini was the heir to Udolpho and that Montoni was her distant – but nearest – relative. Montoni courted her, but the passionate Laurentini loved someone else. Montoni departs in high dudgeon; soon after, Laurentini mysteriously disappears. Montoni returns, claiming Udolpho as his property. Emily's extreme surprise at the door to the chamber being left open underpins the suspicion that it contains damning evidence of Montoni's culpability in Laurentini's 'disappearance', a hunch strengthened by another of Emily's 'linkages'. Having heard Annette's garbled version of Laurentini's past, Emily's

> thoughts recurred to the strange history of Signora Laurentini and then to her own strange situation, in the wild and solitary mountains of a foreign country, in the castle, and the power of a man, to whom, only a few preceding months, she was an entire stranger . . .'
>
> (*MU*, 240)

Although the 'strange situation' sounds like the female Gothic's version of marriage, Emily's position is quite other: Montoni is now her 'parent'. The same property laws that ensured that Montoni inherited from Laurentini on the advent of her 'death' pertain here. Through his marriage to her aunt, Montoni stands to gain Emily's fortune, should she 'disappear'. Emily links her suspicion of what happened to Laurentini to her fears of what might happen to her.

We now have this possible link between the 'spectacle' in Udolpho and the glimpsed words of her father's MS papers: both disclosures reveal something about Emily's status. If the supposition raised by Emily's 'glimpse' into the MS proved true (that her father had had an affair), then her status would be altered directly: as an illegitimate child Emily's property rights would be placed in jeopardy. In the case of the other 'discovery', these very property rights jeopardise her. Within Udolpho's Gothic society 'lifting the veil' reveals to Emily (through the mirror image of Laurentini's 'body') that her status is that of property, either to be bartered away – as Montoni attempts to do – or discarded, put out of sight, once her entitlements have fallen within the net of male acquisitiveness. In both cases, the ambiguity of 'witness' continues to resonate: as someone gaining an illicit glimpse of male power behind the arras, Emily is a transgressive spectator; at the same time she 'witnesses' acts that transgress against her – and Laurentini's – natural rights.

And yet the more the reader strives to connect the apparently unconnected, the more gaps open up around the edges. What possible similarities could there be between the benevolent St Aubert and the evil Montoni? The linkage appears to be fortuitous, part of Emily's random thought processes. And yet the text suggests otherwise: the veiled picture and the hidden words are linked by 'an odd kind of coincidence'. Coincidences are by definition 'odd': to speak of a 'predictable coincidence' taxes the word's common meaning. In this respect 'an odd kind of coincidence' takes on the character of a double negative, with method now showing through the random association: this is what makes the coincidence 'odd'. The mental paradigm with which Radcliffe would be working underlines the point. According to the tenets of associationism, memories are linked in the mind according to three basic principles: similarity, difference, and – the relevant one – contiguity. Distinct data may find themselves stored contiguously – accidentally adjacent – in the mind: in this case they would be, literally, coincidental. Oddly coincidental suggests there is more to the connection than simple 'contiguity'.

If the reader stands back from *Udolpho*, and compares it with *The Romance of the Forest*, Radcliffe's previous novel, the connection made by Emily's 'unconscious' mind becomes somewhat clearer. In their plotting the two romances are mirror images of each other (having similar details in reversed order). In *Romance* Adeline discovers, and reads, her father's secret manuscript; what she learns leads to the exchange of a bad father (the Marquis de Montalt) for a good, idealised one (the brother he murdered). In *Udolpho* Emily discovers, but does not read, her father's secret manuscript; but she does catch a glimpse, the evidence of which threatens the opposite exchange, of an ideal father (St Aubert as she knew him) for a bad one (St Aubert as he appears in his secret history). What the 'odd kind of coincidence' does is disclose the link in Emily's unconscious mind between St Aubert the 'bad' father, and Montoni, her new surrogate father. The veiled 'picture' and the glimpsed sentence in the manuscript are the literal traces of paternal vices, one of lust, the other of greed. In both cases the victims are women, the one dishonoured, the other murdered.

Of course we eventually learn that Emily does not think exactly like this, or at least, not consciously: the ego-ideal represented by the benevolent St Aubert does not crumble. Once we finally know the Marchioness de Villeroi's story – how she was poisoned by her husband and Laurentini – it becomes clearer that the words glanced at by Emily probably refer to this ghastly episode, and certainly not to an adulterous affair between her father and the Marchioness. This knowledge also provides a new explanatory link for the odd coincidence, as both manuscript and 'picture' imply murder.

And yet the reader has been led to believe differently, as has Emily. One of the unappreciated subtleties of Radcliffe's art is her ability to equip her heroines with a psychological subtext. Her heroines are not fainting cyphers of conventional femininity, but have an inner life. But whereas her contemporary Jane Austen pushed forward the art of creating subtext through dialogue or ironic indirection, Radcliffe created hers through textual – hermeneutic – clues. The final winding-up of *Udolpho*'s mysteries dispels Emily's worries:

> she was released from an anxious and painful conjecture, occasioned by the rash assertion of Signora Laurentini, concerning her birth and the honour of her parents. Her faith in St. Aubert's principles would scarcely allow her to suspect that he had acted dishonourably; and she felt such reluctance to believe herself the daughter of any other, than her, whom she had always considered and loved as a mother, that she would hardly admit such a circumstance to be possible; yet the likeness, which it had been frequently affirmed she bore to the late Marchioness, the former behaviour of Dorothée ... the assertion of Laurentini, and the mysterious attachment, which St. Aubert had discovered, awakened doubts, as to his connections with the Marchioness, which her reason could never vanquish, nor confirm.
>
> (*MU*, 663)

The tense of the last phrase suggests that these suspicions had been preying on Emily's mind for a considerable period; and yet they have only been made explicit once she finds herself in a position to banish them. But they have been implicit. They are expressed in Emily's superstitious fears, when her mind races, and flies to wild conjectures, or when odd kinds of coincidences intrude upon her mind. Indeed, in the last sentence, the language explicitly equates the struggle to resist the 'contagion' of superstition with Emily's effort to control her rising suspicions regarding her father's moral standing. The phrasing is the same in both cases: we hear of doubts her 'reason could never vanquish, nor confirm'. Superstitious fears and thoughts that transgress against the paternal ideal are identified as one and the same thing.

Emily's superstitious fears, her unconscious thought processes, and her transgressive impulses, are joined. Appropriately enough, the link is first made when Emily ventures to burn her father's papers, an act that simultaneously invokes obedience (she burns them according to her father's will) while holding out the temptation to transgress (the papers record her father's secret thoughts). Superstition overwhelms her as she approaches her dread task. As she enters the closet in which the papers were concealed she feels an 'emotion of unusual awe' (*MU*, 102). Her mind, weakened by melancholy, succumbs:

> It was lamentable, that her excellent understanding should have yielded, even for a moment, to the reveries of superstition, or rather to those *starts of imagination* which deceive the senses into what can be called nothing less than momentary madness.
>
> (*MU*, 102; my italics)

During this moment she believes she sees 'the countenance of her dead father' (*MU*, 103). The face appears again as she retrieves the papers from beneath the floorboards. Distracted, her

> eyes involuntarily settled on the writing of some loose sheets, which lay open; and she was unconscious, that she was *transgressing* her father's strict injunction, till a sentence of dreadful import awakened her attention and her memory together. She hastily put the papers from her; but the words, which had roused equally her *curiosity* and *terror*, she could not dismiss from her thoughts.
>
> (*MU*, 103; my italics)

This mixture of *curiosity* and *terror*, which Radcliffe later calls 'purely sublime' (*MU*, 248), most intensely attends her two moments of partial, and 'false' decipherment. Here, where she gains an 'unconscious' glimpse into her father's papers, and later when she lifts the veil on the mysterious 'picture'. Her decipherments are false, because we eventually learn that it is not Laurentini's body behind the veil, nor do the glimpsed words confess an adulterous relationship between her father and the Marchioness de Villeroi. And yet these *starts of the imagination* – when her curiosity and terror are most intensely aroused – truly reflect Emily's 'unconscious': they let us know what is going on in Emily's mind beneath the self-censorship of propriety. For instance, we eventually learn that the figure behind the black veil is a waxen *memento mori*, one depicting an implicitly male body in an advanced state of decay. Emily misinterprets – 'projects' – its gender and identity in a moment of imaginative terror. Such projections clue us into the structure of Emily's unconscious mind.

And as we have seen, Emily's moments of 'false' decipherment – of literal and figurative discovering – are also transgressive. In Emily's mind hers are rebellious acts, ones contravening her father's and Montoni's injunctions. St Aubert's spectral face fixes Emily in its regard in recriminatory anticipation of Emily's disobedience. Emily's 'superstitious' fantasy discloses her unconscious desire, her unacknowledged guilty purposes revealing themselves as her father's spectral body, the party injured by her secret intentions. Emily hears a footstep pacing the gallery outside the apartment containing the veiled (and transgressively viewed) picture; seeing a masculine figure 'all the horrors of that chamber rushed upon her mind' (*MU*, 384), but it is not – as she fearfully expects – Montoni. In both cases the transgressive act of 'lifting the veil' on 'paternal' secrets is preceded by patriarchal spectres.

We are apt to find the device of the fainting heroine risible, so familiar has it become. But as we have seen, Radcliffe does not use the device casually. Her heroines' fainting spells dramatise subtextual conflicts, which frame the psychologies of her heroines while forming the bases of her themes. Emily loses consciousness when presented with knowledge or desires forbidden to her; but this would not be so if St Aubert had not planted himself, as censor, within her mind. The narrator assures us that Emily welcomes this; but insofar as this censorship is linked to superstitious terror, patriarchal spectres and the irrational, it loses its moral authority. As a result the text becomes dynamic: we no longer have a moral code we are meant to infer, but a conflict we are invited to interpret.

In the last chapter I used the chiasmus 'romance of origins: origins of romance' to organise my thoughts on one of the important issues of *The Romance of the Forest*. The manuscript Adeline discovers romanticises her origins, supplanting her brutal 'father' with an ideal one. At the same time the episode of the secret manuscript duplicates in miniature the wider conditions of the woman writer, where the disciplines of propriety enforce concealment. We observe Adeline 'discovering' a secret script idealising her origins. But the text framing this discovery invites a twofold recognition: firstly, that the need to romanticise origins is an originating impulse of romance, and secondly, that this need to 'romanticise' is a consequence of repression. Adeline's secret manuscript, her 'romance of origins', discloses the existence of profound cultural factors where gender, identity, desire and social conformity all coalesce into the significant shape of the female Gothic. Moreover, to the degree that *The Romance of the Forest* discloses this process of origination, so it transforms 'romance' itself from an anodyne genre into something with aesthetic depth.

In *The Mysteries of Udolpho* the explained supernatural fulfils a similar dynamic, only turned inside out. *The Romance of the Forest* begins with a wicked father and ends with an idealised one (possibly fantasised). *The Mysteries of Udolpho* begins the other way round, with an idealised father who in moments of supernatural terror is linked with a wicked one (Montoni). Emily's fantasies, her superstitious moments when her mind races, typify 'romance' creativity, and it is here that we find an uncensored view of patriarchy.

As we have seen, the principal way in which Emily's superstitions furnish us with such an uncensored view is to collapse the difference between 'patriarchal Udolpho', presided over by the acquisitive Montoni, and la Vallée, the pastoral seat of sensibility and benevolence with its paternal guardian, St Aubert. The mystery of Udolpho (the veil) is uncannily linked to the mystery of La Vallée (the manuscript). The situation is actually more complex in that we have two apparent opposites (Udolpho and La Vallée) and a mediating term, Chateau-le-Blanc. In Chateau-le-Blanc the two 'mysteries' physically interconnect. Emily believes the body behind the veil to be Laurentini's, whereas Laurentini actually haunts the Chateau-le-Blanc in expiation of the Marchioness's murder, the shocking event alluded to (it ultimately seems) in the manuscript at La Vallée.

Chateau-le-Blanc also mediates between La Vallée and Udolpho thematically. Udolpho offers us a vision, so to speak, of patriarchy red in tooth and claw. Emily's lifting of the veil, in a fit of curiosity and terror, on a 'horrible spectacle' that leaves her senseless, is subsequently re-enacted in a bid to escape. Conducted through the labyrinthine dungeons and corridors of Udolpho she stops by a curtained recess: 'she wished, yet dreaded, to lift it, and to discover what it veiled: twice she was withheld by the recollection of the terrible spectacle her daring hand had formerly unveiled in an apartment of the castle' (*MU*, 348). The suspicion that it hides her murdered aunt nerves her hand and indeed there is a bloody, disfigured corpse behind the arras. Emily once again faints in horror, ostensibly because it is Madame Montoni's body. Again Emily is wrong: it is actually the corpse of one of Montoni's bandits. But thematically it is revealing, for it refigures Emily's central fear that, like Laurentini and her aunt, she will be used for her property, and once that is possessed, discarded.

The particularities of Madame Montoni's history compound the meanings of this repetition of the figure of the veil. Emily's aunt is another incontinent woman, in her case, verbally so. Her logorrhoea, propelled by pride, makes her an obvious target for Montoni: she ends her life locked away, gagged, the verbal flow stopped. As in Laurentini's case (as first imagined by Emily), the veil of sensibility undergoes a sinister reversal of meaning: rather than the safeguard of feminine modesty the 'veil' (and the values it metonymically implicates) becomes a form of imprisonment, something complicit in the material exploitation of women. After they have been divested of their property, the 'bodies' of Laurentini and Madame Montoni are – or so Emily momentarily imagines – discreetly veiled, stopped-up, silenced. The surface moral drift of the romance may suggest that, somehow, Madame Montoni is to blame for what happens to her. Her ridiculous vanity and lack of sensibility certainly make her unsympathetic. But in the context of Udolpho her lack of sensibility is less a failing of morality, and more a failing of craft. According to the tenets of sensibility, the feeling female heart is also an introverted one; introverted, at least, until touched by a heart it can trust, at which point a mutual

lowering of the ramparts may occur (as, for instance, between
Captain Benwick and Louisa Musgrove in Jane Austen's
Persuasion). Emily's sensibility is part of her caution; her insensible
aunt, by contrast, is incautious. Her petty vanities leave her
defenceless. As a result she is simple prey for male adventurers
such as Montoni. For Emily, her aunt's stifled voice holds a particular terror, for it is analogous with her own form of incontinence,
her unstoppable imagination. Just as her aunt cannot control her
mouth, Emily cannot rein in her fantasy; and just as Madame
Montoni's actual voice may be stifled, so may Emily's inner 'voice'.

In this respect the terrible spectacle of Madame Montoni's murdered body becomes cautionary indeed. Emily's bid to escape is
ironically inapposite, for her deliverer, Barnardine, does not assist
her out of altruism, because he has been suborned to deliver Emily
into the custody of Morano. This transaction mockingly echoes
dynastic marriage, as does Emily's aunt's with Montoni, for both
'alliances' turn on the exchange of property: Montoni marries for
land, while Barnardine delivers Emily for money. Indeed, Madame
Montoni's murdered, veiled body (an image, we remember, conjured by Emily) serves as an emotional correlative of patrilineal,
patriarchal union, the terminus of what Mary Wollstonecraft called
being 'Bastilled' in marriage (Wollstonecraft 1980: 154–5). The
careful use of 'horror' and 'terror' also guides us subtextually to
Emily's fears. The self-subverting sublime of horror is based on
fear of physical injury. Radcliffe reserves the word horror for
Emily's confrontations with the veiled 'picture', her aunt's shrou-
ded 'corpse', or encounters with Montoni. The *horrifying* mysteries
of Udolpho repeatedly point to the mutilation of the female body,
as opposed to the *terrors* of La Vallée, which turn more on viola-
tions of the mind.

La Vallée promises, superficially, the antithesis of Udolpho's
patriarchal horrors. It is not simply that Emily's parents have
scandalised their relatives by marrying for love rather than money
and social position. St Aubert clearly belongs to the new social
order. He is anti-aristocratic, provincial by choice, bourgeois, a
proponent of 'disciplined sensibility' and companionate marriages.
As such he helps figure the familiar Radcliffean 'Gothic cusp',
where the old order surrenders to the new. Moreover, the educational tenor of his language does not dwell on the importance

of submission to parental wishes – on the need to sacrifice desire for the sake of 'alliance' and patrilineage – but on a self-discipline that would vouchsafe his child's autonomy. His is a language of personal liberation, albeit one paradoxically achieved through restraint.

Chateau-le-Blanc, then, mediates between Udolpho and La Vallée in several ways. As a topographical representation of the Gothic cusp, both orders overlap. The Marchioness de Villeroi's pre-marital love affair looks back to La Vallée and its cult of sensibility and companionate marriages. At one point it is rumoured that she and her dynastically undistinguished lover had actually married, but that family pressures had subsequently forced her into a feudal alliance with the Marquis de Villeroi. The Marquis, in turn, has his figurative origins in Udolpho, for it is from there, and a sexual liaison with Laurentini, that he has recently come. Udolpho's patterns of courtship and marriage are the 'feudal' ones of loveless, dysfunctional alliances, of convenience, property, lust and murder. The marriage of St Aubert's sister and Villeroi is the forced union of disparate worlds, the strife of the Gothic cusp rendered in marital terms. As regards plot, the Chateau-le-Blanc is the triangulation point between Udolpho and La Vallée for it is there that the mysteries of both houses are resolved.

The title of the romance is thus eloquently partial, for the mysteries of La Vallée are as important as the mysteries of Udolpho. Of course, it is possible to read Chateau-le-Blanc as a middle ground where the antithesis La Vallée/Udolpho is reconciled; but by the same token the idealism of La Vallée is darkened by the shadow of Udolpho, which now overlaps the hitherto discrete ground of St Aubert's pastoral, 'anti-patriarchal' retreat. If Emily's conscious mind succeeds in keeping La Vallée and Udolpho separate, her unconscious mind, with its 'odd coincidences', clearly does not. Here the image of St Aubert's anti-patriarchal retreat is as tenuous as the mask of his own probity at the moment of Emily's troubling glance into her father's secret history.

Like her earlier romances, Radcliffe structures *The Mysteries of Udolpho* around a search for identity, and in doing so she rings the changes on previous motifs. We have already seen how *Udolpho* inverts the plot structure of *The Romance of the Forest*. A *Sicilian*

Romance is also re-worked. There, as we saw, Mazzini subjects
Louisa to live burial. Insofar as Julia's identity is linked to the
discovery of her mother, the father may be said to be the keeper
of his daughter's secrets. Mazzini maintains his power over Julia
by keeping her mother, and, by implication, her own identity, in
the dark. Insofar as they have a common origin Julia's ignorance
and superstitiousness are literally connected, for it is her mother's
desperate bangings that the uniformed Julia misinterprets as supernatural phenomena.

Udolpho shifts this complex of ideas into the figurative through
the device of St Aubert's manuscript. The reader and Emily are
both invited to believe that secrets material to Emily's identity
are concealed in St Aubert's papers. As it turns out the mysteries
of the manuscript are really those of Udolpho: the papers relate
the death of St Aubert's sister, a death having its origins in the
untrammelled world of Montoni's feudal castle, a place both geo-
graphically and temporally on the further side of the Gothic cusp.
Udolpho's denouement snips the subversive knot tying La Vallée
and Udolpho together, but before it does there is a great deal of
uncertainty, and it is this uncertainty that generates the contagion
of superstition infecting Emily's mind. In the end news of Emily's
'true' mother (news material to her identity) is not concealed
in St Aubert's manuscript; but in the interim Emily's suspicions
regarding St Aubert (that his manuscript does harbour secrets
impinging on her social status) defamiliarise her world, rendering
it 'supernatural'.

In other words Emily's social identity is constituted through
paternal nurture, through her internalisation of St Aubert's anti-
aristocratic, anti-feudal and anti-patriarchal values, with their
stress on disciplined sensibility, measured benevolence and regu-
lated passions. As the mysteries of La Vallée and Udolpho elide
the differences – in Emily's unconscious – between St Aubert and
Montoni, so her 'identity' (and the paternal authority on which it
is based) comes under threat, a threat projected onto the world
around her as a sense of 'strangeness', or, if you like, the supernatural.

Reading *Udolpho* in this way keys us into a final subtextual
element: Emily's motive in relinquishing Valancourt. Superficially,
Emily is being a good girl to the last, renouncing the object of her

desires on the paternal advice of the Count de Villefort, the 'step-father' of the intermediary Chateau-le-Blanc. But insofar as Emily's mind is conditioned by the unvoiced possibility that St Aubert's anti-patriarchal values are illusory – a possibility collapsing the differences between her father and step-father, St Aubert and Montoni – so it becomes reasonable to assume that Valancourt is being tested. Where, between St Aubert and Montoni, does Valancourt actually fall? The rumours Emily hears regarding Valancourt's behaviour in Paris – his gambling, card-sharping and womanising, indeed his 'taste for every vicious pleasure' (*MU*, 507) – suggest that he is a secret Montoni. By general report Valancourt spends his days in Paris with 'a set of men, a disgrace to their species, who live by plunder and pass their lives in continual debauchery' (*MU*, 505). Just as St Aubert's manuscript apparently relates secrets that destabilise Emily's ideal image of him, so do the Parisian rumours undermine her image of Valancourt.

Emily's protracted refusal to listen to Valancourt's attempts at self-exculpation may thus be interpreted as a reasonable, self-interested period of trial: Valancourt must prove by his hopeless devotion that he really loves Emily for herself, and not her property. He must disprove the rumour that he is an acquisitive, predatory male (in short, a Montoni), while establishing his credentials as a 'companionate' husband.

There are other subtextual hints that in testing Valancourt Emily is asserting herself rather than bowing to 'parental' pressure to be a sensible, obedient girl. Emily takes news of Valancourt's gambling calmly enough; it is when she hears about his mistress that she faints. Later, the kindly, maternal Theresa urges that Valancourt has suffered enough, and that Emily is throwing away her happiness, but Emily stubbornly refuses to listen (*MU*, 637). What the reader is invited to deduce here is Emily's jealousy, the blow received by her *amour propre*. In many ways Emily's treatment of the repentant Valancourt looks forward to Jane Eyre bringing Rochester to heel, gaining the whip hand over her lover, so seeking marriage on terms of her own, and not her lover's, making.

In this respect we should not think of Emily as a passive subject upon whom the supernatural is visited; nor should we think of her as an undesiring blank. The supernatural is a consequence of Emily's active, desiring — if subconscious and subtextual — encounter with the world. The supernatural comes upon her as she tests the pastoral values of La Vallée against the 'worldly' ones of Udolpho; as they are shaken, so the world is made strange. But this itself is a sign of her secretive quest.

It is through the figural that Radcliffe is able to produce an anatomy of her culture's deep structure. She achieves this in *The Mysteries of Udolpho* by bringing together the sexual politics of sensibility and the supernatural through this simple *donneé*: a young girl in a patriarchal setting cannot control her imagination. In her next romance the gender of her fantasist changes; so, too, her political focus.

8

Radcliffe's politics:
The Italian

The Bastille of France, notwithstanding all its horrors, was never, perhaps, to be compared, in the rigour of usurped jurisdiction, with the court of Inquisition, in Spain . . .
Review of *The Authentic Memoirs and Sufferings of Dr. William Stahl*, 1789, trans. 1791, in *Critical Review* III, 1791

When he is clad like a magistrate, in his Black Robe, he looks like a shade come from the *Acheron*. It is hard to tell whether his Hat, his Wig, his Eyebrows, his eyes, his face, or his gown is blackest . . . His countenance is hideous . . . – no man, tho' ever so undaunted, can avoid being seiz'd with Horror at the sight of it. He has a dreadful Authority, a frightful look, a dreadful malice, and an insatiable avarice.
Constantin de Renneville on M. d'Argenzon, Commissary for the Bastille (Renneville 1715: 49)

But, as *Whigs*, [the Revolution Society] exulted over the demolition of the Bastille, and over the still more important downfall of Systematic Tyranny. That Revolution has given a wholesome lesson to *Tories*, and a salutory lessen to *Tyrants* . . . by teaching them, that . . . no length of oppression can ever eradicate from the human heart, the immutable Principles of Natural Justice.
A Letter From Earl Stanhope, to the Right Honourable Edmund Burke: Containing a Short Answer to His Late Speech on the French Revolution (Stanhope 1790: 26)

The Italian (1797) was the last novel produced by Radcliffe during her lifetime. Three years had lapsed since the publication of *The Mysteries of Udolpho*, two since her book of travel writing, *A Journey Down the Rhine*. Given the frantic pace of Radcliffe's early career – five books in six years – the two allotted to the relatively slim *Italian* gives the impression that this was a final, considered text, one putting her earlier work in a measured, self-conscious perspective.

Viewing *The Italian* purely in terms of plot strengthens the impression. Salient features from Radcliffe's earlier story-lines are recycled in this one text. Most prominently there is the conflict between the demands of alliance and romantic love, with Vivaldi's and Ellena's desires running counter to the Marchesa's feudal pride. As an analogue to the main plot Ellena is incarcerated within a convent through the Marchesa's machinations and is offered the familiar 'choice of evils'; in this case, of either marrying a stranger (thus relinquishing Vivaldi) or taking the veil, a dilemma dramatised, once again, as the threat of literal 'live burial' (*I*, 126). We have the device of the 'two fathers' familiar from the previous two romances: here a malevolent patriarch appears to be the heroine's father until the final revelation discloses the true one to be benevolent and paternal, if also usurped. There is the usual close brush with incest/murder, the two conflated in the scene where Schedoni parts the 'lawn' of his 'daughter's' breast in preparation of penetrating her with his 'poinard', only to discover his own portrait around her neck, itself a recognition device familiar from earlier Radcliffe fictions. The actual discovery of the mother – Olivia by Ellena – looks back to *A Sicilian Romance*, while the explicit identification of the Marchesa's class consciousness as feudal bigotry recalls Radcliffe's first text, *The Castles of Athlin and Dunbayne*.

The Italian may indeed be a self-conscious retrospective; of that there is no way of knowing. And yet it is not, as the above plot review may lead us to conclude, a simple continuation of her earlier themes. On the contrary, *The Italian* marks a new departure in Radcliffe's fiction. There are two immediate, telling discontinuities. The main action concerns, not a heroine in flight from a vile patriarch, but a hero persecuted (albeit indirectly) by his mother. Secondly, the action is brought up to the verge of modern times. Indeed, we are given an actual date: 'About the year 1764, some English travellers in Italy . . . happened to stop before the portico of the Santa Maria del Pianto' (*I*, 1). We learn that the tale we are about to hear concerns the events surrounding an extraordinary confession made within the church 'several years' before. As the text dates this confession as 1752, the actual conclusion, to which the narrative takes us, must have occurred shortly before the arrival of the English tourists. So a neat symmetry confronts us: the fictional time of Radcliffe's last romance ends in the year of her own birth.

Radcliffe may have been having a quiet joke. More significant, however, is Radcliffe's progressive move towards the present. Each succeeding romance appears to take place at a time subsequent to the last. We earlier saw how Radcliffe's middle romances appeared to establish radical credentials by situating their events during the 'Gothic cusp', the period around the beginning of the seventeenth century when the medieval and modern periods were felt to overlap – the one ending, the other just beginning – hence, typically, the flight of modern heroines of sensibility from their feudal fathers. This 'reading' of the past was implicitly liberal and potentially radical because it chimed with the views of those supporting the French Revolution, who saw the present as a similar historical juncture, where feudal prerogatives and abuses would pass away in favour of a new benevolent order founded on the rights of man. One 'cusp' was the mirror of the other; as Radcliffe's romances ended with the modern representatives of sensibility triumphant, then, so she could be construed as endorsing progressive forces now.

So the question becomes: in moving her settings nearer the present, does Radcliffe take her work out of the ideological frame of the 1790s, or further into it? Is abandoning the Gothic cusp an act of conservative, or liberal, intent? Or is it – on the contrary – apolitical?

In answering this question I will be approaching *The Italian* in a way quite different from my earlier discussions of Radcliffe's texts. In particular, I will be looking more narrowly at Radcliffe's ideological and political meanings. In each chapter I have sought to examine a different aspect of Radcliffe's art. I have reserved the immediately ideological for the *The Italian* because it invites just such an approach. *The Italian* is a different kind of text. In it the heroine is not overly predisposed to the 'spectral', is not given to 'superstition', to the imaginative excesses of sensibility. As we shall see, the hero Vivaldi occupies the 'feminine' role of fantasist. The difference is crucial.

In the chapter on the aesthetic background I warned against a common preconception in earlier Radcliffe criticism. Classic Gothic texts by male writers – such as those by Matthew Lewis, James Hogg or Charles Maturin – were seen to stage the conflict between desire and morality, id and super-ego, Orc and Urizen, with a stark clarity. Radcliffe's, by comparison, seemed cushioned with sensibility. But my argument has been that Radcliffe's texts have an agenda of their own. 'Sensibility' ought not to be seen as Radcliffe's sop to propriety, nor should we regard her texts as the products of conventional, feminine timidity. For Radcliffe, sensibility was not a fashion accessory. On the contrary, it was an important fictional instrument, one that expanded the scope of her writing. Her heroines' proneness to sensibility – to imaginative excess – created the conditions for what I have called the figural: the inscription of 'dream' texts within the main narrative, texts inscribing meanings alternative to the rational ones of the 'explained' supernatural. This hermeneutic tension in turn encoded a conflict between the conventional and the transgressive, while the theme of secretive 'feminine fancy' added the self-reflexive issue of the woman writer. For Radcliffe to strip away her heroine's predisposition to the phantasmal was therefore to alter profoundly the direction of her fiction.

Several explanations for this change of direction come to mind. The political and aesthetic atmosphere had intensified alarmingly. By mid-decade sensibility was under assault from all political sides. The terror in France provoked intense reaction in England. Tory wits blamed French bloodshed on sensibility (among all other things faddish and foreign). William Canning's witty report from *The Anti-Jacobin* is a typical indictment:

Sweet child of sickly FANCY! – Her of yore
From her lov'd *France* ROUSSEAU to exile bore;
And, while midst lakes and mountains wild he ran
Full of himself, and shunn'd the haunts of man,
Taught her o'er each lone vale and Alpine steep
To lisp the story of his wrongs, and weep;
Taught her to cherish still in either eye,
Of tender tears a plentiful supply,
And pour them in the brooks that babbled by; –
– Taught by nice scale to meet her feelings strong,
false by degrees, and exquisitely wrong; –

– For the crush'd beetle, *first*, – the widow's dove,
And all the warbled sorrows of the grove; –
Next for poor suffering *Guild*; and, *last* of all,
For parents, Friends, a King and Country's fall.

The Anti-Jacobin; or, Weekly Examiner (9 July 1798)

The string of casual insinuations and accusations includes egotism, effeminacy, irrationalism, ('babbled') and a tragi-comic misplaced morality. In one respect the motivation for attacking sensibility was simple xenophobia: all things French were lumped together as poisonous cultural cargo and blamed for the catastrophic turn in Paris, blamed regardless of logical consistency or historical probability. Thus wits like Canning would in the same breath cite both indiscriminate emotional gush and excessive rationalism – both weepy Rousseau and dusty Voltaire – as the responsible malefactors. But their cultural paranoia was not without ideo-logical method. Sensibility was attacked for being implicitly anti-hierarchical, for presupposing a democracy of feeling hearts; more-over, it was perceived to empower women while dis-empowering men (by encouraging them to be teary, uxorious and weak).

From the radical perspective the charge sheet was equally exten-sive. Sensibility was seen as a fashionable affectation which masked establishment inaction: it invited the rich to purge their moral qualms with a few benevolent tears rather than to attack inequality systematically. In Mary Wollstonecraft's words, 'Sensibility is the *manie* of the day, and compassion the virtue which is to cover a multitude of vices . . .' (Wollstonecraft 1790: 5). It also privileged obscurantist 'common-sense' over analysis, instinctive feeling over deep-digging reason. Finally, from a feminist point of view, far from empowering women sensibility turned them into objects of sensuality. Sensibility's seminal texts – Richardson's *Clarissa* and Rousseau's *Eloisa* – gave 'a sanction to the libertine reveries of men', as Wollstonecraft colourfully put it (Todd 1977: 227); even as the language of these male writers reproved the violation of modesty it dwelt avidly on the fascinating charms of outraged chastity. Worse, not only did sensibility construe women as objects of sensuality, it encouraged them – through the excessive cultivat-ion of non-rational charms – to be in themselves sensual objects.

To gain a sense of how quickly the ideological topography changed during the stressful period of the French Revolution and

the ensuing terror one need only recall that prior to 1789 comba-
tants of the 1790s such as Burke and Wollstonecraft would have
held a similarly positive attitude towards sensibility: roughly, that
it was an index of the age's improving manners. Radcliffe's career
registers sensibility's shifting fortunes. Whereas *The Romance of
the Forest* stood four-square behind Rousseau and sensibility –
especially through the figure of La Luc, a character modelled on
Emile's ideal 'Vicar du Savoyard' (Chard 1986: xxiii) – *Udolpho*
hedges its bets. The clearly insensible Madame Montoni accuses
Emily of flaunting her 'boasted sensibility'. Emily 'mildly' replies
that she would not ' "boast of sensibility – a quality, perhaps, more
to be feared, than desired" ' (*MU*, 281). In this Emily echoes her
father's warning that ' "all excess is vicious", including that of
sensibility which must end in ' "selfish and unjust passion" ' (*MU*,
20). Emily establishes her sensibility by 'mildly' reproving her
egregious aunt; St Aubert evinces his by benevolently advising his
daughter against sensibility's excesses. In *Udolpho* one proves one's
sensibility by denying one has it.

In 1794 it seemed possible to pre-empt the charges against
sensibility (such as those soon to be brought by the *Anti-Jacobin*)
through such sophistical paradoxes as *Udolpho*'s. By 1797 matters
were more difficult; witness the following, direct assault on Radcliffe:

> I, allude, Sir, principally to the great quantity of novels with which
> our circulating libraries are filled, and our parlour tables covered, in
> which it has been the fashion to make *terror* the *order of the day*, by
> confining the heroes and heroines in old gloomy castles, full of spectres,
> apparitions, ghosts, and dead men's bones . . .
>   A novel, if at all useful, ought to be a representation of human life
> and manners, with a view to direct the conduct in the important
> duties of life, and to correct its follies. But what instruction is to be
> reaped by the distorted ideas of lunatics, I am at a loss to conceive . . .
> is the corporeal frame of the female sex so masculine and hardy, that
> it must be softened down by the touch of dead bodies, clay-cold hands,
> and damp sweats?
>
>   *Spirit of the Public Journals* (1797: 227–8)

In case anyone missed the connection between the Gothic romance
and the events in France, the article was entitled 'Terrorist Novel
Writing'. As a footnote makes clear, *The Mysteries of Udolpho* was

foremost in the reviewer's sights. As is often the case with ideological counter-attacks, the charges brought against *Udolpho* are contradictory. Emily's 'masculine' resourcefulness in exploring the gory byways of Udolpho prompts the call for more sensibility in the representation of femininity; but the reviewer has just indicted sensibility for the excesses of Emily's imagination. As we saw, Emily's 'distorted ideas' are also her most transgressive ones. In this light the injunction to stick to probable representations 'of human life and manners' appears sinister: it is as if Radcliffe were being warned against trespassing onto ideologically illicit territory.

In addition to being labelled the literary equivalent of a *sans-culotte*, Radcliffe had to endure the further embarrassment of Matthew Lewis. Radcliffe must have found publication of *The Monk* in 1796 extremely unhelpful. With scandalous brio *The Monk* demands to have it all ways. It pillories sensibility as the worst form of foreign hypocrisy and mocks its pretensions as a literary form; it also offers us, for our approval, stereotypical figures of sensibility. De Sade thought Lewis's *The Monk* the most brilliant of the Gothic novels (Sage 1990: 48), probably for presenting the same lesson as his own *Justine*, that virtue in distress, far from stirring the benevolence of men, merely excites their desires. The more Ambrosio's sister modestly rebuffs him, the more violent her brother's lusts become. A contemporary satire, 'Modern Novels. Inscribed to the Author of *The Monk*', makes the relevant point:

> Now, a romance, with reading debauchees,
>   Rouses their torpid powers, when nature fails;
>   And all these legendary tales
> Are, to a worn-out mind, cantharides.
>
> *Spirit of the Public Journals* (1800: 260)

Cantharides was the 'technical' term for Spanish fly, a supposed aphrodisiac. Radcliffe was now indirectly accused of pornography.

To make matters worse, the literary history of the Gothic novel was rewritten, with Germany now receiving the blame. The *Schauerroman*, meaning, roughly, novels of psycho-sexual excess and violence (such as *The Monk*), were interpreted as primarily German in origin. As one reviewer put it, 'Germany was poured forth into England, in all her flood of sculls and numsculls' (Reiman 1977: 747), to the immediate peril of the nation's youth.

So strongly did this myth take hold that literary scholars have only recently been able to dispel it (Hadley 1978). Or rather, what now seems to be the case is that there was vigorous cross-fertilisation between the German and English novel: the paternity, so to speak, was shared. *The Rovers*, from *The Anti-Jacobin; or, Weekly Examiner*, gives an idea of what 'popular' (at any rate conservative) opinion conceived a German play to be. The work itself is a parody of Schiller's *The Robbers*, which, a footnote explains, put robbery in 'so fascinating a light, that the whole of a German university went upon the highway in consequence of it'. The plot is comically improbable and convoluted; besides funny names it features assassination (of all kinds) and a *ménage à trois*; it 'Tells how Prime Ministers are shocking things, / And *reigning Dukes* as bad as tyrant Kings' (4 June 1798, no. 30: 236). In other words, *The Rovers* is an ordinary tale of murder, radicalism and unconventional sex.

During the reactionary 1790s conservatives sought to demonise the 'Other', figuring it as foreign, where the 'Other' now included sensibility and the Gothic romance. By 1801 the *Anti-Jacobin Review and Magazine* was insinuating that Radcliffe's art was 'rather German than English'. Under these circumstances of gathering reaction one might have expected Radcliffe to move towards the politically anodyne. In fact, she defends not only her art but the aesthetic and ideological values that motivated it (hence *The Italian*'s increased ideological 'visibility'). Radcliffe the 'gentlewoman' remained loyal to the complex of values associated with sensibility (even if the woman writer had begun to express doubts). Nevertheless, the ideological stress of the times required a reworking and re-assessment of her art (Conger 1989). As Radcliffe did so political matters came increasingly to the fore.

The first epigraph to this chapter provides a convenient way into the politics of *The Italian*: 'The Bastille of France, notwithstanding all its horrors, was never, perhaps, to be compared, in the rigour of *usurped jurisdiction*, with the court of Inquisition, in Spain' (my italics). *The Italian* exploits the tendency of the English imagination to identify the Bastille with the Inquisition, both being models of *usurped jurisdiction* differing principally in their degree of rigour.

The Italian's description of the prisons of the Inquisition is significant:

> The carriage having reached the walls, followed their bendings to a considerable extent. These walls, of immense height, and strengthened by innumerable massy bulwarks, exhibited neither window or grate, but a vast and dreary blank; a small round tower only, perched here and there upon the summit, breaking their monotony.
>
> (I, 196)

The description does not match the historical Bastille but it does closely duplicate the features of the Bastille's popular representation – one of high blank walls (cf. Schama 1989: 389–93). The Bastille was frequently used to imprison Protestants and other heretics, so this, too, would have strengthened the equation.

The Italian works its politics by begging the question of what a proper jurisdiction might be. The immediate, ready answer is the juridical practices of a Protestant England, but as this was a period when the nature of the British Constitution was under intense debate, the answer was not an unproblematic one. For instance, the text contrasts the monastery of San Stefano with the convent of the Santa della Pieta. The representation of the first is explicitly anti-Catholic, being a hypocritical institution founded on pride and spiritual and financial covetousness; it is hierarchical, tyrannical, and based on blind obedience to meaningless dogma. The convent of Santa della Pieta, although ostensibly Catholic, actually enjoys a Protestant regime owing to the enlightenment of the Superior, whose 'religion was neither gloomy, nor bigotted; it was the sentiment of a grateful heart offering itself up to a Deity, who delights in the happiness of his creatures; and she conformed to the customs of the Roman church, without supposing a faith in all of them to be necessary to salvation' (I, 300). The contemporary reader would register the Superior's liberal, anti-dogmatic values as Protestant; more particularly, though, her values chime with those of liberal dissenters and other champions of religious toleration. Radcliffe is throwing in her lot – not with the King and church mob – but with provincial and middle-class intellectuals, such as, for instance, Richard Price or Joseph Priestly, who were more often its victims. Religious toleration was not an abstract issue – the Test and Corporation Acts disbarred from public office dissenters and all others refusing to swear loyalty to the established church (Thompson 1968: 29).

The 'constitutional controversy' of the 1790s turned on the issue of innovation. There was a broad agreement as to the origin of the 'British' Constitution: Magna Carta and the Glorious Revolution figured centrally in most accounts. Differences turned on the interpretations of these events. Conservative opinion saw the Constitution as the providential work of ages; accordingly, established practice had hallowed authority. From this point of view, events in France merely pointed up the follies and dangers of innovation. 'Liberals' drew a different lesson from 1215 and 1688. Richard Price's *A Discourse On the Love of Our Country* (published in 1789, the opening salvo of the controversy) is typical. The occasion for the pamphlet was the celebration of the anniversary of the Glorious Revolution, and behind that, the recent revolution in France. Price argued that the king was the representative of the people: 'His sacredness is the sacredness of the community' (Price 1790: 23). The Glorious Revolution enshrined the right to liberty of conscience; the right to resist power when abused; and, most significantly, the right to choose our own governors, to cashier them for misconduct (including the king, the 'chief magistrate'), and to frame a government for ourselves (Price 1790: 34). Although a great work, the Revolution was not 'perfect' (Price 1790: 35); it therefore followed that innovation was positively demanded by the Constitution; only by improvement could the rights and interests it promised be delivered in full.

To speak approvingly of 'rights' situated one 'left' of centre, at the very least, for it signalled a frame of mind in which the Constitution was to be adapted to guarantee those rights, as opposed to the Tory faction, for whom the key notion was reverential, even grateful, subjection to immemorial laws and practices – 'submission, but with free choice', as Coleridge was to put it (Raysor 1936: 8), echoing Burke's 'proud submission', a phrase from the *Reflections* much criticised by radicals such as Tom Paine and Thomas Christie. The expression 'contains a contradiction. A man may be *proud of submitting*, as he may be proud of disgrace, and glory in his shame; but the *act* of submission itself implies *humility*, and can have nothing in it of *pride*' (Christie 1791: 37).

More than any of her previous books, *The Italian* is conditioned by the language of rights and entitlements. The vignette of the Santa della Pieta revealed an enlightened Superior respecting the rights of conscience of those within her order (even as she disguises her liberalism from a repressive central authority). But in this it only reproduces the main thematic thrust of the romance, which centres on a heroine caught up in the emotional and political intricacies of Burke's contradictory 'proud submission'.

With the exception of *The Romance of the Forest*, Radcliffe's previous romances featured a young woman persecuted by the marital wishes of her family, wishes running counter to her own. The exceptions are Adeline and Ellena, for whom matters are quite different – having lost their families, they are relatively free to marry as they wish. But whereas Adeline is preoccupied by the propriety of marrying the man with whom she has 'eloped', Ellena is exercised by issues of rights and self-respect. *The Italian* reverses Radcliffe's customary plot, in that it is now the male suitor who wishes to marry against the wishes of his family. Unencumbered with disagreeable parents wishing to thwart her, Ellena's conflict becomes internalised. She is opposed, not by a 'father' out there, but by scruples, in here. Her struggle is principally between desire and pride. She desperately wishes to marry Vivaldi but is acutely alert to the 'degradation of intruding herself' (*I*, 150) into a family that rejects her. Ellena tells Vivaldi that ' "pride, insulted pride, has a right to dictate, and ought to be obeyed" ' (*I*, 151). She therefore *proudly submits* to the established social order, preferring to renounce Vivaldi than marry him under such humiliating circumstances. But there is also the 'pride of conscious worth' (*I*, 68), which propels her to defend her desires and her rights. Ellena's conflict – and situation – is reminiscent of Elizabeth Bennet's in *Pride and Prejudice*, where desire, identity and class consciousness are bound up together, leading to predictable vacillation:

> [Vivaldi's] unaffected distress awakened all her tenderness and gratitude; she asked herself whether she ought any longer to assert her own rights . . . As she applied these questions, she appeared to herself an unjust and selfish being, unwilling to make any sacrifice for the tranquility of him, who had given her liberty, even at the risk of his life. Her very virtues, now that they were carried to excess, seemed to her to border upon vices; her sense of dignity, appeared to be

narrow pride; her delicacy weakness; her moderated affection cold
ingratitude; and her circumspection, little less than prudence degener-
ated into meanness.

(*I*, 181)

Emily's feelings are a tangle of conflicting impulses: of desire
and pride, deference and self-assertion. One can take the comparison with *Pride and Prejudice* further and say that the Marchesa is
an overblown version of Lady Catherine (although strictly speaking one would have to say that Austen's version of aristocratic
arrogance is an underdrawn version of Radcliffe's). Both remind
us that during the period there was much strife between the
'middling' and upper classes. It was partly a tension between new
mercantile wealth and landed or 'old' money, but it was equally a
conflict between margins and centre, between provincial culture
and urban or 'court' fashion, between a liberal, often dissenting
bourgeoisie bound to strict notions of morality and propriety
(however 'progressively' interpreted) and an old élite, whom they
perceived as luxurious, shallow, immoral and retrogressive. We
see the tension represented in the conflict between Elizabeth
Bennet and Lady Catherine, but also in the bad blood between
Ellena and the Marchesa.

Earlier I said that in *The Italian* the implied opposite of the
Inquisition is English, Protestant, toleration. By the same token,
the implied opposite of the Marchesa's feudal bigotry is the liberal
political culture celebrated by such provincial assemblies as Richard
Price's Revolution Society. For the English, middle-class imagination, the Bastille and the Inquisition were two faces of the same
nightmare, the tyranny of the church and the caprice of the state
being different expressions of a single despotism. The Bastille was
both an Inquisitional prison for Huguenots and a dumping ground
for inconvenient members of the nobility, provided their families
had sufficient clout to secure a *lettre de cachet*, the state's chief
instrument of 'usurped jurisdiction'. To an extent, Vivaldi is just
such a victim. As we saw in Chapter 4, one of the very first
representations of the fall of the Bastille conflated the historical
events with the possibly true, possibly apocryphal, eighteenth-
century story of the man in the iron mask. According to legend,
the eponymous victim was a refractory member of the French

Royal Family. Revolutionary propaganda enlisted the story to support the Bastille's reputation as the epitome of arbitrary state power (a reputation in embarrassing danger of flagging owing to the lack of victimised wretches found among its liberated ruins). The supposition suggests itself because it so brutally dramatised the ability of state power to nullify the individual, literally 'effacing' him. Vivaldi experiences a similar threat, of being helplessly masked as an anonymous power decides his fate. Although the charges brought against Vivaldi are religious in nature, the Inquisition is, ideologically, identifiable with the Bastille, both being cyphers for the excesses of feudalism, of unfettered monarchy.

The Marchesa is the focal point in the novel for anti-monarchical feeling. Against the Marchesa's claims for aristocratic privilege *The Italian* sets the inviolable rights of the person, although honoured more in the continually threatened breach than in the observance. When the abbess of San Stefano menaces Ellena with the choice of taking the veil or a stranger in marriage Ellena claims that ' "the immortal love of justice, which fills all my heart, will sustain my courage no less powerfully than the sense of what is due to my own character" ' (*I*, 84). Vivaldi in his turn flies to the defence of her ' "right of independence" ' (*I*, 142).

Generally, though, the 'rights of man' are honoured most in the continually threatened breach. The society in which Ellena and Vivaldi live is overwhelmingly one of violation. When Olivia is raped by her brother-in-law her only recourse is to marry her abuser; when he stabs her, her best option is to take refuge in a convent, leaving her children to her sister. The confessional serves as an instrument of church policy where dogma is policed; and if that fails, the Inquisition waits to violate the mind via the frailties of the flesh.

As an antistrophe to Vivaldi and Ellena's language of the rights of man we hear Marchesa and her confessor – the evil monk Schedoni – descant on the rights of privilege. Or rather, although they appear to support the same end, they do so from different directions. Schedoni marvels that the state should neglect to provide the death penalty for those class interlopers who would sully a noble line through unsanctioned marriage: ' "Justice does not the less exist, because her laws are neglected", observes Schedoni. "A sense of what she commands lives in our breasts; and when we fail to obey that sense, it is to weakness, not to virtue, that we yield" ' (*I*, 168). The Marchesa, 'not yet familiar with atrocious guilt', fears to admit to herself the crime alluded to by Schedoni – the murder of Ellena – 'yet, so acutely susceptible was her pride, so stern her indignation, and so profound her desire of vengeance, that her mind was tossed as on an tempestuous ocean' (*I*, 169). Schedoni leads her on through taunts: ' "My daughter! can it be possible that you should want courage to soar above vulgar prejudice, in action, though not in opinion?" ' (*I*, 172). Caught between passion and conscience the Marchesa momentarily leans towards conscience when a requiem reawakens her dormant sensibility; empathising with the newly dead she exclaims 'And to this condition would I reduce a being like myself' (*I*, 177). Schedoni is contemptuous:

> 'Behold, what is woman! . . . The slave of her passions, the dupe of her senses! When pride and revenge speak in her breast, she defies obstacles, and laughs at crimes! Assail but her senses, let music, for instance, touch some feeble cord of her heart, and echo to her fancy, and lo! all her perceptions change . . . O, weak and contemptible being!'
>
> (*I*, 177–8)

Schedoni speaks the language of philosophical libertinage in accents reminiscent of De Sade's blasphemous free-thinkers. Like De Sade's libertines, Schedoni draws his morality from nature. Custom and law are no more than vulgar prejudices: what is moral in one society is an outrage in another, and vice versa. Indeed, nature reveals a morally anarchic world of self-assertion and power; the enlightened agent will do whatever serves his ends, and at whatever costs, for there are no divine sanctions, only natural encouragements. The sense of justice that lives in our breasts is the simple imperative of self-aggrandisement.

The Marchesa is willing to soar with Schedoni above 'vulgar prejudice', but for quite different reasons. Far from subscribing to a world of moral relativism, she wishes to believe that aristocratic prerogatives supersede the law of the land; the rights of a noble house take precedent over common statutes. The Marchesa's frame of mind looks back to a medieval one of rigid hierarchies and absolute feudal sovereignty. Her sense of caste conflicts with a residual Christianity, however, hence her mental confusion.

In Radcliffe's reconstruction of an immediate Continental past, philosophical libertinage and the *ancien régime* are shown to form an unholy alliance. The immorality of both is linked to the social instability of the present: the Marchesa longs to recoup lost feudal privileges, while Schedoni employs the new philosophy to repair the consequences of primogeniture and his exclusion from the family estate. Schedoni's 'free-soaring' tune soon changes when he discovers that Ellena is his 'daughter': like any feudal genealogist, he immediately sets about restoring the fortunes of his house. Of course, Schedoni is not inconsistent in any deep sense, as all along his Enlightenment patter does no more than gloss his self-interest.

English readers would have found unexceptionable the contention that free-thinking nobles were part of the decadent stew that rotted the old regime from within. That the Marquis was now Citizen de Sade, magistrate for the revolution, was no more than predictable. In this respect Radcliffe's views were conventional, but she uses them for less conventional purposes. For instance, it is sensibility that humanises the Marchesa. The Tory case was that sensibility and libertinage (both philosophical and sexual) amounted to much the same thing. Radcliffe separates them, and by having the libertine Schedoni sneer at the Marchesa's awakening sensibility Radcliffe makes her case far more effectively than simple words in sensibility's defence – although later the narrator becomes positively waspish in denouncing Schedoni's own 'illusions':

> And, while he confounded delicacy of feeling with fatuity of mind, taste with caprice, and imagination with error, he yielded, when he most congratulated himself on his sagacity, to illusions not less egregious, because they were less brilliant, than those which are incident to sentiment and feeling.
>
> (*I*, 289)

One also catches the accents of an attack on the 'common sense' wielded by Tory critics to bludgeon liberal innovators – and women writers – into silence.[1]

---

[1] For instance, the author of 'Terrorist Novel Writing' conceives his task as recalling women writers 'to the old boundaries of common sense' (*Spirit of the Public Journals*, 1797: 227).

Radcliffe does more than simply oppose sensibility to the diabolical rationalisms of Schedoni and the Marchesa. Sensibility
humanises the Marchesa, but more than that it makes her 'democratic'. Her response to the requiem for the dead looks back to
the 'graveyard' school of poetry, which stressed the equalising
tendencies of contemplating the great leveller. The Marchesa's
awakening sensibility calms her passions, and with her passions
the social bigotry which constitutes her aristocratic nature. Here
she begins to approach Vivaldi's and Ellena's language of inalien-
able human rights.

A deep-running ambiguity now begins to confront the reader.
Schedoni's cynical statement that a sense of what justice commands
'lives in our breasts' may be taken as a swipe at the innate rights
of man and therefore as a back-handed, Burkean defence of the
organic accretions of law. Outside precedent there is only a Sade-
ian, atheistical world of self-assertion and moral anarchy, of
'natural rights'. To consult what lives in our breasts is to risk
liberating whatever beast that lurks there. But it is precisely to an
innate sense of justice that Vivaldi and Ellena constantly appeal.
For sensibility to work its progressive influence its observers have
to consult the benevolent instincts within their own breasts. But
the text places in question the universal existence of such instincts.
In the absence of such a dependable instinct one's only recourse is
to the law, to the statutes and precedents that guarantee our liberty.
But this Burkean view runs counter to the pro-innovation accents
of Vivaldi and Ellena's appeals to the rights of man. The political
logic of sensibility is both encouraged and countered.

It is tempting to dismiss Radcliffe's vacillation as typical liberal
fence-sitting; and yet, during this period of reactionary hysteria,
when all around radicals were busy breaking their 'squeaking
trumpets of sedition', to remain vacillating took real courage.
Earlier I noted that for the first time since *The Castles of Athlin
and Dunbayne* Radcliffe chose a temporal setting outside the Gothic
cusp. I then posed the question of what this choice signalled
regarding Radcliffe's political intent. My answer is that it indicated
Radcliffe's re-affirmation of liberal, dissenting, bourgeois values
(this at a time when upstanding members of the community
considered the purpose of dissenters to be 'to undermine and blow
up the constitution' (*Anti-Jacobin Review and Magazine*, 1798: 626)).

In Chapter 3 we saw how, prior to the 1790s, the myth of the Goth largely supported a Whiggish interpretation of English history. I then argued that women writers took advantage of the unimpeachable – even bland – politics of the Goth to secure ideological advantages. Indeed, the more potent the advantage, the more the Goth was idealised as our common chivalric ancestor. But in the 1790s the constitutional controversy re-infused 'Gothic' with an explicitly contentious ideological meaning. As we saw, Burke's intervention was the key, as his chivalric romance of Marie Antoinette and glorification of tradition opened the way for radicals to fight back by labelling Burke's politics as feudal and Gothic. For instance, Thomas Christie accuses Burke of cherishing 'the principles of Gothic feudality', of 'consecrating in his writings the unclassic jargon of lawyers, monks and sophists of the middle ages' (Christie 1791: 4). For radicals, 'Gothic' was a wholly pejorative term, one indicating feudal despotism. Christie invites his reader to consider the case of *'ancient France'* where a 'great and enlightened people' were deprived

> of almost all the advantages Nature had given them, by an oppressive and arbitrary Government: – without *agriculture*, for the people (who are the cultivators) were despised and kept in a state of the lowest servitude: – without *commerce*, for it was reckoned dishonourable: – without *liberty*, for the life and property of every individual was constantly at the mercy of a minister, or of his mistress: – without *laws*, for where arbitrary will can suspend any thing, there the laws are a mere fiction: and lastly, without *morals*, for these depend on laws and a fixed constitution. How could there be morals in a country, where the whole government consisted of a system of oppression, from the highest down to the lowest ranks of society – where talents and worth availed nothing against interest and favour – where the only road to power and success was to flatter the Great; to encourage their vices, and to be a partaker in them – where no man trusted to the goodness of his cause, but to the patronage of some great man to support it – In fine, where women are nominally excluded from the Throne, and yet the country was really governed by a set of prostitutes?
>
> (Christie 1791: 85)

In describing the Gothic vices of the *ancien régime* in France Christie is also frying fish closer to home: his ultimate aim is to roast reactionary English opinions. But this was in 1791. The typical radical strategy was to secure the high moral ground by first interpreting the true nature of the British Constitution, and then to argue that the revolutionary elements in France wanted no more than the same liberties and rights vouchsafed to Britons. Any who opposed this reasonable and indeed patriotic view were stigmatised as sunk in Gothic bigotry, as heartless defenders of feudal oppression. But by 1797 it had long since become clear that the object of the French Revolution was not an English-style constitutional monarchy but out-and-out republicanism. In 1791 Christie sneers at English reactionaries: 'When any mention is made of *reform, improvement*, or *change* of any kind whatever, their feeble or frighted imaginations immediately conjure up the horrors of anarchy, riot, mobs, murders, burning, &c.' (Christie 1791: 22). Alas, for Christie, the alarmists were proved right. By 1797 a wider public appetite for innovation had quite died out, and yet Radcliffe, in centring her fiction on court machinations, closely reproduces in her fictional society Christie's portrait of French monarchical abuse. By situating her fiction in the recent past Radcliffe deprives herself of an historical fig-leaf. This is not criticism by analogy; this is criticism direct. In her depiction of the Marchesa and her circle Radcliffe does not join in Burke's idealising gloss of Continental feudalism, of Whiggish chivalry; rather she echoes Christie's acerbic, radical views of the evils attendant upon aristocratic, Gothic abuses.

There is, however, a counter-argument. By 1797 the heat had gone out of the controversy. There was now something like a reactionary consensus where France was seen to be rotten, root and branch, past and present. Of course the *ancien régime* was corrupt; it was never like Britain. To attack French aristocratic abuse was unexceptionably patriotic.

The difficulty with this view is that *The Italian*'s setting is not France. There is a generic similarity between the society described in *The Italian* and the French *ancien régime*, but so was there between it and the numerous principalities England was presently allied with against France. As a depiction of Britain's allies *The Italian* was more likely to put ardour into a French than a British arm.

My point is not that *The Italian* was calculated to embarrass the British war effort. *The Italian* resonates, not with British war policy, but with English class politics. The logic of the Gothic cusp had been the supercession of the feudal by the modern: despotic, patriarchal abuse would be put behind us, and sensibility would reign. Relocating the text in the near present unfastens this cosy view. We are now dealing, not with things as they were, and how they might be, but with things as they are. In this respect *The Italian* provides us with a displaced representation of England and 'Englishness'. The war with France required national unity. The popular press's patriotic contribution to the war effort included a discourse on 'The Character of a True Briton':

> The True Briton is the child of virtue and of reason. The one he loves by natural disposition; the other guides him in the practice of her dictates. From the strength of his reason, he is a zealous friend to order; by the virtuous ardour of his spirit, he is the adorer of Liberty. Without the due restraint of law, he fears he might be vicious; without the energy of freedom, he feels he should be mean. He would neither have his evil tendencies indulged, nor his virtuous impulses repressed.
>
> *Spirit of the Public Journals* (1799: 144)

Systematic antitheses box in the true Briton, who becomes something of a disciplined 'mean'. In *The Italian* Ellena and Vivaldi also belong to a middling class, in a twofold manner. Fictionally, they inhabit a middle ground between the Marchesa's world of aristocratic corruption and a lower world of peasants and servants. Symbolically, though, they are 'middle class', irrespective of their fictional background. That is to say, the text implicitly defines Englishness as a middle-class quality, which it further interprets as the condition of 'sensibility'. It is through sensibility that Ellena and Vivaldi express themselves as human agents, ones capable of responding to the dictates governing the 'True Briton'. The condition of being a servant, or an 'aristocrat', is insensibility, an indifference to the stimuli that move Ellena or Vivaldi.

In this respect the Marchesa and Paulo are alike in their Otherness. The depth of the Marchesa's feudal pride places her outside the carefully balanced framework of instinct and rationality identified in 'The True Briton'. *The Italian*'s implicit message here is that aristocratic mores are essentially 'un-English', are foreign and threatening. On the face of it Paulo appears to be a different case, for he is governed by at least one instinct conservative commen-

tators interpreted as profoundly 'British': the deferentiality of the
lower orders. *Moderate Politics: Devoted to Britons* (1791) opines:

> Providence has happily, in pity to mankind, giving [sic] those of lowest
> degree, who compose the bulk of a state, that natural disposition
> to content, which leads them, when honestly left to themselves, to
> acquiesce in that mode of succession which wiser men than themselves
> recommend for the general good.
>
> (*Critical Review* 1791: 428)

Paulo has this happy faith in the wisdom of his superiors.
Indeed, Paulo is so devotedly loyal and subordinate that he appears
less as a human being and more as an anthropomorphised dog,
practically wetting himself with joy at every sight of his master
(Todd 1982). The rhetoric of *Moderate Politics* construes the con-
tented lower orders as British, discontented ones as foreign. The
double-bind of Paulo's representation is that he is only permitted
within the magic circle of Englishness if he is doggedly loyal;
but this very loyalty dehumanises him, renders him 'Other' and
'insensible'. In the case of both *The Italian* and *Moderate Politics*,
'fear of the mob' colours their representations of the lower orders.

The Italian's ostensible politics is thus of provincial, dissenting,
middle-class culture. It trusts in a British instinct for liberty, but
only within the confines of an historically hallowed constitution;
it regards English aristocratic mores as a betrayal of Englishness,
but can only contemplate the lower orders approvingly through
the pastoral fiction of the loyal servant; it believes in the freedom
of conscience, trusting that all free consciences will be Protestant
ones; it lays its faith in the democratising, improving effects of
sensibility, but in the end sees sensibility as – by definition – a
middle-class quality.

This sketch of a politics hedged in by wishes and fears may
strike us as typically craven liberal fence-sitting, but in this historical context it was a brave defence of threatened freedoms. When
pressed *The Italian* reveals a radical edge. It sharpens the contrast
– present in Radcliffe's earlier books – between the marriage mores
of the aristocracy and the middle class. The arranged 'alliances' of
the former effectively stripped women of essential rights,
whereas the 'companionate' ideal of bourgeois marriage stressed a
degree of mutuality, respect and power. In the history and charac-

ter of Olivia and the Marchesa de Vivaldi we witness the effects of marriage as feudal institution. The Marchesa has internalised the power structure that shaped her destiny, and compulsively seeks to impose it in turn; Olivia has escaped internalising those marriage values which have seen her legally bound to her own rapist, but the reverse side of the coin is that this leaves her a disempowered victim. Ellena and Vivaldi's relationship is in explicit contrast to the tyrannical horrors of 'alliance', and is much closer to the pattern of 'marriage' envisioned by contemporary radical feminists, such as Wollstonecraft. Moreover, Ellena and Vivaldi's courtship is conducted through the language of rights, and this, too, as we have seen, is radically tinged.

But as is usually the case with Radcliffe, her most powerful and subtle thinking is deeply embedded within her use of fictional form. Beneath the surface inflections cueing us into contemporary ideological meanings we find a more telling – but also more abstract – treatment of the theme of power.

The framing narrative thematically opens up the text in a way quite different from Radcliffe's previous prologues. A group of travellers happen to stop at the portico of the Santa Maria del Pianto, where they observe a sinister-looking man, partially muffled, with an eye which seemed 'expressive of uncommon ferocity' (*I*, 1). One of the travellers, a chauvinistic Englishman, expresses patronising contempt on learning that this man is an assassin enjoying the sanctuary of the church. The text then focuses on the building's sublime interior, and then on the confessional. The Englishman once again observes the assassin, but instead of coolly appraising him, as before, he turns his eyes in fearful submission, and hastily quits the church.

The narrative has moved from the portico of the church to its interior; that is to say, from a tourist's view of Italian culture to a view from within. Here power is not a matter of 'laws' *per se* (as the Englishman believes), but of customs and institutions. In particular, the sublimity of the church and the confessional are revealed as instruments of social power (the *Italian*'s subtitle is, significantly, *The Confessional of the Black Penitents*). The Englishman ceases to observe the assassin from without – as if the muffled

figure were some sort of curious exhibit – but from within the
same cultural frame; and here the balance of power shifts.

This shift is registered in the politics of looking. Looking, and
its variants, is a recurring theme of the romance (Miles 1993:
171–9). The first chapter opens with Vivaldi straining to get a
glimpse of the veiled Ellena, who has just come from church. The
scene is a direct reprise of the opening paragraphs of Matthew
Lewis's *The Monk*, in which two young cavaliers dwell upon the
attractions of the modest Antonia. Lewis's text transgressively
dwells upon voyeurism, on the sensualisation of sight. The narrative oversteps the mark in its fascinated observance of Antonia's
charms. Later, we observe Ambrosio's visual seduction when Matilda holds up a poinard to her naked breast, and again when
Matilda demonically conjures up a vision of a nude Antonia for
Ambrosio's delectation.

Lewis's text is transgressive in the sense that it subverts the
politics of modesty (and, by extension, sensibility) through excess.
The implicit references here are to the 'ideal presence' of Henry
Home, Lord Kames, an important figure in the Scottish Enlightenment and author of the influential *Elements of Criticism* (1762).
Although 'ideal presence' was Kames's coinage, the concept itself
belonged to the deep structure of eighteenth-century aesthetics.
The leading idea of ideal presence is the ability of fiction – poetry
and drama as well as romances – to create an impression of reality
so intense that readers or spectators find it easy to lose themselves
in the illusion. Kames saw this as a providential aspect of human
nature, for he linked 'ideal presence' to another common idea of
the period: that as observers we have innate moral instincts which
will lead us to abhor spectacles of vice, while greeting scenes of
benevolence with warm, melting approval. Ideal presence was, as
it were, the improving engine of sensibility.

Further to this, the ideal subject-matter for ideal presence was,
as we have seen, virtue in distress. The logic of modesty construed
the feminine as a visually affecting object, all the more affecting
if caught in moments of chaste repose or despicable outrage. As
we saw in earlier chapters, Radcliffe had explored this cultural
construction of the feminine. Lewis, through his intervention, laid
bare the pretensions of Kamesian ideal presence and 'virtue in
distress'. In Lewis visually affecting scenes of outraged virtue serve

only to titillate; or if they do move the fictional viewer, they do so by mobilising his or her baser appetites.

Radcliffe's response to Lewis's transgressions was not to flee in horror; rather she responded by exploring the power inherent in culturally determined ways of seeing. *The Italian* advances a politics of looking by formulating its own version of what film theorist Laura Mulvey has influentially termed the 'male gaze' (Mulvey 1975). Radcliffe does this by arranging for the tables to be turned on the male gazer; Vivaldi, who initially expresses his dominance by wishing to peer beneath Ellena's veil finds himself 'veiled' in turn by the Inquisition. Blindfolded, and brought before the Inquisitors' scrutiny, he now finds himself the object of power. Within the dungeons of the Inquisition, and powerless to resist its tricks, he gives himself over to the spectral, to the 'contagion' of superstition. When reminded of his mental weakness by Schedoni, Vivaldi 'blushes'. He has, in effect, been 'feminised'.

Within *The Italian* looking is not an innocent activity. And that is because there is always a mismatch in power and status between those who look, and those who are looked upon. As in the prologue, this power is revealed as a function of cultural institutions and practices, such as the confessional, the 'sublime' architecture of the church itself, or, indeed, sensibility.

In recent years German reader-response critics have advanced the view that the Gothic novel owed its popularity to the manner in which it provided a vicarious sense of control for a readership who otherwise felt themselves powerless (cf. Conger 1989; Richter 1988 and 1989). When the European bourgeoisie looked about them during the revolutionary decade, they discovered themselves caught 'amidst the shocks of contending factions, the wreck of surrounding governments, and the general desolation of the civilized world' (*Anti-Jacobin Review and Magazine* 1798: I, iii). In particular, they found themselves imprisoned in the wreckage of an old order without the liberating promise of a new one. But within the realm of the Gothic novel – as David Richter puts it – doors mysteriously fly open, releasing the imprisoned subject blissfully into a new, liberating dawn.

If so, then we have another angle on Radcliffe's powers of enchantment, for as we have seen, she is the great prose poet of the Gothic cusp, of that imagined transition from a decadent to a vital, new order. And yet, with *The Italian*, it is as if Radcliffe were forced to take stock of her art, measuring her own complicity in the power structures with which she had engaged.

In 1788 Mary Wollstonecraft gave this definition of sensibility:

> I should say that it is the result of acute senses, finely fashioned nerves, which vibrate at the slightest touch, and *convey such clear intelligence to the brain, that it does not require to be arranged by the judgment*. Such persons instinctively enter into the character of others, and instinctively discern what will give pain to every human being.
>
> (Quoted in Conger 1989: 116)

Two years later she attacks Burke for endorsing a 'sentimental jargon' that has 'never received the *regal* stamp of reason':

> A kind of mysterious instinct is *supposed* to reside in the soul, that instantaneously discerns truth, without the tedious labour of ratiocination. This instinct... has been termed *common sense*, and more frequently *sensibility* ... it has been *supposed* ... to reign paramount over the faculties of the mind, and to be an authority from which there is no appeal.
>
> (Wollstonecraft 1790: 64–5)

It is easy to see why Wollstonecraft has turned rationalist within the space of two years. Burke's 'common sense' entrenches the status quo; as sensibility ostensibly shares common sense's instinctive quality, the two must fall together, and with them the hierarchical authority they unthinkingly endorse (a view backed up through metaphor: the mind should be ruled not by accustomed authority – e.g. the king – but by reason).

Radcliffe's opinions do not go through such a spectacular reversal, but they are re-examined. In particular, *The Italian* takes to an extreme the 'sub-textual' doubt registered in her earlier romances as to the validity of sensibility as both the instrument and the character of a dawning new age. Within the walls of the Inquisition the feminised Vivaldi is not delivered through sensibility; his sensibility, rather, is a symptom of his incarceration. His are the 'instincts' of the powerless. It is not simply that the veiled Vivaldi is forced to submit to the gaze of others, in the way that formerly the heroines were forced to; we also see, in his new proneness to superstition – his susceptibility to the spectral tricks of the Inquisition – a re-representation of the 'origins of romance'.

Within the 'patriarchal' walls of the Inquisition, the 'feminized' Vivaldi turns fabulist, as Adeline does in her cell in the ruined abbey.

Does Radcliffe anticipate the subtleties of modern criticism? Is she here re-viewing her own role as the Great Enchantress, as the provider of narratives whereby the powerless are (but only within the vicarious realm of fiction) empowered? Judging from *The Italian* alone, the render might find it hard to say. But as I trust I have shown, one sees in the run of her career Radcliffe's increasing self-consciousness as a romancer, a self-consciousness stimulated by her fictional apprehension of the subtle realities of power. While the 'gentlewoman' may have preferred the romance of origins, the 'authoress' progressively deepened her analyses into the originating impulses that produced just such romances. In the end it is not a question of which is the true Radcliffe, the 'woman writer' or the 'proper lady'. Both are 'Radcliffe', both sides of a single dynamic. One misses much if one lets oneself be beguiled by the soothing – if also soporific – tones of the gentlewoman. The reverse is also true, but it has been the 'gentlewoman' whose notes have been most (in)attentively listened to by critics. Seeing Radcliffe's career as a whole helps sharpen the ear so one catches the dissenting accents of *The Italian*, together with the sexual-political importance of the reversal of gender, 'gaze' and power implicit in Vivaldi's 'feminisation'. Lewis tastelessly brought out the latent eroticism of the modesty that had conditioned the representation of Radcliffe's earlier heroines. Radcliffe responded, not with denial, but by widening the frame. *The Italian* is not just the most political of Radcliffe's romances, it is also the most 'sexual-political'. In place of Lewis's satire, Radcliffe investigates sensibility as a site of power, one that obtains regardless of gender. And so it is that Vivaldi recapitulates the careers of Radcliffe's early heroines within the confines of a conspicuously patriarchal Inquisition.

Conclusion

It was a misfortune to any man of talent to be born in the latter end of
the last century. Genius stopped the way of Legitimacy, and therefore it
was to be abated, crushed, or set aside as a nuisance. The spirit of
monarchy was at variance with the spirit of the age. The flame
of liberty, the light of the intellect, was to be extinguished with the
sword – or with slander, whose edge is sharper than the sword. The
war between power and reason was carried on by the first of these
abroad – by the last at home. No quarter was given (then or now) by
the Government-critics, the authorised censors of the press, to those
who followed the dictates of independence, who listened to the
tempter, Fancy. Instead of gathering fruits and flowers, immortal
fruits and amaranthine flowers, they soon found themselves beset not
only by a host of prejudices, but assailed with all the engines of power,
by nicknames, by lies, by all the arts of malice, interest and hypocrisy,
without the possibility of their defending themselves 'from the pelting
of the pitiless storm', that poured down upon them from the strong-
holds of corruption and authority ... the poets, the creatures of sympathy, could not stand the frowns both of king and people.

William Hazlitt, *The Spirit of the Age* (1910: 203)

As we saw in the epigraph with which this study began, by the
end of the decade Ann Radcliffe discovered herself increasingly
caught up in the 'pelting' of – to use her own phrase – 'the storms
of power'. In Chapter 2 I raised the question of why, at the
height of her fame, and at the age of only thirty-three, Ann
Radcliffe suddenly stopped publishing. I want to conclude my
study of Radcliffe's romances by suggesting that William Hazlitt
comes closest to giving us an answer.

For many readers it will doubtless seem fanciful to include
Radcliffe among Hazlitt's list of radical casualties, among the

progressive talents snuffed out by the virulence of the 1790s reaction. But if so it will only be because of Radcliffe's lingering – but undeserved – reputation for unexamined conservatism. Edmund Burke's rueful assessment that the balance of the intellect was on the side of the Jacobins has been emphatically endorsed by posterity: the early Romantic literary canon, to a man, is composed of writers who in one way or another, at one time or another, sought to lift Hazlitt's 'flame of liberty'. To be stigmatised with conservatism, in this instance, must therefore be fatal to any literary reputation, for it is to be smeared with the greasy advantages of 'Legitimacy'.

One way of thinking about what I have done in this book is to see it as mounting a case against this view, and for Radcliffe as one of Hazlitt's stymied geniuses, as a writer who, from the depths of dissenting culture, ought to prevail against 'the spirit of monarchy'. Here I would remind the reader of how, again and again, Radcliffe returns to her favoured *mise-en-scène* of a moment of passage from a feudal to a modern world, where the latter is conditioned by benevolence, sensibility, companionate relationships and (comparatively speaking) equality. As Hazlitt reminds us, in the 1790s this was enough to incur assaults from the 'engine of power'.

The sophisticated sceptic will of course grant the apparent liberalism of Radcliffe's themes before pointing to the irredeemable conservatism of her form. In her endings and explanations eighteenth-century rationalism is re-imposed and with it a rejection of the Romantics' fundamental belief in the radical, shaping power of the imagination.

Here the issue of gender is inescapable. For the woman writer, the ideological circumstances – the cultural pressures and realities – were in varying degrees different from those obtaining for men. It is in this respect anachronistic to look in vain for the woman Romantic rising up, like Blake's Orc, to smash Urizen's discursive structures; to write in the same way – and in accordance with the same agendas – as male writers.

As I have argued all the way through, Radcliffe's radicalism is to be found in her subtext, in the transgressive thoughts hazarded by her heroines in moments of supernatural terror, in the counter-stories embedded in the main narrative, in displaced allusions and figures. The tension between Radcliffe's surface narrative, which appears to go in a conservative direction, and her subtext, which moves in quite other ways, is the source of Radcliffe's aesthetic dynamism. We cannot know whether Radcliffe saw herself as a writer deliberately withdrawing from the public gaze, from the 'frowns both of king and people'. But to an extent that is not my argument. I do not believe that the curtailment of Radcliffe's public career was a simple case of a writer wilting in a repressive atmosphere. My argument, rather, is that ideological contention deprived Radcliffe of the imaginative conditions necessary for her art. Her writing thrived because its deepest purposes were allowed to remain covert. She prospered because of – not in spite of – the stresses between the proper lady and the woman writer. The ideological dispute noted by Hazlitt threatened to lay bare the latent 'radicalism' of her work. The authorised censors of the press were quick to sniff out anything that might be construed Jacobinical, and a lot of Radcliffe could be so construed. In such an atmosphere of militantly policed reaction the ideologically dubious could not remain subtextual. The creative tension between the gentlewoman and the authoress which had earlier sustained Radcliffe was now broken.

Further reading

This section has four basic aims: 1) to acknowledge the critical sources that have influenced me most, together with a short indication of how they have influenced me; 2) to structure bibliographical information in a convenient fashion; 3) to indicate the standard references to standard topics that would otherwise have cluttered the text; and 4) to give some indication of recent work on Radcliffe. There are currently available several excellent bibliographies on the Gothic novel, on both primary and secondary texts: Dan McNutt's *The Eighteenth-Century Gothic Novel* (1975), and more recently Frederick Frank's *The First Gothics: A Critical Guide to the English Gothic Novel* (1987) and *Gothic Fiction: A Master List of Twentieth-Century Criticism and Research* (1988). Given how easily accessible information on Radcliffe and the Gothic is I have limited references to work done in the last ten years or so, except where the first three purposes dictate otherwise. I have divided the entries by chapter and (where appropriate) thematically for ease of reference. Full publishing details may be found in the bibliography.

Chapter 1: The Great Enchantress

ENCHANTMENT

The issue of 'enchantment' – the predisposition of readers to be enchanted by particular literary works – is one of the most intractable critical questions. I have been influenced, and helped, by the work-in-progress of David Richter ('The reception of the Gothic novel in the 1790s' [1988] and 'The unguarded prison [1989]) and

Terry Castle ('The spectralization of the Other in *The Mysteries of Udolpho* [1987] and 'Phantasmagoria: Spectral technology and the metaphorics of modern reverie' [1988]).

Richter has employed the methodology of German reader-response criticism to gain a purchase on a shift in reading habits he tentatively identifies as occurring towards the end of the eighteenth century: 'a shift from the reading for information, and for the sake of entry into a verisimilar world otherwise inaccessible to the reader, toward reading as an escape from the world one inhabits into an inward locus of fantasy' (1988: 121). Richter is both enticed by the prospect that this shift may be the 'result of changes in modes of economic production' (131), and chastened by the difficulty of proving it.

Terry Castle covers very similar territory, but tries to contextual-ise it by encompassing it within a history of the imagination. In her essay on *The Mysteries of Udolpho* (1987), Castle links 'spectralization' in Radcliffe to an erasure of boundaries between real and unreal, life and death, produced by sociological changes in practices of – and attitudes towards – dying. The work gains by being read in tandem with her 'Phantasmagoria' essay (1988). In 1798 in Paris Etienne-Gaspard Robertson staged the first *fantas-magorie*, in which, in a darkened pavilion outfitted in the manner of Radcliffe, members of the audience's dead relatives came to life again through the astounding technology of the 'magic lantern'. Castle's concern is with the shift in the meaning of 'phantasma-goria', from literal to figurative show. The *fantasmagorie* was no sooner invented than it was internalised as 'phantasmagoria', the bizarre mental theatre of the deranged imagination. Castle links this to the fate of the supernatural, which was no sooner expunged from our religious beliefs than it reappeared as the tendency of the mind to be haunted by 'ghosts', 'spectres', 'phantoms'. Castle's point is that we have become habituated to this 'displaced super-naturalism', and that it has a history worth attending to.

Both Castle and Richter approach their subjects in a mood of tentative speculation. There is, I think, widespread agreement that the late eighteenth century witnessed a shift in the practices of the imagination along the lines Castle and Richter suggest. What one makes of this is another, more difficult matter. Whether Radcliffe was the 'product' of this shift, or whether she helped produce it (or both) is also almost impossible to tease out. Whatever the case, both Richter and Castle see Radcliffe as centrally involved in the formation of new ways of reading, and in this I follow them.

THE GOTHIC ROMANCE

Two more or less recent developments have transformed the critical approach to Gothic fiction. The first followed as the consequence of Eve Kosofsky Sedgwick's *The Coherence of Gothic Coventions* (1980). Rather than seeing Gothic novels as the product of endlessly recycled conventions, Sedgwick argued that they possessed a hidden coherence. In particular, she focused on boundaries in the Gothic, interpreting the genre's typical features – the castle, live burial, the veil – as representations of somatic spaces articulating two central anxieties: 1) the fear of invasion, of being helpless to prevent the transgression of the boundary between self and other (essentially Emily's plight in the unlockable room in Udolpho); and 2) its obverse, the fear of being unable to cross the boundary between self and other (as for instance, in live burial). Sedgwick's book was influential because it provided a form of figurative interpretation that went beyond simple Freudian allegory, and secondly, because her approach made it possible to read the Gothic as registering anxieties regarding the integrity of the self: in Sedgwick's view, the Gothic was primarily about the 'fragmented subject'.

The second development came about as a result of the work of the Russian critic Mikhail Bakhtin. Bakhtin focused on the novel, but he has influenced attitudes to fiction in general, including Gothic romance. A presiding critical attitude had been that a work ought to be unified, whereas Bakhtin stressed the desirable quality of multiple dissonant voices within fiction. This dissonance – or 'heteroglossia' – is for Bakhtin the source of the novel's aesthetic energy, a liberating view for students of Gothic romance, which is nothing if not 'disjunctive'. Elizabeth Napier's *The Failure of Gothic* (1987) provides a good example of the traditional approach; for the other, see Jacqueline Howard, *Reading Gothic Fiction: A Bakhtinian Approach* (1994). See also Jeffrey Cox's introduction to *Seven Gothic Dramas: 1789–1825* (1992). Mikhail Bakhtin's major works include *Rabelais and his World* (1972) and *Problems of Dostoevsky's Poetics* (1973).

Both 'developments' are anticipated in David Punter's still influential *The Literature of Terror* (1980), which should also be consulted for its analysis of Radcliffe's reading public. As regards recent studies, Eugenia Delamotte's *Perils of the Night* (1990) helpfully expands on Sedgwick while providing an exceptionally detailed study of 1790s Gothic conventions and Radcliffe's use/ transformation of them. Victor Sage's *Horror Fiction in the Protestant Tradition* (1988) should be consulted by anyone interested in the theological politics of Gothic fiction, while Kate Ferguson Ellis's *The Contested Castle* (1989) follows Mary Poovey's seminal essay 'Ideology in *The Mysteries of Udolpho*' (1979) in situating the Gothic in the ideological stresses of late eighteenth-century capitalism. For Radcliffe's Gothic 'sources' see Ellis; for her influence on later writers see J. M. S. Tompkins' *The Work of Mrs. Radcliffe* (1921) and Marilyn Butler's 'The Woman at the Window' (1980).

RADCLIFFE'S CONSERVATISM

The view that Radcliffe was an instinctive – even unthinking – conservative is widespread. After noting Lowry Nelson's comment that Radcliffe's novels 'now seem more like childish fantasies than evocations of primal horror', David Durrant typically (and influentially) comments: 'It is not because she is puerile, however, but because she is philosophically traditional, that her novels fit modern definitions of the gothic so badly. She is not a forerunner of the romantic movement, but the staunch foe of its most salient characteristics' (Durrant 1982: 519). An egregious expression of this view is to be found in Michael Taylor's essay 'Reluctant Romancers' (1991). Taylor finds *The Mysteries of Udolpho* 'spectacularly silly' (90); Radcliffe herself is not so much an unselfconscious romancer as she is a stupefyingly complacent one (95). The premise behind the comments of both Durrant and Taylor is that Radcliffe instinctively held to the rationalist tenets of the Enlightenment. See also Charles C. Murrah, 'Mrs. Radcliffe's landscapes' (1984); April London, 'Radcliffe in context' (1986); and B. M. Benedict, 'Pictures of conformity' (1989).

REPRESENTING THE FRENCH REVOLUTION

As we have seen from the Walter Scott and William Hazlitt quotations, the view that Radcliffe's romances somehow reflect events in France has been a commonplace since her own day. Even so, there has been surprisingly little work on just how her work did represent contemporary events in France. For the standard work on the subject, see Ronald Paulson, *Representations of Revolution* (1983); for the political meanings of 1790s fiction in general, see Gary Kelly, *The English Jacobin Novel* (1976).

FOUCAULT ON THE GOTHIC

For a further discussion of Michel Foucault's reading of the late eighteenth century and its relation to the Gothic, see my *Gothic Writing* (1993); for Foucault directly on the Gothic novel, see Simon During, *Foucault and Literature* (1992), and Chloe Chard, Introduction to *A Romance of the Forest* (1986).

In *Gothic Writing* I principally look at Foucault's *Madness and Civilization* (1967) and *The History of Sexuality* (1979); both Chard and During discuss Foucault's essay 'Language to Infinity' (1977).

Chapter 2: The gentlewoman and the authoress

RADCLIFFE'S BIOGRAPHY

All students of Radcliffe are indebted to the pioneering work of Clara McIntyre (1920) and J. M. S. Tompkins (1921). Although they began with the same limited resources – the *Annual Biography and Obituary* for 1824 and the memoir Thomas Noon Talfourd appended to *Gaston de Blondeville* (1826) – they both assemble an impressively deep body of contextual knowledge. Aline Grant's *Ann Radcliffe* (1951) remains the only biography to date. Although she, too, has researched Radcliffe's milieu in impressive depth, very little is added to our knowledge beyond what is already present in McIntyre and Tompkins. The most recent introduction is E. B. Murray's *Ann Radcliffe* (1972).

My discussion of this issue in relation to sensibility is heavily dependent upon Mary Poovey's *The Proper Lady and the Woman Writer* (1984).

Chapter 3: The aesthetic context

FEMALE GOTHIC

There is now a substantial body of criticism on the female Gothic. For recent examples, see Kate Ellis, *The Contested Castle* (1989); Tamar Heller, *Dead Secrets* (1992), and Alison Milbank, *Daughters of the House* (1992). The phrase itself was coined by Ellen Moers; see her *Literary Women* (1977). For earlier contributions, see Margaret Doody, 'Deserts, Ruins, Troubled Waters: Female Dreams in Fiction and the Development of the Gothic Novel' (1977); Sandra Gilbert and Susan Gubar, *The Madwoman in the Attic* (1979); Eva Figes, *Sex and Subterfuge* (1982); Juliann Fleenor's important collection *The Female Gothic*, with its many essays on the subject (1983); Claire Kahane's seminal article 'The Gothic mirror' (1985), which influentially focused on the representation of the mother in the Gothic; and Frances Restuccia 'Female Gothic writing' (1986).

For a sample of the work this criticism was reacting against, see Lowry Nelson jr, 'Night Thoughts on the Gothic Novel' (1963); Robert Hume 'Gothic versus Romantic' (1969); Robert Hume and Robert Platzner ' "Gothic versus Romantic": A Rejoinder' (1971); and Leslie Fiedler, *Love and Death in the American Novel* (1966).

PICTURESQUE AND SUBLIME

For standard reference works on the sublime see Samuel Monk, *The Sublime* (1960) and Thomas Weiskel's difficult but challenging *The Romantic Sublime* (1976). For a short, clear introduction to the sublime in the eighteenth century, see Martin Price, 'The sublime poem' (1969); for the sublime and the Gothic novel, see David Morris 'Gothic Sublimity' (1985). Malcolm Ware's *Sublimity in the Novels of Ann Radcliffe* (1963) is informative, if of limited critical interest.

The related grouping of the picturesque, the pictorial, and landscape has stimulated more criticism on Radcliffe than almost any other aspect of her work. See Angela Keane (1994); Benedict (1989); Murrah (1984); Rhoda L. Flaxman, 'Radcliffe's dual modes of vision' (1986); Jean H. Hagstrum, 'Pictures to the heart' (1984); John Thompson, 'Seasonal and Lighting Effects in Ann Radcliffe's Fiction' (1981). For the most helpful essay on Radcliffe's sources and her use of them, see Charles Kostelnick, 'From picturesque view to picturesque vision' (1985). Daniel Cottom's *The Civilized Imagination* (1985) contains an extremely useful study of Radcliffe's relation to the taste of the period.

For a discussion of landscape in a wider economic context, see John Barrell, *The Dark Side of the Landscape* (1980), and Ann Bermingham, *Landscape and Ideology* (1987).

ASSOCIATIONISM, SENSIBILITY AND TRAVEL-WRITING

Despite the importance of associationism for eighteenth-century aesthetics there has been little in the way of recent work on the subject, certainly not in terms of a student guide. For example Pat Rogers, *The Eighteenth Century: The Context of English Literature* (1978), is relatively light on the subject. But Basil Willey, *The Eighteenth Century Background* (1940), and M. H. Abrams, *The Mirror and the Lamp* (1953), offer extremely useful introductions. For further reference, see Martin Kallich's series of essays (1945, 1946, 1947). Don Locke's *A Fantasy of Reason* (1980) lucidly introduces the work of the radical philosopher William Godwin; Locke also covers the relationship between associationism and Godwin's radicalism.

On sensibility there have been a number of excellent and accessible works. See especially Janet Todd, *Sensibility: An Introduction* (1986) and R. F. Brissenden, *Virtue in Distress* (1974). For the political overtones of sensibility, see Marilyn Butler, *Romantics, Rebels and Reactionaries* (1987).

For Radcliffe and travel-writing see Chloe Chard (1986).

Chapter 4: The historical context

RADICAL POLITICS

E. P. Thompson's *The Making of the English Working Class* (1968) remains an invaluable guide. For literary-historical works on the radical politics of the period, see Iain McCalman, *Radical Underworld* (1993); Jonathan Mee, *Dangerous Enthusiasm* (1992); David Worral, *Radical Culture* (1992); Ronald Paulson (1983). On the French Revolution itself, see Simon Schama, *Citizens* (1989) for an informative, provocative, revisionist chronicle.

THE MYTH OF THE GOTH

The standard work on the subject – the myth of the Goth and the political uses to which it was put – is Samuel Kliger's *The Goths in England* (1952). Kliger's book is an invaluable resource for anyone interested in the latent ideological meanings of Gothic writing. For a more recent contribution, see R.J. Smith, *The Gothic Bequest* (1987). For the Goth/Oriental opposition, see Kliger and Gary Kelly, 'From Gothicism to Romantic Orientalism' (1989a).

Chapter 5: Early works

Relatively little work has been done on Radcliffe's early romances; the best remains that published by the Arno Press in 1980 in their 'Gothic Studies and Dissertations' series. For details, see Frank (1988). Recent criticism touching upon Radcliffe's first two works includes Marilyn Butler (1980), Kate Ellis (1989) and Alison Milbank (1993).

For the gendering of the picturesque and sublime in Romantic poetics, see Phil Cox, *Gender, Genre and Romantic Poetry: An Introduction* (1995). For the gendering of the sublime, see Linda Kauffman, *Gender and Theory* (1989).

For a still very reliable guide to how Radcliffe's readership interpreted her imitations of Claude and Salvator Rosa, see J. M. S. Tompkins (1921).

Chapter 6: In the realm of the figural

Freud's essay on the uncanny has proved extremely influential in the formulation of the 'fantastic' (Freud 1958); see in particular Tzvetan Todorov, *The Fantastic: A Structural Approach to a Literary Genre* (1973); and Rosemary Jackson, *Fantasy: The Literature of Subversion* (1981).

For the complex issue of whether Freud explains the Gothic, or the Gothic explains Freud, see Peter Thorslev jr, *Romantic Contraries* (1981) and Terry Castle (1987 and 1988).

For an introduction to Freud, see Richard Wollheim, *Freud* (1971); for an accessible commentary on Jacques Lacan, see Terry Eagleton, *Literary Theory: An Introduction* (1983).

Chapter 7: The hermeneutics of reading

The Mysteries of Udolpho is, critically, the best served of Radcliffe's Works. Mary Poovey's essay (1979), examining the role of ideology in *Udolpho*, is probably the single most influential piece written on Radcliffe in recent years. Her central thesis is that Radcliffe's text reveals a latent contradiction in the cult of sensibility: although sensibility offered to empower women by locating feminine talents at the heart of cultural improvement, these same 'talents' limited the ability of women to act meaningfully in the areas that most affected their lives: economic reality and male acquisitiveness.

The explained supernatural receives considerable critical attention, usually in terms of the uncanny: see M. L. Carter, *Specter or Delusion* (1987) and D. L. Macdonald, 'Bathos and repetition' (1989). The conflict between the rational and irrational is also seen as registering a dread of sex: see Coral Howells, *Love, Mystery, and Misery* (1978), Tori Haring-Smith, 'The Gothic Novel' (1982) and Juliann Fleenor (1983), whose collection contains several essays on the topic.

Bette B. Roberts (1989) writes usefully on *Udolpho* and the 'horrid novels' mentioned in *Northanger Abbey*. Coral Howells' essay 'The pleasure of the woman's text' (1989), with its focus on *Udolpho*'s ambiguous doublings, comes closest to my own approach.

Chapter 8: Radcliffe's politics

That *The Italian* is a re-working of Matthew Lewis's *The Monk* is commonly accepted: for an excellent discussion see Syndy M. Conger, 'Sensibility restored' (1989). For a general consideration of the politics of Gothic romance, see Emma Clery (1992), who also argues for the latent radicalism of Radcliffe. In her view Radcliffe's romances 'tell of the fiction of reality', and with it, by implication, of the ' "right" of patriarchy' (81). M. M. Hennelly jr's essay 'The slow torture of delay' (1987) argues that *The Italian* replicates Inquisitional practices in its narrative structure, while Janet Todd's essay on the manservant in *The Italian* (1982) is a useful guide to the class politics of Radcliffe's romance.

Bibliography

Abrams, M. H. (1953) *The Mirror and the Lamp: Romantic Theory and the Critical Tradition*. Oxford and New York: Oxford University Press.

The Age of Prophecy! Or, Further Testimony of the Mission of Richard Brothers. By a Convert. (1795) London.

Aikin, A. L. and Aikin, J. (1773) *Miscellaneous Pieces, in Prose*. London: J. Johnson.

Allott, M. (1959) *Novelists on the Novel*. Repr. London: Routledge, 1975.

Altick, T. D. (1957) *The English Common Reader: A Social History of the Mass Reading Public, 1800–1900*. Chicago: University of Chicago Press.

Anderson, H. (1982) 'Gothic heroes' in R. Folkenflik (ed.), *The English Hero, 1660–1800*, Newark: University of Delaware Press, 205–21.

Annual Biography and Obituary for the year 1824. (1824) VIII. London: Longman, Hurst, Rees, Orme, Brown & Green.

The Anti-Jacobin; or, Weekly Examiner.

The Anti-Jacobin Review and Magazine; or, Monthly Political and Literary Censor.

Austen, J. (1972) *Northanger Abbey*. Harmondsworth, Middlesex: Penguin. Originally published 1818.

Baker, E. (1929) *The Novel of Sentiment and the Gothic Romance*. V of *The History of the English Novel*. New York: Barnes & Noble.

Bakhtin, M. (1972) *Rabelais and his World*. Trans. H. Iswolsky, Cambridge, Mass.: MIT Press.

—— (1973) *Problems of Dostoevsky's Poetics*. Trans. R. W. Rostel. Ann Arbor: Ardis.

Barrell, J. (1980) *The Dark Side of the Landscape: The Rural Poor in English Paintings, 1730–1840*. Cambridge: Cambridge University Press.

Beattie, J. (1783) *Dissertations Moral and Critical*. II of *The Philosophical and Critical Works of James Beattie*. Repr. Hildesheim and New York: Georg Olms Verlag, 1974.

Beer, G. (1982) ' "Our unnatural No-voice": the heroic epistle, Pope, and women's Gothic', *Yearbook of English Studies*, 12: 125–51.

Benedict, B. M. (1989) 'Pictures of conformity: sentiment and structure in Ann Radcliffe's style', *Philological Quarterly*, 68(3): 363–77.

Bermingham, A. (1987) *Landscape and Ideology: The English Rustic Tradition 1740–1860*. London: Thames and Hudson.

Birkhead, E. (1921) *The Tale of Terror: A Study of the Gothic Romance*. London: Constable.

Bogel, F. (1984) *Literature and Instability in Later Eighteenth-Century England*. Princeton: Princeton University Press.

Brissenden, R. F. (1974) *Virtue in Distress: Studies in the Novel of Sentiment from Richardson to Sade*. London and Basingstoke: Macmillan.

British Critic (1796) Review of *Camilla*. VII: 527.

—— (1796) Review of *Historical Anecdotes of Heraldry and Chivalry*. (London: Robson, 1795) VII: 448.

—— (1798) Review of *The Works of Tobias Smollet*. XII: 61.

—— (1799). XIII.

Brooks, P. (1973) 'Virtue and terror: *The Monk*', *ELH* 40: 249–63.

Bronfen, E. (1992) *Over Her Dead Body: Death, Femininity and the Aesthetic*. Manchester: Manchester University Press.

Brothers, R. (1794a) *A Revealed Knowledge, of the Prophecies and Times. Book the First*. London.

—— (1794b) *A Revealed Knowledge of Prophecies and Times, Particularly of the Present Time, the Present War, and the Prophecy Now Fulfilling. The Year of the World 5913. Book the Second*. London.

—— (1796) *Notes on the Etymology of a Few Antique Words*. London: G. Riebeau.

Burke, E. (1887) *A Philosophical Inquiry Into The Origin of Our Ideas of The Sublime and Beautiful*. London: Cassell & Company. Originally published 1757.

—— (1910) *Reflections on the Revolution in France*. London: J. M. Dent. Originally published 1790.

Butler, M. (1980) 'The woman at the window: Ann Radcliffe in the novels of Mary Wollstonecraft and Jane Austen', *Women and Literature*, 1: 128–48.

—— (1981) *Romantics, Rebels and Reactionaries: English Literature and its Background, 1760–1830*. Repr. Oxford: Oxford University Press, 1987.

—— (ed.) (1984) *Burke, Paine, and the Revolution Controversy*. Cambridge: Cambridge University Press.

—— (1987) *Jane Austen and the War of Ideas*. Rev. edn. Oxford: Clarendon Press.

Butt, J. and Carnall, G. (1979) *The Mid-Eighteenth Century*. Oxford: Oxford University Press.

Calet, J. J. (1789) *A True and Minute Account of the Destruction of the Bastille*. Trans. from the French, by an English Gentleman. London: W. Browne and J. Warren.

Cantor, P. A. (1984) *Creature and Creator: Myth-making and English Romanticism*. Cambridge: Cambridge University Press.

Carter, M. L. (1987) *Specter or Delusion? The Supernatural in Gothic Fiction*. Ann Arbor: UMI Research Press.

Castle, T. (1987) 'The Spectralization of the Other in *The Mysteries of Udolpho*' in Laura Brown and Felicity Nussbaum (eds), *The New Eighteenth Century: Theory, Politics, English Literature*, London and New York: Methuen, 237–53.

—— (1988) 'Phantasmagoria: spectral technology and the metaphorics of modern reverie', *Critical Inquiry*, 15:26–61.

Chard, C. (1986) Introduction to *The Romance of the Forest*. Oxford: Oxford University Press.

Christianity, The Only True Theology: or, An Answer to Mr. Paine's Age of Reason. By a Christian. London: F. & C. Rivington and J. Mathews. (No date)

Christie, Thomas (1791). *Letters on the Revolution in France and on the New Constitution Established by the National Assembly; Occasioned by the Publications of the Right Hon. Edmund Burke, N.P., & Alexander de Colonne, Late Minister of State*. Dublin: J. Johnson.

Clery, E. J. (1992) 'The Politics of the Gothic Heroine in the 1790s' in P. W. Martin and R. Jarvis (eds.), *Reviewing Romanticism*, London and Basingstoke: Macmillan, 69–85.

Colton, J. (1976) 'Merlin's Cave and Queen Caroline: Garden Art as Political Propaganda', *Eighteenth-Century Studies*, 10: 1–20.

Conger, S. M. (1989) 'Sensibility Restored: Radcliffe's Answer to Lewis's *The Monk*' in K. W. Graham (ed.), *Gothic Fictions: Prohibition/Transgression*, New York: AMS Press, 113–49.

Cottom, D. (1985) *The Civilized Imagination: A Study of Ann Radcliffe, Jane Austen, and Sir Walter Scott*. Cambridge: Cambridge University Press.

Cox, J. (ed.) (1992) *Seven Gothic Dramas, 1789–1825*. Athens, Ohio: Ohio University Press.

Cox, P. (1995) *Gender, Genre and Romantic Poetry: An Introduction*. Manchester University Press (forthcoming).

Crease, J. (1795) *Prophecies Fulfilling; or, the Dawn of a Perfect Day; with Increasing Light Breaking Forth into all Directions, addressed to all Scoffing Sectarians and Others, who, in the Plenitude of their folly, Despise and Reject Richard Brothers; as the Jews also Despised and Rejected Jesus Christ*. London: G. Riebeau.

Critical Review (1791a). Review of *The Authentic Memoirs and Sufferings of Dr. William Stahl* (1789, trans. 1791) III.

—— (1791b). *Review of Moderate Politics; Devoted to Britons*. (Walker: 1791) III: 427–30.

—— (1792a). Review of *Historical Sketch of the French Revolution*. (Debrett: 1792) IV: 443.

—— (1792b). Review of *The Romance of The Forest*, by Ann Radcliffe. IV: 458–60.

—— (1792c). Review of *Rights of a Free People. An Essay on the Origin, Progress and Perfection of the British Constitution, with an Historical Account of the various Modifications of Monarchy. From the Norman Invasion to the Revolution*. (Debrett, 1791) V: 166.

—— (1795a). XIII.

—— (1795b). Review of *A Journey Made in the Summer of 1794*, by Ann Radcliffe. XIV: 241–44.

—— (1796). XVI. Review of *An Antiquarian Romance*, by Governor Parnall. XVI: 146.

—— (1798). Review of *The Italian, or The Confessional of the Black Penitents*. XXI: 166–70.

—— (1798). Review of *An Inquiry into the Present Conditions of the Lower Classes, and the Means of Improving It*, by Robert Acklam Ingram. (Debrett: 1797) XXIV: 117.

De Bruyn, F. (1987) 'Hooking the Leviathan: The Eclipse of the Heroic and the Emergence of the Sublime in Eighteenth-Century Literature', *The Eighteenth Century: Theory and Interpretation*, 28: 195–215.

Delamotte, E. C. (1990) *Perils of the Night: A Feminist Study of Nineteenth-Century Gothic*. New York and Oxford: Oxford University Press.

Demophilius (1776) *The Genuine Principles of the Ancient Saxons, or English Constitution. Carefully Collected from the Best Authorities*. Philadelphia: Robert Bell.

Doody, M. A. (1977) 'Deserts, Ruins, Troubled Waters: Female Dreams in Fiction and the Development of the Gothic Novel', *Genre*, 10: 529–72.

Drake, N. (1800) *Literary Hours, or Sketches Critical and Narrative*, 2nd edn., 2 vols. Repr. New York: Garland Publishing, 1970.

Duff, W. (1767) *An Essay on Original Genius And Its Various Modes of Exertion in Philosophy and the Fine Arts, Particularly in Poetry*. Repr. Gainesville, Florida: Scholars' Facsimile & Reprints, 1964.

—— (1774) *Critical Observations on the Writings of the Most Celebrated Geniuses in Poetry, Being a Sequel to the Essay on Original Genius*. London, Repr. Delmar, New York: Scholars' Facsimiles & Reprints, 1973.

During, S. (1992) *Foucault and Literature: Towards a Genealogy of Writing*. London: Routledge.

Durrant, D. (1982) 'Ann Radcliffe and the Conservative Gothic', *SEL*, 22: 519–29.

Eagleton, T. (1983) *Literary Theory: An Introduction*. Oxford: Basil Blackwell.

Ellis, K. F. (1989) *The Contested Castle: Gothic Novels and the Subversion of Domestic Ideology*. Urbana and Chicago: University of Illinois Press.

Elwood, Mrs. (1843) *Memoirs of the Literary Ladies of England*. 2 vols. London: Henry Colburn.

European Magazine (1788). XIII.

—— (1789). XVI.

—— (1794). XXV.

Fairchild, H. N. (1928) *The Noble Savage: A Study in Romantic Naturalism*. New York: Columbia University Press.

Fawcett, M. L. (1983) '*Udolpho*'s Primal Mystery', *SEL*, 23: 481–94.

Fiedler, L. A. (1966) *Love and Death in the American Novel*. Rev. edn. New York: Stein and Day.

Figes, E. (1982) *Sex and Subterfuge; Women Writers to 1850*. London and Basingstoke: Macmillan.

Flaxman, R. L. (1986) 'Radcliffe's Dual Modes of Vision' in M. A. Schofield and C. Macheski (eds.), *Fetter'd or Free? British Women's Novelists, 1670–1815*, Athens, Ohio: Ohio University Press, 124–33.

Fleenor, J. E. (ed.) (1983) *The Female Gothic*. Montreal: Eden Press.

Foot, M. and Kramnick, I. (1987) *The Thomas Paine Reader*. Harmondsworth, Middlesex: Penguin.

Foucault, M. (1967) *Madness and Civilization: A History of Insanity in the Age of Reason*. Trans. Richard Howard. Repr. London: Tavistock, 1987.

—— (1970) *The Order of Things: An Archeology of the Human Sciences*. Repr. London and New York: Tavistock/Routledge, 1989.

—— (1977) 'Language to Infinity' in D. F. Bouchard (ed.), *Language, Counter-Memory, Practice: Selected Essays and Interviews*, Ithaca, New York: Cornell University Press.

—— (1979) *The History of Sexuality: Volume I, An Introduction*. Trans. Robert Hurley. Repr. Harmondsworth, Middlesex: Penguin, 1981.

Frank, F. S. (1987) *The First Gothics: A Critical Guide to the English Gothic Novel*. New York and London: Garland.

—— (1988) *Gothic Fiction: A Master List of Twentieth-Century Criticism and Research*. London: Meckler.

Freud, S. (1958) 'The "Uncanny" '. Originally published 1919. Collected in Benjamin Nelson (ed.), *On Creativity and the Unconscious: Papers on the Psychology of Art, Literature, Love, Religion*. Trans. Joan Riviere. New York: Harper & Row.

—— (1984) 'Beyond the pleasure principle'. Originally published 1920. Collected in *On Metapsychology: The Theory of Psychoanalysis*, XI of *The Pelican Freud Library*. Harmondsworth, Middlesex: Penguin.

Gentleman's Magazine (1823) 'Ann Radcliffe'. XCIII: 87–8.

Gerard, A. (1774) *An Essay on Genius*. London and Edinburgh: W. Strachan, T. Cadell & W. Creech.

Gilbert, S. M. and Gubar, S. (1979) *The Madwoman in the Attic: The Woman Writer and the Nineteenth-Century Literary Imagination*. New Haven and London: Yale University Press.

Graham, K. W. (ed.) (1989) *Gothic Fictions: Prohibition/Transgression*. New York: AMS Press.

Grant, A. (1951) *Ann Radcliffe: A Biography*. Denver: Alan Swallow.

Gregory, J. (1774) *A Comparative View of the State & Faculties of Man with Those of the Animal World*. 6th edn, 2 vols. London: J. Dodsley.

Grosse, K. (1968) *Horrid Mysteries*, ed. Devendra P. Varma. London: Folio Press. Originally published 1796.

Hadley, M. (1978) *The Undiscovered Genre: A Search for the German Gothic Novel*. Berne, Frankfurt am Main and Las Vegas: Peter Lang.

Haggerty, G. E. (1989) *Gothic Fiction/Gothic Form*. University Park and London: The Pennsylvania State University Press.

Hagstrum, J. H. (1984) 'Pictures to the Heart: The Psychological Picturesque in Ann Radcliffe's *The Mysteries of Udolpho*', *Green Centennial Studies: Essays Presented to Donald Greene in the Centennial Year of the University of Southern California*. Charlottesville: University Press of Virginia, 434–41.

Hamilton, P. (1983) *Coleridge's Poetics*. Oxford: Basil Blackwell.

Haring-Smith, T. (1982) 'The Gothic Novel: A Tale of Terrors Tamed', *Gesellschaftswissenschaftlich*, 31 (8): 49–55.

Harrison, L. (1916) *A Lover of Books: The Life and Literary Papers of Lucy Harrison. Written and Arranged by Amy Greene*. London, Paris and Toronto: J. M. Dent & Sons.

Hartley, D. (1794) *Arguments on the French Revolution and the Means of Peace*. Bath: R. Cruttwell.

Hazlitt, W. (1907) *Lectures on the English Comic Writers*. London, New York and Toronto: Oxford University Press. First published 1818.

—— 1910 *The Spirit of the Age; or, Contemporary portraits*. London and New York: J. M. Dent & Sons. First published 1825.

Heller, W. T. (1992) *Dead Secrets: Wilkie Collins and the Female Gothic*, New Haven and London: Yale University Press.

Hennelly, M. M. jr (1987) ' "The Slow Torture of Delay": Reading *The Italian*', *Studies in the Humanities*, 14(1): 1–17.

Holland, N., and Sherman, L. (1977) 'Gothic Possibilities', *New Literary History*, 8: 278–94.

Home, H., Lord Kames (1751) *Essays on the Principles of Morality and Natural Religion*. Repr. Ann Arbor, Michigan and London: University Microfilms International, 1981.

—— (1774) *Elements of Criticism*. 5th edn., 2 vols. Edinburgh and London: Kincald, Creech, Bell, Johnston & Cadell.

Howard, J. (1994) *Reading Gothic Fiction: A Bakhtinian Approach*. Oxford: Clarendon Press.

Howells, C. A. (1978) *Love, Mystery, and Misery: Feeling in Gothic Fiction*. London: Athlone Press.

—— (1989) 'The Pleasure of the Woman's Text: Ann Radcliffe's Subtle Transgressions' in K. W. Graham (ed.), *Gothic Fictions: Prohibition/Transgression*. New York: AMS Press.

Hume, R. (1969) 'Gothic versus Romantic: A Revaluation of the Gothic Novel', *PMLA*, 84: 282–90.

Hume, R. and Platzner, R. L. (1971) ' "Gothic versus Romantic": A Rejoinder', *PMLA*, 86: 266–74.

Hurd, R. (1811) *The Works of Richard Hurd*. Repr. vol. II Hildesheim and New York: Georg Olms Verlag, 1969.

—— (1911) *Letters on Chivalry and Romance*, ed. Edith J. Morley. London: H. Frowde.

Ireland, W. H. (1799) *The Abbess: A Romance*. 4 vols. London: Earle and Hemet.

—— (1805) *Gondez, The Monk: A Romance of the Thirteenth Century*. 4 vols. London: W. Earle & J. W. Hucklebridge.

Jackson, R. (1981) *Fantasy: The Literature of Subversion*. London and New York: Methuen.

Johnson, C. L. (1988) *Women, Politics, and the Novel*. Chicago: University of Chicago Press.

Kahane, C. (1985) 'The Gothic Mirror' in S. N. Garner *et al.* (eds.), *The (M)other Tongue: Essays in Feminist Psychoanalytic Interpretation*. Ithaca and New York: Cornell University Press.

Kallich, M. (1945) 'The Association of Ideas and Critical Theory: Hobbes, Locke, and Addison', *ELH*, 12: 290–315.

—— (1946) 'The Association Criticism of Francis Hutcheson and David Hume', *Studies in Philology*, 49: 644–67.

—— (1947) 'The Association of Ideas and Akenside's *Pleasures of the Imagination*', *Modern Language Notes*, 62: 166–73.

Kauffman, L. (1989) *Gender and Theory: Dialogues on Feminist Criticism*. Oxford: Basil Blackwell.

Kavanagh, J. (1863) *English Women of Letters: Biographical Sketches*. 2 vols. London: Hurst and Blackett.

Keane, A. (1994) 'Resisting Arrest: the National Constitution of Picturesque and Gothic in Radcliffe's Romances; *News from Nowhere: Theories and Politics of Romanticism* (I).

Kelly, G. (1976) *The English Jacobin Novel*. London and New York: Longman.

—— (1989a) 'From Gothicism to Romantic Orientalism', *Ariel*, 20 (April): 3–18.

—— (1989b) *English Fiction of the Romantic Period, 1789–1830*. London and New York: Longman.

Kermode, F. (1983) *The Classic: Literary Images of Permanence and Change*. Cambridge, Mass.: Harvard University Press.

Kiely, R. (1972) *The Romantic Novel in England*. Cambridge, Mass.: Harvard University Press.

Kliger, S. (1952) *The Goths in England: A Study in Seventeenth and Eighteenth Century Thought*. Cambridge, Mass.: Harvard University Press.

Knight, R. P. (1808) *An Analytic Inquiry Into The Principles of Taste*. 4th edn. London: T. Payne & J. White.

Kostelnick, C. (1985) 'From Picturesque View to Picturesque Vision: William Gilpin and Ann Radcliffe', *Mosaic: A Journal for the Interdisciplinary Study of Literature*, 18(3): 31–48.

Lee, S. (1783–85) *The Recess: A Tale of Other Times*. 3 vols. Repr. New York: Arno Press, 1972.

A Letter to the Reverend John Erskine, D.D., One of the Ministers of Edinburgh: On the Dangerous Tendency of his Late Sketches of Church-History: By His Countenancing The Authors, and Promoting the Designs, of the Infamous Sect of the Illuminati (1798). Edinburgh: J. Moir.

Lewis, M. G. (1973) *The Monk: A Romance*, ed. Howard Anderson. Repr. Oxford: Oxford University Press, 1986.

Life of Joseph Balsamo, Commonly Called Count Cagliostro: Containing the Singular Adventures of that Extraordinary Personage, From His Birth, Till His Imprisonment in the Castle of St. Angelo. To Which are Added, The Particulars of his Trile before the Inquisition, The History of His Confessions Concerning Common and Egyptian Masonry, and Variety of Other Interesting Particulars (1792). Trans. from the Original Proceedings published at Rome by order of the Apostolic Chamber. Dublin: P. Byrne *et al*.

Linguets (1783) *Memoirs of the Bastille. Containing A Full Exposition of the Mysterious Policy and Despotic Oppression of the French Government. In the Interior Administration of that State-Prison*. Trans. from the French. London: Kearsly & Spilsbury.

Locke, D. (1980) *A Fantasy of Reason: The Life and Thought of William Godwin*. London: Routledge & Kegan Paul.

London, A. (1986) 'Ann Radcliffe in Context: Marking the Boundaries of *The Mysterious Udolpho*', *Eighteenth-Century Life*, 10: 35–47.

Longueil, A. E. (1923) 'The Word "Gothic" in Eighteenth-Century Criticism', *Modern Language Notes*, 38: 453–60.

Lowth, R. (1835) *Lectures on the Sacred Poetry of the Hebrews*. Trans. G. Gregory. 3rd edn. London: Thomas Tegg & Son.

Macdonald, D. L. (1989) 'Bathos and Repetition: The Uncanny in Radcliffe', *Journal of Narrative Technique*, 19(2): 197–204.

Madoff, M. (1979) 'The Useful Myth of Gothic Ancestry', *Studies in Eighteenth-Century Culture*, 9: 337–50.

McCalman, I. (1993) *Radical Underworld: Prophets, Revolutionaries, and Pornographers in London, 1795–1840*. Oxford: Clarendon Press.

McIntyre, C. (1920) *Ann Radcliffe in Relation to her Time*. New Haven: Yale University Press.

McNutt, D. J. (1975) *The Eighteenth-Century Gothic Novel: An Annotated Bibliography of Criticism and Selected Texts*. Folkestone, England: Dawson.

Mee, J. (1992) *Dangerous Enthusiasm: William Blake and the Culture of Radicalism in the 1790s*. Oxford: Oxford University Press.

A Memoir of Mr. Justice Talfourd, by a Member of the Oxford Circuit (1854). London: Butterworths.

Milbank, A. (1992) *Daughters of the House: Modes of the Gothic in Victorian Fiction*. London: Macmillan.

—— (1993) Introduction to *A Sicilian Romance*, by Ann Radcliffe. Oxford and New York: Oxford University Press.

Miles, R. (1993) *Gothic Writing 1750–1820; A Genealogy*. London: Routledge.

Moers, E. (1977) *Literary Women*. London: W. H. Allen.

Monk, S. (1960) *The Sublime: A Study of Critical Theories in XVIII-Century England*. Ann Arbor: The University of Michigan Press.

Montagu, E. (1810) *An Essay on the Writings and Genius of Shakespeare Compared With The Greek and Dramatic Poets With Some Remarks Upon the Misrepresentations of Mons. De Voltaire. To Which are Added, Three Dialogues of the Dead*. 6th edn. London: R. Priestly.

Montague, E. (1807a) *The Demon of Sicily, A Romance*. 4 vols. London: J. F. Hughes.

—— (1807b) *Legends of a Nunnery: A Romantic Legend*. 4 vols. London: J. F. Hughes.

Monthly Review (1801). Review of *Rimualdo; or, The Castle of Badajos. A Romance*, by W. H. Ireland. XXXIV: 203–04.

Morris, D. B. (1985) 'Gothic Sublimity', *New Literary History*, 16: 299–319.

Mortimer, E. (1808) *Montoni: or, The Confessions of the Monk of St. Benedict, A Romance*. 4 vols. London: J. F. Hughes.

Mulvey, L. (1975) 'Visual Pleasure and Narrative Cinema', *Screen*, 16 (3): 6–18.

Murrah, C. C. (1984) 'Mrs Radcliffe's Landscapes: The Eye and the Fancy', *University of Windsor Review*, 18: 7–23.

Murray, E. B. (1972) *Ann Radcliffe*. New York: Twayne.

Napier, E. (1987) *The Failure of Gothic: Problems of Disjunction in an Eighteenth-Century Literary Form*. Oxford: Clarendon Press.

Nelson, L. jr (1963) 'Night Thoughts on the Gothic Novel', *Yale Review*, 52: 237–57.

Nicolson, M. H. (1963) *Mountain Gloom and Mountain Glory: The Development of the Aesthetics of the Infinite*. New York: W. W. Norton & Co.

Nollen, E. (1984) 'Ann Radcliffe's *A Sicilian Romance*: A New Source of Jane Austen's *Sense and Sensibility*', *English Language Notes*, 22(2): 30–7.

Paine, T. (1791–92) *The Rights of Man*, in M. Foot and I. Kramnick, *The Thomas Paine Reader*. Harmondsworth, Middlesex: Penguin.

Paulson, R. (1983) *Representations of Revolution, 1789–1820*. New Haven and London: Yale University Press.

Percy, T. (1906) *Percy's Reliques of Ancient English Poetry*. 2 vols. Repr. London: J. M. Dent, 1910. Originally published 1765.

Piozzi, H. L. (1801). *Retrospection; or, A Review of the Most Striking and Important Events, Characters, Situations, and Their Consequences. Which the Last 1800 Years have Presented to the View of Mankind*. 2 vols. London: Stockdale.

Poovey, M. (1979) 'Ideology in *The Mysteries of Udolpho*', *Criticism*, 21: 307–30.

—— (1984) *The Proper Lady and the Woman Writer: Ideology as Style in the Works of Mary Wollstonecraft, Mary Shelley, and Jane Austen*. Chicago and London: University of Chicago Press.

Porter, R. (1982) *English Society in the Eighteenth Century*. Repr. Harmondsworth, Middlesex: Penguin, 1988.

Price, M. (1969) 'The Sublime Poem: Pictures and Powers', *Yale Review*, 58: 194–213.

Price, R. (1790) *A Discourse on the Love of Our Country, Delivered on November 4, 1789, At the Meeting-House in the Old Jewry, To the Society for Commemorating the Revolution in Great Britain*. 3rd edn. London: T. Cadell.

Priestley, J. (ed.) (1775) *Hartley's Theory of the Human Mind, on the Principle of the Association of Ideas: with Essays Relating to the Subject of It*. London: J. Johnson.

—— (1777) *A Course of Lectures on History and Criticism*. London.

—— (1791) *Letters to the Right Hon. Edmund Burke, Occasioned by his Reflections on the Revolution in France*. Birmingham.

Punter, D. (1980) *The Literature of Terror: A History of Gothic Fiction from 1765 to the Present Day*. London and New York: Longman.

Quarterly Review (1814). Review of *Remorse. A Tragedy.*, by S. T. Coleridge (London: 1814). XI, April and July: 177–90.

Radcliffe, A. (1789) *The Castles of Athlin and Dunbayne: A Highland Story*. Repr. New York: Arno Press, 1972.

—— (1993) *A Sicilian Romance*, ed. Alison Milbank. Oxford: Oxford University Press. Originally published 1790.

—— (1986) *The Romance of the Forest: Interspersed With Some Pieces of Poetry*, ed. Chloe Chard. Oxford: Oxford University Press. Originally Published 1791.

—— (1980) *The Mysteries of Udolpho, A Romance: Interspersed With Some Pieces of Poetry*, ed. Bonamy Dobrée. Repr. Oxford: Oxford University Press. Originally published 1794.

—— (1795) *A Journey Made in the Summer of 1794, Through Holland and the Western frontier of Germany, With a Return Down the Rhine: To Which Are Added Observations During a Tour to the Lakes of Lancashire and Westmoreland, and Cumberland*. London: G. G. and J. Robinson.

—— (1981) *The Italian, or The Confessional of the Black Penitents. A Romance*, ed. Frederick Garber. Oxford: Oxford University Press. Originally published 1797.

—— (1826) 'On the Supernatural in Poetry', *New Monthly Magazine*, 16: 145–52.

—— (1826) *Gaston de Blondeville; or, The Court of Henry III, Keeping Festival in Ardenne: A Romance and St Albans Abbey: A Metrical Tale, To Which is prefixed a Memoir with Extracts from her Journals*, 4 vols. London: H. Colbourn.

Railo, E. (1927) *The Haunted Castle: A Study of the Elements of English Romanticism*. London: E. P. Dutton.

Raysor, T. M. (ed.) (1936) *Coleridge's Miscellaneous Criticism*. London: Constable.

Reeve, C. (1785) *The Progress of Romance Through Times, Countries and Manners*. Colchester: W. Keymer.

—— (1977) *The Old English Baron: A Gothic Story*, ed. James Trainer. Oxford: Oxford University Press. The novel was originally published in 1777 as *The*

Champion of Virtue. A Gothic Story; the second edition, with the present title, was published in 1778.

Reiman, D. H. (ed.) (1977) *The Romantics Reviewed*, I. New York and London: Garland Publishing.

Renneville, C. de (1715) *The French Inquisition: or, the History of the Bastille in Paris, the State Prison in France*, trans. from the original at Amsterdam. London.

Restuccia, F. L. (1986) 'Female Gothic Writing: "Under Cover to Alice" ', *Genre*, 18: 245–66.

Richter, D. H. (1988) 'The Reception of the Gothic Novel in the 1790s', in Robert W. Uphans (ed.), *The Idea of the Novel in the Eighteenth Century*. East Lansing, Michigan: Colleagues Press, 117–37.

—— (1989) 'The Unguarded Prison: Reception Theory, Structural Marxism, and the History of the Gothic Novel', *The Eighteenth Century: Theory and Interpretation*, 30: 3–17.

Roberts, B. B. (1989) 'The Horrid Novels: *The Mysteries of Udolpho* and *Northanger Abbey*' in K. W. Graham (ed.), *Gothic Fictions: Prohibition/Transgression*, New York: AMS Press, 89–111.

Robison, J. (1797) *Proofs of a Conspiracy Against all the Religions and Governments of Europe, Carried on in the Secret Meetings of Free Masons, Illuminati, and Reading Societies*. Edinburgh.

Rogers, P. (ed.) (1978) *The Eighteenth Century: The Context of English Literature*. London: Methuen and Co.

Rosenberg, J. D. (1979) *The Genius of John Ruskin*. Boston and London: Routledge & Kegan Paul.

Rothstein, E. (1974) 'The Lessons of *Northanger Abbey*', *University of Toronto Quarterly*, 44: 14–31.

—— (1975–76) ' "Ideal Presence" and the "Non-Finito" in Eighteenth-Century Aesthetics', *Eighteenth-Century Studies*, 9: 304–32.

Rousseau, J.-J. (1784) *Eloisa: Or, A Series of Original Letters. A New Edition: To Which Is Now First Added, The Sequel of Julia; or, The New Eloisa*. 4 vols. London: H. Baldwin.

—— (1974) *Emile*. Trans. Barbara Foxley. London: J. M. Dent. Original French publication 1762.

Sade, Marquis de (1965) *The Complete Justine, Philosophy in the Bedroom, and Other Writings*. Trans. Richard Seaver and Austyn Wainhouse. New York: Grove Press Inc.

Sage, V. (1988) *Horror Fiction in the Protestant Tradition*. London and Basingstoke: Macmillan.

—— (ed.) (1990) *The Gothick Novel: A Casebook*. London; Macmillan.

Said, E. (1978) *Orientalism*. New York: Pantheon Books.

Saintsbury, G. (1906) *A History of Nineteenth Century Literature (1780–1900)*. London: Macmillan & Co.

Schama, S. (1989) *Citizens: A Chronicle of the French Revolution*. Harmondsworth, Middlesex: Penguin.

Schofield, P. (1992) 'British Politicians and French Arms: The Ideological War of 1793–1795', *History*, 77: 183–201.

Schroeder, N. (1980) '*The Mysteries of Udolpho* and *Clermont*: The Radcliffean

Encroachment on the Art of Regina Maria Roche', *Studies in the Novel*, 12: 131–43.

Sedgwick, E. K. (1980) *The Coherence of Gothic Conventions*. New York, Repr. New York and London: Methuen, 1986.

Sharpe, W. (1775) *A Dissertation Upon Genius*. Repr. Delmar, New York: Scholars' Facsimiles & Reprints, 1973.

Smith, C. (1971) *Emmeline, the Orphan of the Castle*, ed. Ann Henry Ehrenpreis. Oxford: Oxford University Press. Originally published 1788.

Smith, R. J. (1987) *The Gothic Bequest: Medieval Institutions in British Thought, 1688–1863*. Cambridge: Cambridge University Press.

Spacks, P. M. (1989) 'Female Orders of Narrative: *Clarissa* and *The Italian*' *Rhetorics of Order/Ordering Rhetorics in English Neoclassical Literature*, Newark: University of Delaware Press, 158–71.

Spirit of the Public Journals. Being an Impartial Selection of the Most Exquisite Essays & Jeux D'Esprits (1797–1800). I–IV.

Stanhope, E. (1790). *A Letter From Earl Stanhope, to the Right Honourable Edmund Burke: Containing a Short Answer to His Late Speech on the French Revolution*. London.

Stoler, J. A. (1980) *Ann Radcliffe: The Novel of Suspense and Terror*. New York: Arno Press.

Stone, L. (1979) *The Family, Sex and Marriage: The Family and Marriage in England, 1500–1800*. Harmondsworth, Middlesex: Penguin.

Taylor, M. (1991) 'Reluctant Romancers: Self-Consciousness and Derogation in Prose Romance', *English Studies in Canada*, 17(1): 89–106.

Thompson, E. P. (1968) *The Making of the English Working Class*. Harmondsworth, Middlesex: Penguin.

Thompson, G. (1791) *The Spirit of General History, In a Series of Lectures, From the Eighth to the Eighteenth Century*. Carlisle.

Thompson, G. R. (ed.) (1974) *The Gothic Imagination: Essays in Dark Romanticism*. Pullman, Washington: Washington University Press.

Thomson, J. (1981) 'Seasonal and Lighting Effects in Ann Radcliffe's Fiction', *Journal of the Australasian Universities Language and Literature Association*, 56: 191–200.

Thorslev, P., jr (1981) *Romantic Contraries*. New Haven: Yale University Press.

Todd, J. (ed.) (1977) *A Wollstonecraft Anthology*. Bloomington and London: Indiana University Press.

—— (1982) 'Posture and Imposture: The Gothic Manservant in Ann Radcliffe's *The Italian*', *Women and Literature*, 2: 25–38.

—— (1986) *Sensibility: An Introduction*. London & New York: Methuen.

Todorov, T. (1973) *The Fantastic: A Structural Approach to a Literary Genre*. Trans. Richard Howard. Cleveland and London: The Press of Case Western Reserve University.

Tompkins, J. M. S. (1921) *The Work of Mrs. Radcliffe and its Influence on Later Writers*. Repr. New York: Arno Press, 1980.

—— (1932) *The Popular Novel in England, 1770–1800*. London: Constable.

Tracy, A. B. (1980) *Patterns of Fear in the Gothic Novel, 1790–1830*. New York: Arno Press.

Tschink, C. (1795) *The Victim of Magical Delusion: or, the Mystery of the Revelation* of P–L: A Magico-Political Tale. Founded in Historical Fact. Trans. Peter Will. London: G. C. & J. Robinson.

van Leeuwen, F. (1982) 'Female Gothic: The Discourse of the Other', *Revista Canaria de Estudios Ingleses*, 4: 33–44.

A View of the Relative State of Great Britain and France at the Commencement of the Year 1796. (1796). London: J. Debrett.

Volney, C. F. (1819) *The Ruins: or a Survey of the Revolutions of Empires*. London: J. Davison.

Walpole, H. (1791) *The Mysterious Mother: A Tragedy*. Dublin: J. Archer, W. Jones and R. White.

—— (1968) *The Castle of Otranto, A Gothic Story* in *Three Gothic Novels*, ed. Peter Fairclough. Repr. Harmondsworth, Middlesex: Penguin. Originally published 1765.

Ware, M. (1963) *Sublimity in the Novels of Ann Radcliffe*. Uppsala and Copenhagen.

Warner, Richard (1789) *Hampshire Extracted from a Domes-day Book: with an Accurate English Translation; A Preface; and an Introduction*. London.

Warton, J. (1782) *An Essay On the Genius and Writings of Pope*. 4th edn., 2 vols. Repr. Farnborough, Hants.: Gregg International, 1969.

Warton, T. (1762) *Observations On The Fairy Queen of Spenser*. 2nd edn., 2 vols. London and Oxford: R. & J. Dodsley and J. Fletcher.

—— (1778 and 1781) *The History of English Poetry From the Eleventh Century to the Seventeenth*. Repr. London: Alex Murray & Son, 1890.

Weiskel, T. (1976) *The Romantic Sublime: Studies in the Structure and Psychology of Transcendence*. Baltimore: John Hopkins University Press.

Willey, B. (1940) *The Eighteenth-Century Background: Studies in the Idea of Nature in the Thought of the Period*. Repr. London: Chatto and Windus, 1980.

Williams, I. (ed.) (1968) *Sir Walter Scott; On Novelists and Fiction*. London: Routledge & Kegan Paul.

—— (ed.) (1970) *Novel and Romance, 1700–1800: A Documentary Record*. London: Routledge & Kegan Paul.

Wolff, C. G. (1972) 'A Mirror for Men: Stereotypes of Women in Literature', *The Massachusetts Review*, Winter/Spring: 201–18.

—— (1983) 'The Radcliffean Gothic Model: A Form for Feminine sexuality', in J. E. Fleenor (ed.), *The Female Gothic*, Montreal: Eden Press, pp. 207–23.

Wollheim, R. (1971) *Freud*. Glasgow: Fontana.

Wollstonecraft, M. (1790) *A Vindication of the Rights of Men, in a Letter to the Right Honourable Edmund Burke, Occasioned by His Reflections on the Revolution in France*. London: J. Johnson.

—— (1980) *Mary and The Wrongs of Woman*, ed. Gary Kelly. Oxford: Oxford University Press. Originally published in 1788 and 1798, respectively.

—— (1985) *A Vindication of the Rights of Woman*. Repr. Harmondsworth, Middlesex: Penguin. Originally published 1792.

Worrall, D. (1992) *Radical Culture: Discourse, Resistance and Surveillance, 1790–1820*. New York and London: Harvester Wheatsheaf.

Index